aurora metro press

Founded in 1989 to publish and promote new writing, the company has specialised in new drama and fiction, winning recognition and awards from the industry.

Charles Way: Plays for Young Performers
ISBN 0-9536757-1-8 £9.95

Black and Asian Plays Anthology
introduced by Afia Nkrumah **ISBN 0-9536757-4-2 £9.95**

Six Plays by Black and Asian Women Writers
ed. Kadija George **ISBN 0-9515877-2-2 £7.50**

Graeae Plays 1 new plays redefining disability, selected and introduced by Jenny Sealey **ISBN 0-9536757-6-9 £12.99**

Best of the Fest. new plays celebrating 10 years of London New Play Festival ed. Phil Setren **ISBN 0-9515877-8-1 £12.99**

Seven plays by women, female voices, fighting lives.
ed. Cheryl Robson **ISBN 0-9515877-1-4 £5.95**

Balkan Plots, plays from Central and Eastern Europe, introduced by Gina Landor **ISBN 0-9536757-3-4 £9.95**

Eastern Promise, 7 plays from Central and Eastern Europe eds. Sian Evans and Cheryl Robson **ISBN 0-9515877-9-X £11.99**

Mediterranean plays by women. ed. Marion Baraitser
ISBN 0-9515877-3-0 £9.95

A touch of the Dutch: plays by women. ed. Cheryl Robson
ISBN 0-9515877-7-3 £9.95

THE PAUL HAMLYN FOUNDATION

YOUNG BLOOD

AURORA METRO PRESS

We gratefully acknowledge financial assistance from the Paul Hamlyn Foundation and The Prince's Trust.

With thanks to: Gillian Wakeling, Alison Spiby, Lyric Theatre, Hammersmith, Ollie Anamashawan, Vicky Ireland, Kathy Everett, Jo Belloli, London Bubble Youth Theatre, Nick Mosley, Anna Wallbank, London Drama and Jon Owen.

ISBN 0-9515877-6-5   Printed by Anthony Rowe, Chippenham

PLAYS FOR YOUNG PERFORMERS

The Girl who fell through a hole in her Jumper
by Naomi Wallace and Bruce McLeod

The Search for Odysseus
by Charles Way

Darker the Berry
by J. B. Rose

Geraniums
by Sheila Yeger

Out of their Heads
by Marcus Romer

AURORA METRO PRESS

Sally Goldsworthy

From 1990 -1996 she was director of the London Bubble Youth Theatre in Peckham South London where they made plays in tents, halls, streets and occasionally theatres. She has directed plays for many companies including most recently Cardboard Citizens Theatre Company, London Bubble Theatre Company, The Women's Theatre Workshop and Kew Gardens. From 1992 - 1995 she was member of the Executive Committee for the National Association of Youth Theatres and represented Youth Theatres on the Advisory Council of the National Campaign for the Arts. Since 1996 she has been Head of Education at the Lyric Theatre Hammersmith.

Whilst editing **Young Blood** she has had two sons Gabriel and Frankie.

Cheryl Robson

Worked for the BBC for several years, before founding the Women's Theatre Workshop and Aurora Metro Press. She has developed, produced and published the work of many UK and international women writers. She teaches Creative Writing at Middx. University and completed her MA in Playwriting Studies at Birmingham University in 1991.

Plays include: **Scream and Dream** (84), **O Architect!** (89) *Critics Choice,* **The Taking of Liberty** (92) Winner of the South London Playwriting Competition, **Simply Hostile** (94) ACGB Option Award, **Versus** (96) ACGB Writers Bursary.

Productions for WTW include: **Low in the Dark** by Marina Carr (Theatro Technis), **Veronica Franco** by Dacia Maraini (Oval House), **Libration** by Lluisa Cunille (The Gate), **Joined at the Head** by Catherine Butterfield (Man in the Moon Theatre), **Tucson** by Lisa Perrotti with the Red Room (Finborough Theatre) *Critics Choice.*

Contents

Introduction by Sally Goldsworthy   9

The Girl who fell through a hole in her Jumper   17
by Naomi Wallace and Bruce McLeod

The Search for Odysseus   49
by Charles Way

Darker the Berry   123
by J. B. Rose

Geraniums   203
by Sheila Yeger

Out of their Heads   271
by Marcus Romer

Introduction

by Sally Goldsworthy

Young Blood started out as a quest to meet my own personal needs as a director. For six years I ran the London Bubble Youth Theatre and whilst we devised many shows, sometimes the group wanted to work on what they would call - 'a proper script, where you get to hold bits of paper.' No problem, I thought and off I went to find the perfect script for a group of twenty, 13 - 17 year olds in Peckham, South London. We weren't asking too much; quality writing, good stories, large casts and lots of parts for young women. I knew that such plays existed, I'd even seen them but finding them in print proved to be impossible.

Once I started looking, I realised I wasn't the only one with this problem. The one cry I kept hearing from teachers, youth theatre directors and F.E. Lecturers was: 'We want to do new plays but where are they?' So the idea for this anthology was born; to publish some of the most interesting, challenging, contemporary writing for young performers in one volume, to extend the life of the plays beyond their first production and to make them available to young people throughout the UK.

To develop performing skills young people need to work on the best scripts available; to have the opportunity to explore the ideas, form and language of exceptional writers. Young people in schools, youth theatres and colleges need to work on plays that excite, stretch and inspire them. The response from young people to the final selection has been remarkable. Several have been chosen by students to be performed as part of their GCSE practical exams. *Darker the Berry* and *Geraniums* have already had full productions by Youth Theatre companies. *The girl who fell through a hole in her jumper*, *Out of their heads* and *The Search for Odysseus* have been professionally produced by Young Peoples' Theatre companies in Yorkshire,

London and Wales and further productions are planned in Germany and West Yorkshire.

The last fifteen years have seen a dramatic change in the fortunes of both theatre companies performing for young people in schools and youth clubs and in the use of drama in schools. During the 1970's and early 80's Theatre in Education companies were commissioning some of the most exciting young writers in the country. Writers such as Noel Greig, Bryony Lavery, Diane Samuels and Nona Shepherd all developed their craft writing for young people and still write for them. Watford T.I.E. and Belgrade T.I.E., both companies that did much to nurture new writing, have ceased to exist, due to funding cuts in the 1980's as have M6, the Cockpit Arts Project and many others. Many of those left, continue to make sure that young people have the opportunity to experience high quality theatre. Companies such as Theatre Centre, Roundabout T.I.E., Made in Wales and Tag Theatre Company still regularly commission new plays but all companies are stretched to breaking-point, making long-term strategy planning a virtual impossibility. In the current climate a commission for a cast of five is considered to be a luxury.

Recently, there has been a lot of rhetoric about new funding commitments particularly through the Lottery Arts for Everyone scheme enabling young people to have more access to the arts both as participants and audiences. It is early days but it will take more than a few large grants to well-known organisations to reverse the destructive tide of the last 15 years. There need to be changes to ensure that the money actually gets to young people and the companies who are working with them and not to support glossy applications written by consultants. Funders need to support young people as artists, to enable groups and individuals to experiment and take risks so that they are able to create their own theatrical language. Only then can theatre remain a dynamic part of our cultural life.

In the last few years there have been some notable exceptions of professional productions exploring the issues and concerns of young people. *Disco Pigs* by Edna Walsh from the Irish Company Corcadorca at the Bush Theatre, Jonathan Harvey's *Babies* and Sarah Kane's *Blasted* both at the Royal Court Theatre and Iain Bank's *The Wasp Factory* at the West Yorkshire Playhouse and the Lyric Theatre, Hammersmith, all recent examples of plays that were new, exciting and had something important to say. These productions received rave reviews, sometimes created controversy but importantly, they performed to packed houses. Not only are plays for and about young people exciting, they can also be good business at the box office. If theatre is to continue as a contemporary art form, it desperately needs the energy and ideas of a new generation of artists and audiences. The plays in this collection are not about building the audiences of the future but about what needs to be written and shown on stage *now*.

Chances for young people to perform have gone three steps forward and two steps back. When the National Curriculum was introduced in 1995, teacher specialists were horrified to discover that Drama didn't have a place in the core curriculum. This meant that schools had no obligation to continue teaching Drama as a subject in its own right. The English curriculum included elements of drama but many teachers feared that as an optional subject, Drama would disappear completely from the timetable. The loss of many specialist advisors and inspectors has also left Drama teachers feeling vulnerable and unsupported. In fact, Drama or Theatre Studies is now one of the most popular courses studied at GCSE. Since 1995 the number of young people studying Drama at Key Stage 4 has risen by 154% - not bad for an optional subject.

A positive move has been the growing number of Btec and Degree courses in the Performing Arts. As more and more young people have the opportunity to develop performing arts skills, the lack of exciting published scripts has become a major problem. As one lecturer recently remarked: 'There's a limit to how many times I can do *The Crucible* and remain sane.' *Young Blood* will provide students and lecturers with five new plays to work on.

As with all sections of the arts, youth theatres have been struck by funding crises. Many have faced the double whammy of losing funding from both local authorities and Regional Arts Boards. Despite this and with the support of the National Association of Youth Theatres, many have continued to grow from strength to strength across the UK. There are opportunities for young people to become involved in a range of events from regular weekly sessions to summer schools and spectacular collaborations with international artists. Two recent shows that have left a lasting impression are the Royal Court Young People's Theatre production of *My House in the Bush of Ghosts* produced by Odu Thnes from Nigeria and Lewisham Youth Theatre's production of Richard Cameron's *Almost Grown* as part of the National Theatre's BT Connections programme. Whatever the future holds, youth theatre is here to stay and the young people who attend and run them are hungry to perform relevant and challenging material.

This selection is a purely personal one. I have included plays that excite me and that I would like to work on with a group of young people. All of the plays in this collection have a unique theatrical vision. Publishing these plays enables them to have life beyond the first production. Where previously they have only been performed in one area they can now be presented by groups anywhere in the UK. The idea of a group in Scotland performing J.B. Rose's work, originally written for a group of young people in Deptford is one that everyone involved in this collection finds exciting. What writer wouldn't welcome hundreds of productions of their plays?

The Plays

The Girl who fell through a hole in her Jumper by Naomi Wallace and Bruce McLeod is the wonderful story of Noil, a young girl who accidentally falls into a strange and fantastical world where nothing is quite what it seems. Set at the end of a hole in Noil's jumper, the play is a classic adventure story proving that a girl is as capable as any boy of solving riddles and confronting tyrants. Along the way Noil meets a Mirror searching for an identity, a keen but not very talented musical Crumb and the monstrous exiled It-nose. Using humour, Naomi Wallace and Bruce McLeod have created a brilliant imaginary world with a strong role model for young women. The play provides young performers with a great opportunity to work on a non-naturalistic script.

Charles's Way's *The Search for Odysseus* is an imaginative re-telling of a classic myth with enormous contemporary relevance. It is not seen through the eyes of the conquering hero but through those of his son, who sets out to find him. Telemachus is no blood-thirsty hero but an awkward and angry adolescent who is searching 'west and west again to the edge of the world.' Why has his father abandoned his family? In this rite of passage story he learns that becoming an adult is a messy and complicated business. Both the language and the imagery have a unique poetic quality, providing a fantastic opportunity for the performers to create a spectacular, visionary world of islands, monsters and abandoned women and children. In 1995 it was nominated Best Children's Play by the Writers Guild.

Darker the Berry by J.B. Rose also deals with rites of passage but in a completely different style. A comedy set in Jamaica, it is a story about class, belonging, mother/daughter relationships and growing up. Most of all, it is about a rich and vibrant community struggling with poverty. Writing in patois, J.B. Rose has created a set of characters who young people will recognise from their own communities. Norma is a young girl who refuses to be beaten into submission by her stepmother, who favours her natural daughter Esther. *Darker the Berry* is J.B. Rose's first full-length play and reflects the experiences of many first generation African Caribbean immigrants in the UK - the stories of the parents and grandparents of many young people today. It offers young people the chance to work on a play that explores their own cultural heritage.

Geraniums by Sheila Yeger again explores the issues of choice - both personal and political. The play describes the Battle of Cable Street from the point of view of a group of young Jewish men and women. With historical accuracy, Sheila Yeger has recreated London's East End in 1936 - a world of sweat shops, boxing rings and heated political meetings. The actual Battle of Cable Street offers a moving theatrical moment, as Harry and Zelda form part of a barricade to stop Mosley's blackshirts from passing. It also presents a fantastic challenge to youth groups to recreate a major moment in British history. *Geraniums* is not simply a political play, many of the characters also face personal dilemmas; should Zelda follow her heart and marry Jimmy or stay true to her religion? The play also draws parallels with the present through Claire, Zelda's young granddaughter, who is involved in political action in the 1990's and finds herself fifty years on, facing the same moral choices.

Marcus Romer's *Out of their Heads* explodes the myths and prejudices surrounding the subject of drugs and substance misuse. Three friends start on a trip that takes them way beyond anything they ever expected. It is a powerful play with strong, brutal language and images. Centring around the drug scene, the play explores friendship and betrayal. How did Jelly end up in intensive care? Can Mandy really trust Devoy? Avoiding moralising, the play is an honest portrayal of why young people take drugs. The play contains no easy answers and may offend some people by showing that the issue is far more complicated than many claim. The final scenes have a compelling black humour.

The play was originally written for Pilot Theatre Company and toured with a fully integrated soundtrack. Marcus Romer's script provides groups with a chance to perform a play which exactly captures the language and culture of the current club scene.

How to use this anthology

The plays in *Young Blood* are set in many different places; Jamaica, ancient Greece, London's East End, the club scene and a world at the end of a hole in a jumper. These are plays about love, racism, absent fathers, leaving home, betrayal, drugs. Above all, in one way or another, each of them involves journeys and choices. Choices about who to love, where to live and what to be. You can use the plays or extracts of them to explore a particular issue or to look at that issue from a different angle. Each of the plays uses a different theatrical style, from the naturalism of *Geraniums* to the surreal world of The *Girl who fell through a hole in her Jumper* and the fast filmatic style of *Out of their Heads*.

This collection doesn't include production or teachers' notes. There are no fixed rules about how to use the plays. Produce the whole play to a paying audience or work on scenes. Play about with the casting. Double parts or have six people playing the same character. The most important thing is to have fun with the language, characters and staging so that young people enjoy working on the plays. All of the plays in this collection have a unique theatrical vision. Combine that with the energy, commitment and imagination of a group of young people and the results will definitely be worth watching!

The Girl who fell through a hole in her Jumper

by Naomi Wallace and Bruce McLeod

The Girl who fell through a hole in her Jumper

Our intention in *Girl* was to poke fun at the traditional fairytale/panto adventure and formulas whilst using them as a convenient and fun way of making a whole slew or stew of serious points. Mixing the everyday with the larger-than-life, we wanted Noil to very obviously take on authority and 'common sense,' and to do so with a zest and energy below which bubbles rebellion. And this of course is what the play is all about: rebellion. Very straightforward, and full of frivolity and friendship. As such, the play should have speed, use a lot of space (especially Noil), and be ready for improvisation in the face of a rebellious audience.

Notes for the director:

Noil: It is important that Noil is not portrayed as cute, shy or girlish. She is a smart and courageous girl, not afraid to speak her mind; she is never silly or frivolous.

Crumbs-in-Pockets: While he is the narrator, by no means should he be played as omnipotent or overshadow Noil in any way. Crumbs is a jolly, harmless musician, if not a bit of an egoist. But, when things get scary, he is more of a coward than the rest of the characters.

The characters of **Roach**, the **Mirror**, **It-nose** and the **Windows** and **Doors** can be played by either male or female actors.

While costumes for the other characters may take many forms, Noil must not be dressed in any 'cute' outfit, and certainly not in a dress or skirt. She is on an adventure, and should be dressed accordingly.

Naomi Wallace and Bruce McLeod

The Girl who fell through a hole in her Jumper

by Naomi Wallace and Bruce McLeod

First performed at the Old Red Lion Theatre, Islington as part of the London New Play Festival in 1995.
Directed by Donal O'Mathuna.
Designer Nicola Tedman.

Noil, a young girl	Sophie Stanton
Crumbs-in-Pockets, the narrator	Richard Kill
Lord Principal Plagueworthy	Andrew Callaway
Roach, Lord PP's loyal servant	John Atkins
The Mirror	Lee Walters
The Windows	Jon Barnett
The Doors	Jon Barnett
It-nose	Lee Walters

SCENE 1

Place: At the end of the hole in Noil's jumper.
Onto the bare stage stumbles Noil with an enormous jumper over her head. We only see half of her body as her upper half is caught and covered by the jumper. She struggles with the jumper, trying to pull it over her head. We hear her parents' voices telling her to hurry up and finish dressing or she'll be late for school. As Noil struggles, she becomes very frustrated.

NOIL   Aaaarrrrgggghhhh! I can't get this horrible jumper over my head! I can't do it! I can't do it! I feel so mad! I hate getting dressed! Everyone yelling for me to hurry up, hurry up!

PARENTS' VOICES Hurry up Noil! We're waiting for you!

NOIL *(stands still a moment with the jumper still hiding her face)*
See what I mean? *(begins struggling again)* I feel so stupid stuck
in here like this. Stupid, stupid, stupid. How am I going to figure
a way out? Hey? What's this? There's a hole in my jumper. A big
hole in my jumper. And it's getting bigger. And bigger. *(beat)*
What's in that big hole? Ooooooooooooops.

Lights fade. We hear Noil's voice in the dark.

NOIL   I'm falling. Falling. Falling.

*We hear a large thud. Then silence. Lights up on Noil sitting
sprawled on the stage. The jumper is gone.*

NOIL   I fell.

The narrator, Crumbs-in-Pockets, has appeared.

CRUMBS-IN-POCKETS *(sings)*Once upon a time a child
                    while getting dressed for school
                    fell through a hole in a jacket.

NOIL   Not a jacket, you! It was a jumper. I fell through a
       jumper.

CRUMBS-IN-POCKETS *(sings)* Once upon a time a child
                    while getting dressed for school
                    fell through a hole in a jumper.

NOIL   Right.

CRUMBS-IN-POCKETS *(sings)* Well, this child was a boy child
       and he -

NOIL *(interrupts)* Wait a minute.

CRUMBS-IN-POCKETS *(sings)* And this boy, he went -

NOIL   A girl! This child was a girl *(spells)* G.I.R.L.

CRUMBS-IN-POCKETS A girl?

NOIL   Right.

CRUMBS-IN-POCKETS Excuse me, but this is a magical
adventure story and adventure stories are supposed to be about
boys.

NOIL   Who says?

CRUMBS-IN-POCKETS Well, I'm not sure. *(to public)* That's
what I was told by ... by ... by someone very important out there.

NOIL   Do you believe everything you're told?

CRUMBS-IN-POCKETS Yes ... I mean no ... of course not.

NOIL   Right. Let's start again. I fell through the hole, not
my brother, so this story is about me.

CRUMBS-IN-POCKETS And me. So you have to guess my name
... Hint: I have a cousin named bread. I was born in a pocket. I
sprinkle all over the table and floor when you eat.

NOIL   Hmmm ...Crumbs?

CRUMBS-IN-POCKETS That's half of my name. The rest is in
my ... *(nears public and pulls at his pockets)* I bet you can't
guess!?

NOIL   Pockets? Crumbs-in-pockets. That's your name.

CRUMBS-IN-POCKETS Hello. That's me. My sister's name is
Crumbs-in-cupboard. My brother's name is Crumbs-in-bed.

NOIL   Aren't you a bit ... large to be a Crumbs-in-pockets?

CRUMBS-IN-POCKETS I was the crumbs in the pockets of a
Giant.

NOIL   Oh. Are there giants here?

CRUMBS-IN-POCKETS *(speaks with terror)* Oh yes. Lots of
them, and other scary beasties and things that hiss and spew and

slither and slobber and scratch and spit. *(begins laughing meanly)*
(Noil backs away from him)

CRUMBS-IN-POCKETS So you better get on home, girlie. You're
wasting my time. Send your brother my way. Then I can get on
with this story.

NOIL   Look. I'm here and I'm all you've got and if you
don't want to use me in your story you can go stuff your crumbs
in whosever pockets you choose because I'm leaving.

CRUMBS-IN-POCKETS So what's your name?

NOIL   Lion. Spelled backwards.

CRUMBS-IN-POCKETS *(strums and sings)*
              Once upon a time
              there was a girl named
              Lion-spelled-backwards.

NOIL   Lion spelled backwards is N.O.I.L. My name is
Noil.

CRUMBS-IN-POCKETS Well, Noil, if you're going to be in this
adventure you'd better get started. You'll have to find your way
home.

NOIL   I know. But how?

CRUMBS-IN-POCKETS Through the magic door.

NOIL   How do I find the magic door?

CRUMBS-IN-POCKETS Ah. That's the adventure. And this is
going to be a very dark, decomposing, dastardly, dimply
adventure.

NOIL   And dangerous?

CRUMBS-IN-POCKETS Maybe you should quit.

NOIL   How else am I going to get home?

CRUMBS-IN-POCKETS Alright. But don't say I didn't warn you.
*(He strums wildly. Then we hear boots marching, heavily. Noil is
frightened and hides)*

NOIL   What's that sound?

CRUMBS-IN-POCKETS That sound? Scared are you?
(We hear Roach's voice commanding off-stage)

ROACH   Tock-tick, tock-tick, tock-tick.
(Crumbs-in-Pockets, suddenly scared, hides behind Noil)

Windows and Doors enter, marching and pulling a large clock behind them.

NOIL *(to Crumbs)* Isn't that clock moving a bit fast?

CRUMBS-IN-POCKETS Time flies.

ROACH *(off-stage)* Tock-tick. Tock-tick. Faster! Faster! Tock-tick.

NOIL   Tock-tick?

CRUMBS-IN-POCKETS Tock-tick.

NOIL   Isn't it tick-tock?

CRUMBS-IN-POCKETS Not for these soldiers.

NOIL   Why are they marching? They don't seem very
happy.

CRUMBS-IN-POCKETS Ask them?

NOIL *(comes out of hiding)* Why are you marching?
(The Doors and Windows keep marching and don't hear her. She has to dodge them so they don't march over her)

CRUMBS-IN-POCKETS *(comes out of hiding)* You see? You're not forceful enough. Where's your brother?

NOIL *(shouts)* Hey you bundle of wood and nails. Noil is talking to you.
(Doors and Windows screech to a halt, banging and clanking into each other)
That's better. Now who are you and why are you marching and pulling that clock?

DOOR ONE   We're the doors ...

WINDOW ONE ... and windows ...

DOOR TWO   ... that must march ...

WINDOW TWO ... as Lord PP commands.

DOOR ONE   PP stole us. Says he owns us.

WINDOW ONE He tore us from our fixtures.

WINDOW TWO Ripped us away from our sills, stole our views.

DOOR TWO   Broke our knockers and bells.

WINDOW TWO We'll probably end up as firewood.

CRUMBS-IN-POCKETS Stop feeling sorry for yourselves. Noil is here to free you.

NOIL   Wait a minute. Why do I have to free them? My parents told me never to stick my nose into other people's business.

DOOR ONE   So you won't help us?

NOIL   Sorry. I have to work on getting home.

WINDOW TWO She won't help us.
(The Windows and Doors begin weeping and wailing. Crumbs cries too)

DOOR ONE *(to public)* Isn't this a sad story? Come on, cry with us. No. No. Don't laugh. Cry! Boo-hoo. Come on. Boo-hoo.

NOIL   Please. Stop crying. *(shouts)* Stop! *(silence)*
I'm sorry you're sad. But it's not my business. Here. Let me dry your ... window panes ... and knobs. *(she wipes their tears)*
Please. Tell us your story.
(Doors and Windows sing their song, Crumbs accompanies them)

> ### Song of Serving and Obedience
> March, March, March
> The windows and doors march
> The Big question is
> Why do they march so much?

CRUMBS-IN-POCKETS *(speaks)* It's really quite simple. Listen up. Hup two, three, four.

ALL WINDOWS AND DOORS *(continue singing)*
>March, March, March
>We must do as we're told
>We must feed PP's fire,
>Because he's always cold!

CRUMBS-IN-POCKETS *(speaks)* How do you get people to do as they're told? Keep them marching. Hup, two, three, four.

ALL WINDOWS AND DOORS *(continue singing)*
>March, March, March
>Raise the flags higher
>If you don't do as you're told
>You'll end up on the fire.

CRUMBS-IN-POCKETS *(sings)* If you *do* what you're told, you'll end up on the fire. *(we hear the sound of a whip)*

Roach enters, carrying a slap-stick which he or she uses to keep the Doors and Windows marching.

ROACH   Tock-tick. Tock-tick. Hey, what's going on here, for bugs sake? You're not allowed to stop marching. Not ever. The clock must turn. Tock-tick, tock-tick. That's it, you wood brains. I've got a good mind to feed you to the termites. *(notices public)* Ah ha. What have we here? More troops to turn the clock? Hmmm. A funny set of doors and windows you are. Where's your glass? Where are your knobs? Well, never mind, as long as you can labour for my Lord I don't care what you look like. Well, don't just sit there. *(shouts)* March! *(slaps the stick)* You all now belong to Lord Principal!

NOIL *(smacks Roach on the head)* Hey you, what do you think you're doing shouting at my friends? You shouldn't be snapping your stick at them but thanking them for coming here to sit and watch you, you mean, horrible, little ... What are you?

ROACH *(sings)* More beautiful than a rose I am.
As nimble as a bee
My voice is sweet as honey
And everyone loves me.

NOIL   Are you some kind of a beetle?

ROACH   Some kind of a beetle? How insulting! *(sings)*
I crawl by night, I crawl by day
I never take a coach
I glisten in the moonlight
I am the majestic -

CRUMBS-IN-POCKETS Roach. He's ... She's ... it's a roach. If
she weren't so big I'd squash her under my boot.

NOIL   Aren't you a bit large for a roach?

ROACH   I have to be big otherwise people like him would
step on me.

NOIL   But why are you forcing the Windows and Doors to
march? Can't you see they're unhappy?

ROACH *(circling Noil)* My, my. You are a bold girl, aren't you?
Have you ever thought of marrying an insect, settling down,
raising a few bugs?

NOIL   Who do you work for?

ROACH   Ah, yes. I work for *the* Lord, *the* master, the Big
Bug. *(slaps her stick at the Windows and Doors)* You! Get in
line!

NOIL   Hey! Why don't you just let them go?

ROACH   Sorry. I can't do it. If I don't do what my Lord says
he'll stick a pin, a long shiny pin, right here, through me belly,
and pin me to his wall with all the other bugs who rebelled.
Grumbly Grasshopper rebelled. Now he's in a glass box. Catarra
Caterpillar rebelled and now he uses her body as a pin cushion.

NOIL   You are a coward, Roach.

ROACH   Yes. I am.

NOIL   I don't like cowards.

ROACH   No-one does. I haven't a friend in the world. My own family spits on my feelers when they pass. Sniff, sniff. Sob, sob.

NOIL   It serves you right.

ROACH   But at least I have a stick! *(cracks it)* And I can make things tock and I can make things tick. Get moving, you pile of splinters!   *(herds the Windows and Doors)*
Take your complaints to my Lord. I've got work to do and time to turn.

Roach marches Windows and Doors off, slapping her stick and shouting her tock-ticks. She slaps Crumbs and Noil on the bottom on her way out.

NOIL   I should talk to this Lord. Maybe he can tell me where the magic door is.

CRUMBS-IN-POCKETS You'll have to call his magic name.

NOIL   What's his magic name?

CRUMBS-IN-POCKETS P.P.

NOIL   P.P.?

CRUMBS-IN-POCKETS Yes. Lord P.P.

NOIL *(calls)* Lord P.P. Where are you?

CRUMBS-IN-POCKETS Not like that. Like this: Loooorrrrrdddd PPPPPPPPPPPPPP.

NOIL   He's not coming. Maybe we're not loud enough. Do you think they might help?

CRUMBS-IN-POCKETS No harm in trying.

NOIL *(to public)* Listen, I need to see Lord P.P. because he has got the Windows and Doors enslaved and I have to tell him to set them free. Could you help me call him? Like this: Looooorrrddddd PPPPPPPPPP! Ready?
Loooooooorrrrrrrdddddddd PPPPP PPPPPPPPP!

There is a crash of thunder, lightning. Lord PP enters, in quasi-military dress, followed by a figure dressed as a Mirror. The Mirror will stand to the side of Lord PP and imitate PP's gestures, just as a mirror would.

PP   What? Who? Where? *(booming voice)* Who called me down here? It's freezing!

NOIL AND CRUMBS *(in their fear they point to the public)* They did!

PP   You did? *(now speaks gently to public)* Hello. Hello. My name is Lord Principal Plagueworthy. Some people call me Lord PP. I'm not sure if that's good or bad. Brrrr. It's freezing here.

NOIL   Excuse me, but I need to ask you to

PP *(interrupts)* Please. I don't like questions. Don't you realise who I am? I am very important and very rich. In short, I am - *(takes out a sign from his coat that has V.I.R.P. written on it.)*

CRUMBS-IN-POCKETS A Virp?

NOIL   What's a Virp?

PP   Not a Virp. A V.I.R.P. A Very Important Rich Person. This is my mirror. *(he blows on the Mirror and polishes it with his sleeve)* Whenever I forget how important I am, which happens quite often in fact, I just look into my mirror and see my important face and I am important once more. My father, Lord Potty Pestilent Plagueworthy - that's three P's - when he died, he left me all of this. I own everything, from my castle up there, right down to the pebbles under your feet, including the people, their houses, their children's potties. *(snatches the guitar from Crumbs)* That's mine too. Everything in its proper place; that's two P's. Yes. I have a big job. A really big job. Do you know why? Because I have to spend all my time convincing people like these that it's fair! *(begins to cry)*

NOIL   Why are you crying?

PP   Whenever I speak about myself I'm moved to tears.

NOIL   I'm sorry.

PP *(suddenly forceful)* Ha! You certainly will be. You're just like the others. That's my problem. I call it my Pesky People Problem. That's three P's. *(beat)* You, Crumbs-in-socks, Crumbs-in-clocks, whatever your name is, hanging about and doing nothing all day, get down on your hands and knees and act this story for me or I'll feed your guitar to the fire.
(Crumbs gets down on all fours and acts out PP's lines, which may be miming the action of the words. These are spoken, rather than sung)

> The people cut the wood
> They sow the crops, just like they should
> They harvest their labour
> They hammer and glue
> It's all very hard work and backbreaking too
> They sweat and sweat and sweat
> and I get and get and get.

(Crumbs collapses. PP tears a button from Crumbs's shirt)
Whatever they make. Hmmmm. Nice button.
(Lord PP steps on and over Crumbs's body and the Mirror follows) It's not unfair. In my very important opinion, I'm always cold and getting colder all the time. I need tons of wood to keep my fire burning. My fireplace is as big as a house! Since I've chopped down all the trees in my forest -

NOIL *(interrupts)* You've started using the windows and doors as kindling.

PP   Exactly. And now the Pesky People are complaining that they're freezing because I've taken all their windows and doors. *(to public)* Hey, what are you all staring at, you preposterous pip-squeaks? I've a mind to get you all marching. Yes, yes. Lots of troublesome little pesky people out there. Strong little legs! Hmmmmm. Maybe ...

NOIL *(steps on and over Crumbs, who is still lying on the floor)* Look here, Lord PP, the Doors and Windows aren't yours. Thief! *(she bumps him on the nose)*

PP   Oh my. Another rebel. *(circles her)* But, you're not a boy.

CRUMBS-IN-POCKETS That's what I said.

PP   No. You're a girl. A rebellious girl. Doubly dangerous. Maybe even triply dangerous. *(to Crumbs)* What's her name? *(Noil shakes her head for Crumbs not to tell)*

CRUMBS-IN-POCKETS I'll tell you if I can have my guitar back. *(Lord PP snaps his fingers and the Mirror gives the guitar back)* Noil. Her name is Noil. *(to Noil)* Sorry, but I can't sing without my guitar.

PP   Noil. That's lion, spelled backwards. I like it. Well, Noil, if you're a girl then you must marry. *(he suddenly drops to his knees, Mirror does the same, imitating him)* Will you, Noil, marry me, Lord Principal Plagueworthy? You will have gold and diamonds. You will have an enormous castle to live in, to sweep and clean. You will have an enormous oven to cook in.

NOIL   Are you crazy?

PP   I beg your pardon?

NOIL   I wouldn't marry you if you were the last PP on earth!

PP   But you can't say no. I'm rich and important, etcetera, etcetera, remember?

NOIL   I've got better things to do than wear your jewels and sweep your kitchen.

PP   But all girls want to marry.

NOIL   Who says so?

CRUMBS AND PP *(they point at each other)* He did!

NOIL   Look. I fell through a hole in my jumper and I'm late for school. I have to find the magic door so I can get home. I'm an adventurer, not a marryer.

PP   Then I'll just have to throw you on my fire with the rest of the rebels.

CRUMBS-IN-POCKETS Come on, Noil. All adventure stories end with the girl getting married off.

PP   I'll let you stare into my mirror all day long ... You know ... 'Mirror, Mirror, on the wall, who's the fairest' and all that sort of thing.

NOIL   No.

PP   In twenty-four tock-ticks I'll be back for your answer. I'll marry you or use you for kindling. Either way is fine with me. BBBBrrrr. I'm freezing. Come along, Mirror. It's time for your polish.

PP exits. The Mirror remains, weeping.

NOIL   Why are you crying?

MIRROR   Because I don't have a face. Everyone has a face but me. Look. What do you see when you look at me?

NOIL   I see my face.

MIRROR *(to Crumbs)* What do you see when you look at me?

CRUMBS-IN-POCKETS My ... handsome face.

MIRROR *(sings)* **The Song of the Missing Face**
                    I don't have a face, my head feels like a hole
                    All the faces of Lord PP have scared away my soul

                    In me the world's reflected
                    and it makes me feel dejected

                    Maybe it sounds silly, but I don't want to gaze
                         through glass
                    Always staring at PP's face is a pain in the ...
                    (points to bottom, but doesn't say 'ass')

How will I find a dignified place
without a recognisable face?

MIRROR *(to public)* What do you all see when you look at me?
You see? Everyone sees their face but me when they look at me.
Where is my face? I have no face. Hoo-boo. Hoo-boo.

NOIL   Excuse me. Isn't it boo-hoo?

MIRROR   Thank you. Boo-hoo. Boo-hoo.

PP *(offstage)* Mirror! Hurry up. I need to look at myself.

The Mirror exits, hurrying.

NOIL   Crumbs-in-Pockets. I have to find my way home.
Isn't there something I can do like guess a riddle or kill a dragon?

CRUMBS-IN-POCKETS Oh, I nearly forgot! There are three and a
half things you need to do before you can go home.

NOIL   Crumbs-in-Pockets! What kind of a storyteller are
you if you forget the most important part?

CRUMBS-IN-POCKETS *(to public)* A crumby one?

NOIL   Tell me the three things.

CRUMBS-IN-POCKETS Three and a half things. Ready?
(strums wildly on the guitar)
Number one: You must steal the feather from PP's hat.
Number two: Make It-nose sneeze.
Number three: Break the mirror.
Number three and a half: Never overlook anything, however
small.

NOIL   Number three and a half? That doesn't sound right.

CRUMBS-IN-POCKETS Look. I didn't write this adventure. Just
play along, will you? Stop asking so many questions. Now, don't
forget any of the tasks or you'll be lost here forever.

NOIL   Three and a half things. *(to public)* Will you help me remember them? *(she recites the list again)*

CRUMBS-IN-POCKETS Got it?

NOIL   Got it. Now for the feather. *(to public)* Will you help me call Lord PP again? *(calls)* Loooooord PPPPPPPPP!

Lord PP enters, followed by Roach.

PP   When will the wedding take place?

NOIL   I won't give you an answer until you let me wear your hat.

PP   I can't let you wear my cap. It holds the magic feather.

NOIL *(to public)*   I've got to get that feather!

PP *(as he speaks Noil jumps up and down behind him but can't grab it as he's too tall or keeps moving)* And this magic feather is the only one left in the Kingdom. I had all the other ones burned. Do you know why? Ha! None of your business why.

NOIL *(to public)* I can't get it. He's too tall. Maybe if I can get him to sit down. *(beat)* Lord PP? I hear you can jump higher than anyone in the Kingdom. But I don't believe it.

PP   You don't? Watch this. *(with great seriousness, jumps, once, in the air)*

NOIL   I've seen bugs that can jump higher than that!

PP   Roach! Hoist me! *(Roach stands behind Lord PP and puts her hands on his waist. When he jumps, she helps lift him. Noil urges PP to jump even higher)*

NOIL   Higher! Higher!
(PP finally collapses, exhausted. Noil grabs the feather)

PP   Whew! I think I broke the PP family record for high-jumping. *(to Roach)* To the castle, Roach, for a nap. *(to Noil)* Then I'll be back for your answer.

Roach and Lord PP exit while Roach is speaking.

ROACH   You, know, I really think we should watch out for her. She's a bad bug. I bet her parents were spiders.

NOIL   Well, Crumbs-in-Pockets, I got the feather. *(she puts the feather in the pocket of her overalls, so that it is still visible)* Now for the second task: Make It-nose sneeze. But who is It-nose?*(Crumbs shivers in fear)* Who is It-nose?
(Crumbs backs away) Why are you so scared?

CRUMBS-IN-POCKETS Everyone is scared of It-nose.

NOIL   But why?

CRUMBS-IN-POCKETS Because It-nose everything and everyone. That's why it's in exile, because It-nose.

NOIL   Because it knows what?

CRUMBS-IN-POCKET I just told you. It knows everything. That's why Lord PP made It-nose go far away.

NOIL   Where does It-nose live?

CRUMBS-IN-POCKETS In the horrible, dark forest. The Nosey Forest. But first you have to find the Echo path that leads to the forest and to It-nose.

NOIL   How do I find Echo Path?

CRUMBS-IN-POCKETS You don't find it. It finds you. Just repeat after me:

> Forest, Forest, dark and scary
> With your boney trees so hairy
> Noil must enter, like a breeze
> Find It-nose and make it sneeze

It starts to get dark.

NOIL   Crumbs-in-Pockets?

CRUMBS-IN-POCKETS Nope. This is where I exit. This is your
adventure.

He exits.

NOIL   Crumbs-in-Pockets! Don't leave me alone!
(shadows of trees around her) Don't leave me alone. *(suddenly
her words echo)* Crumbs-in-Pockets! Come back! *(beat)* Hey, I
think I found, found, found it. But it's so dark, dark, dark. I can
hardly see, see, see. *(she crawls along the path)*
How will I know, know, know, when I'm there, there, there?
(she bumps into something) Ouch! I bumped my nose! *(the echoes
have stopped)*

IT-NOSE *(we hear It-nose's voice in the dark. It-nose is very ill-
tempered)* Of course you bumped your noses. You bumped your
noses on my nose.

*Lights up and It-nose is visible. It-nose is a figure whose head is all
nose. It-nose speaks with an abundance of 's' sounds in the words.*

NOIL   Oh! My, what a big ...

IT-NOSE   Don'ts say it! Don'ts say it! 'My, what a bigs noses
you have.' Can't anys of you be a little more originals? Now go
aways. Who gave you permissions to enter nosey forests? Get
outs! Get outs! Get outs!

NOIL   Why are you so angry?

IT-NOSE   Because Lord PPs was afraids of me and he brokes
my sneezer and now I'm defencelesses. What is a noses without
its sneezer?

NOIL   But why is Lord PP afraid of you?

IT-NOSE   Because I knows all about the things he burnses and
hows he's rich because he steals from the poors. I knows he's

bads and should be eaten up by worms. I knows and so I knows too much. If onlys my sneezer weren't broken I'd sneezer him all overs that castle of his.

NOIL   Well, you're in luck because I'm here to make you sneeze. It's my second task. If I don't make you sneeze then I won't be able to find my way home.

IT-NOSE   Leave me alones. You're not smart enoughs to makes me sneeze.

NOIL   Have you tried pepper?

IT-NOSE   Of course I have, and dust and mothballs and pollen.

NOIL   Have you tried a tickle?

IT-NOSE   No I haven't tried a tickle?

NOIL   May I? *(Noil tickles It-nose's nose)* Tickle, tickle, tickle. *(It-nose begins to respond, takes a deep breath and almost lets out a sneeze but the sneeze dies)*

IT-NOSE   Nope.

NOIL   How about this? *(Noil grabs It-nose by the nose and blows on it like a trumpet. It-nose begins again to sneeze but the sneeze dies again)*

IT-NOSE   See? You can'ts do it. You're just likes the others. You're not using your noses.

NOIL   Of course I use my nose. *(sniffs)* I have a very good nose for smelling.

IT-NOSE   Not that nose. Your other nose. *(to public)* Do you know where your nose is? Go on. Points to it. Not that nose you silly sneezers, but your noses. The knows here *(taps head)*. The nose above your noses. Inside your heads.

NOIL   Look, if you're so smart, then how come you lost your sneezer? Give me that nose of yours. *(She grabs it and hangs on)* I'll make you sneeze. *(she spins It-nose in a circle)*

IT-NOSE   Helps. Let go. Ah! My noses!
(Noil quits in frustration. She sits down)

NOIL   I can't make It-nose sneeze. I'll never get home.

IT-NOSE   My poors, poors noses.

NOIL *(to public)*   That's it! Lets use our noses, here, *(points to head)* to figure this out. What can we use to make It-nose sneeze? Think. Think. *(while she thinks, she uses the feather to scratch herself or chew on until the public 'sees' the feather)* The feather? The feather! *(she approaches It-nose who is now fearful and backs away. She runs at It-nose)* Charge!

Noil tickles It-nose's nose. It-nose begins to gasp and pant, preparing for a sneeze. There is a chaotic ruckus of It-nose gasping and gulping air. And then suddenly there is a moment of silence before It-nose lets loose a tremendous sneeze. The wind from this sneeze is loud and throws Noil to her knees.

Now the Windows and Doors enter, battling the wind that is slowing down their march, slowing down the clock until all the Windows and Doors collapse in a heap, exhausted. The wind stops. The clock stops. Silence for some moments.

IT-NOSE *(no longer speaks with extra 's' sounds. It-nose is 'cured')* Has anyone got a tissue?

NOIL   Look! The clock has stopped. You don't have to march anymore!

WINDOW ONE We don't ...

WINDOW TWO ... have to ...

DOOR ONE   ... march anymore?

DOOR TWO   You mean we're ...

WINDOW TWO Free?

DOOR ONE   Free?

WINDOW ONE Free?

NOIL   Yes. The clock is broken. You're free.

DOOR TWO   Hip-Hip

WINDOW ONE Hurrah!

ALL WINDOWS AND DOORS Hip-hip-Hurrah!

NOIL   You better hurry on back to your villages, find the houses you were taken from and start building again.

WINDOW ONE Yes. Yes, there's lots ...

DOOR ONE   ... to do.

DOOR TWO Goodbye. Goodbye.

WINDOW TWO But first let's say

DOOR ONE   Goodbye to this!

They all stomp on the clock as they exit, dragging the remains with them.

NOIL   Well, It-nose, now you have your sneezer back and I have only one more task to do before I can go home. Goodbye It-nose.

IT-NOSE   Goodbye Noil. But remember: *(sings)*
(this song might be sung in a Frank Sinatra style, suggesting It-nose's new freedom)

> Don't forget, don't forget
> You've got a nose, above your nose
> Inside your head, the nose that knows
> So let your sneezer show you ...
> ah, ah, ah, Choo.

Now Goodbye. My sneezer is very tired and I have to go rest it.

It-nose exits.

NOIL   And I must get out of this forest.

Noil crawls again. Lights dim on her as she crawls out of the forest and exits. Lights up on Lord PP at another place on the stage. He is shivering.

PP   What's this terrible wind, this preposterous, punctilious wind? That's two P's. It's never been this cold. Time for some more wood for my fire. Roach!

Roach hurries on.

Bring in some more windows and doors. Chop them up. Throw them on my fire. I've never been this cold before.

Roach exits, then returns dragging the broken clock. When PP sees it, he screams.

My clock! What has happened to my ticker?

ROACH   It got tocked.

PP   Who broke it? I'll roast them alive, I'll -

ROACH   A tremendous wind, all in one blow, knocked us all over. But I did my best, My Lord. There were hundreds of them, swarming all over. *(Roach begins to shadow box)* But I swung to the left, and I swung to the right.

PP   Quiet! You piddling, puddling, posthumous excuse for an insect. You were supposed to protect that ticker with your life. Now how will I know what time it is? How will I know what time to go down to the village to break up the houses and throw them on my fire? *(he beats his own head)* Oh my. Oh me. Oh my. Oh me.

ROACH   Excuse me, Lord PP. But isn't it: Oh me, Oh my?

PP   Not any more it isn't! How will I keep my slaves marching in rhythm without the tock-ticks? Oh, I am so angry I have to look into my mirror to believe just how angry I am. Mirror!

Mirror enters.

Let me look at my face. *(does so)* Yes. Still very important. Even without my ticker. Bring in my Windows and Doors. I'm going to break them board from board, crack their panes, pull out their knobs, bend their sills.

ROACH   They've rebelled sir. They've run off.

PP   What?

ROACH   After the ticker stopped, I couldn't keep them in line, no rhythm for them to march to.

PP   There is only one wind that could have stopped my clock. It-nose's wind. But that's impossible. Only my magic feather can make It-nose sneeze and I have that feather right here. *(feels his hat, then both PP and the Mirror scream at the same time)* Thief! Who stole my feather!

NOIL *(jumps out of hiding, with Crumbs behind her)* I did. And I made It-nose sneeze.

ROACH   I told you she was a bad bug.

NOIL   And now the clock is stopped and the Windows and Doors have rebelled.

PP   Oh, oh, oh, oh. I am mad. I am so mad. So mad.

CRUMBS-IN-POCKETS *(shoves Mirror aside and poses as PP's mirror, whispers)* Just how mad are you, Lord PP?

PP   I'm so made I could ... I could ... *(turns to mirror, sees Crumbs-in-Pockets' face as a reflection of his own image and screams in fright)* AAAhhhh! Whose horrible furious face is that in my mirror? *(Mirror pushes Crumbs away and takes up its proper place beside PP)*

NOIL *(to public)* And now I have to do task number three.

PP   Why I've never seen such a horrible face? Get out of my mirror you horrible face! I want to look at myself, not you!

NOIL   Let's see. I had to break something but I've forgotten what I had to break.

CRUMBS-IN-POCKETS *(whispers to Noil)* Better hurry up.

PP   And not only is it a horrible face, it's an ugly face, a face that no-one would listen to, a face that no-one would obey.

NOIL   I know, let's use our noses to figure this out. *(to public)* Was is a plate? A cup? Can you remember?

CRUMBS-IN-POCKETS *(whispers)* Break it! Break it!

PP *(still shouting at the mirror)* Get out of my face, you ugly, mean face!

NOIL *('hears' the public give her the answer)* That's it. The Mirror! Break the Mirror! *(she raises her fist to strike Mirror, but she freezes and speaks to the public)* But I can't break this mirror. It's not mine. I was told it's bad luck. But my noses tells me I must. Oh, I can't. It's none of my business. But my noses is telling me that maybe we have to break things so that things change. And a change is needed. So I must! *(she breaks the Mirror)*

ROACH   Oh, oh, oh, oh, oh.

MIRROR *(removes the remaining bits of mirror from its face and we now see the Mirror's real face for the first time)* Hello? Hello? *(Mirror feels its own face)* What's this? It's my face. I have a face! Everybody look! I have a face. *(runs to Noil)* What do you see when you look at me?

NOIL   I see your face.

MIRROR *(runs to public)* And what do you see when you look at me? Oh, I'm so happy! Ee-yip! Ee-yip! Ee-yip!

ROACH   Hey, you, isn't it Yip-ee?

MIRROR   Each to one's own, I say. Finally I have my own face. And a very good face it is.

PP   And now I have no mirror. What will I look into when I need to remember how I'm a very important and pretty person? That's still two P's, isn't it? *(he weeps)* Now I'm a nobody. I have no order, no clock, no slaves, no mirror. *(collapses in a heap on the stage)*

Doors and Windows enter, decorated with balloons and party things. They are loud but become quiet when they see the group surrounding the weeping PP.

DOOR ONE   Well I never thought -

WINDOW ONE I'd see the day

DOOR TWO   ... when old Potty PP head ...

WINDOW TWO ... would break down and cry

DOOR TWO   I suppose he's got a heart ...

WINDOW ONE ... after all.

NOIL   He's crying because he can't be a mean, horrible Lord anymore.

CRUMBS-IN-POCKETS He's upset because now he's one of us.

PP   That's right. Now I'm just like the rest of you. Hoo-boo. Hoo-boo. Wait a minute. Is that true? Am I just like the rest of you?

NOIL   Of course you are.

PP   Just like the Pesky People? Then it only follows that I have the same rights as the rest of you.

CRUMBS-IN-POCKETS Oh?

PP   And that means I don't have to live in that freezing castle and chatter my teeth all day and night. That means I can live in a little house like the rest of the Pesky People.

DOOR ONE   Just like ...

DOOR TWO   the rest

WINDOW ONE of us.

PP   But can I at least keep my name?

NOIL   That's up to the Windows and Doors.

PP   Well?

WINDOW ONE *(they huddle to discuss it)* He can keep ...

WINDOW TWO the P's ...

DOOR TWO   but he'll have to drop ...

DOOR ONE   the Lord bit.

NOIL   Take it or leave it.

PP   Drop the Lord in front of my P's? Then I'd only be
Principal Plagueworthy. Ugh. An ugly short name. How about
Pesky Portable Peter? *(they all respond with variations of
'Alright', 'OK', 'I suppose so' etc.)*

MIRROR   Then we'd better be going.

PP   Do you think I could have just a small, small mirror
over my mantelpiece?

Windows, Doors, PP, and Mirror exit, discussing the possibilities.

MIRROR   Well, I have this cousin ...

CRUMBS-IN-POCKETS Well, Noil. I guess the adventure is over
and it's time for you to go home.

NOIL   Yes. I did the three tasks. I stole the feather, made
It-nose sneeze, and I broke the mirror. Now where's the magic
door?

CRUMBS-IN-POCKETS Close your eyes. *(to public)* You too.
Close your eyes and repeat after me: Magical door, magical door,
magical door. Poof ... poof ... poof ...

NOIL   Crumbs-in-Pockets, nothing is happening!

CRUMBS-IN-POCKETS Hmmm. *(beat)* Poof ... Poof ... Poof? It
always worked before.

ROACH   Excuse me, I was wondering what's in this all for
me? The Windows and Doors are free, It-nose found its sneezer,

the Mirror found her face and PP's got a new name. But what about me? What do I get?

CRUMBS-IN-POCKETS Go catch a bug. Can't you see we're busy here?

ROACH   But I am a bug. That's my problem. No-one wants to be friends with a bug. *(she cries)*

NOIL   Stop that, Roach. If you were a little kinder and stopped ordering people around you'd find a friend.

ROACH   Would I?

CRUMBS-IN-POCKETS Might take you a few hundred years.

ROACH   Would you be my friend, Noil?

NOIL   I can't. I don't make friends with bugs.

ROACH   Well, then I guess I'll just go away, maybe sell my body to science. Goodbye ... cruel world ...

NOIL   But I might consider it.

ROACH   Would you?

NOIL   Can you play games? Build a tree house? Do a somersault dive?

ROACH   I can learn!

NOIL   Alright. I'll be your friend. *(when Noil says this we see magical light and the magic door appears)* The magic door! So that's what we forgot. The half! The Three and a half: never overlook anything small. That's you, Roach.

CRUMBS-IN-POCKETS But I wouldn't call him small. Maybe I should change the wording to: never overlook anything, however buggish?

NOIL   Well, this is goodbye. I'm going home.

CRUMBS-IN-POCKETS Goodbye Noil.

ROACH   Wait! Can I come with you?

CRUMBS-IN-POCKETS Sorry, Roach, only Noil can go through the magic door. You belong here.

ROACH   But how will I learn to jump rope if I don't go with her?

CRUMBS-IN-POCKETS Tough crumbs, old bug. Goodbye Noil!

NOIL   Goodbye!

She steps through the magic door and disappears.

ROACH   Wait!

Blackout. We hear Noil struggling in the dark.
Lights up on Noil struggling with her huge jumper.

NOIL   What? This jumper is still stuck on my head? Aaaaaaarrrrrgggghhhh! *(fights angrily with it)*

PARENTS' VOICES Hurry up Noil. You'll be late for school.

NOIL   Aaaaaaarrrrrggggggghhhhhh! Wait a minute. I know I can do it. I just have to take a moment and think, use my knows, careful, think ... They're shouting at me again, telling me to do this, do that. Think Noil. Be calm. I don't want to get lost again. Use your knows. There! *(her head pops through the neck opening)* At last! I'm back!

PARENTS' VOICES Hurry up, Noil. You'll be late for school!

NOIL   I'm ready! *(beat)* Mother, Father, I fell through a hole in my jumper, and I freed the Windows and Doors and I made It-nose sneeze!

PARENTS' VOICES Stop day dreaming, Noil. Come here this instant.

NOIL *(to public)* Day dreaming? Was it all a dream? But what about my new friend, Roach? *(calls softly)* Roach? Roach?

Silence.

NOIL   Well. Maybe it was just a dream after all. I mean, who ever heard of a girl's best friend being a roach?

PARENTS' VOICES Noil?!

NOIL   Coming!

She exits. We hear something clanking then panting. Roach enters, crawling with a piece of the magical door dragging behind her.

ROACH   Magical Door! Magical door my bug bottoms. What kind of magical door collapses just when you're crawling through? *(looks around)* Where's Noil? *(to public)* Did any of you see a girl pass by this way? Which way did she go? Noil? Wait for me!

Roach runs off calling.

CRUMBS-IN-POCKETS *(strums the guitar and enters stage)* And so my friends, that concludes the story of the girl who fell through a hole in her jacket.

NOIL *(offstage)* Jumper, you silly old Crumbs-in-Pockets. The girl who fell through a hole in her jumper.

CRUMBS-IN-POCKETS And so my friends that concludes the story of the girl who fell through a hole in her jumper. So remember: *(sings)*

> If you're always being told what to do
> If you're feeling like a window or a door
> If you're about to cry 'boo-hoo'
> Don't forget, Don't forget -

All cast enter and sing the last part of the song together.
You've got a knows, above your nose
Inside your head, the nose that knows
So let your sneezer show you ...
Ah, ah, ah choo.

NOIL   Make sure you practice that.
ALL   Bye!

Lights down.

End.

Naomi Wallace and Bruce McLeod

Naomi Wallace's latest play is entitled *Pope Lick Creek*. Bruce McLeod is the co-author with Naomi Wallace of *In the Sweat* in the anthology *New Connections* (1997) Faber.

The Search for Odysseus

by Charles Way

The Search for Odysseus.

The play is about a teenage boy searching for a lost Father - its theme is modern and yet timeless. Based on Homer's epic journey poem, *The Odyssey*, in which Odysseus is forced by an angry God to take a long route home after the Trojan war. I have always loved this story; the magic islands with sexy goddesses, fights with one-eyed giants, and sea monsters from the wine dark sea. It's like science fiction from the past. Odysseus' ship could be the 'Starship Enterprise' and Captain Kirk is not unlike Odysseus, a great warrior, a lover of women and above all, a wily fox, a survivor.

There is however, a dark side to the tale, and the nature of Odysseus'character is an ambiguous one. How much does Odysseus really want to get home - perhaps the life of an adventurer has got to him? How heroic are his survival skills, since he seems to leave murder and mayhem wherever he goes? His inquisitive nature, the desire to see over the next horizon can be seen as the proper quest for Western Civilisation to expand its knowledge of the world, but at what cost to others? Homer stresses that Odysseus wants to get home - it's the Gods and Goddesses who stop him - whereas Penelope his wife must use subterfuge not to have other relationships, fending off the advances of a band of suitors. This seems like double standards, ready-made to fit the moral world of Homer's audience. When Odysseus finally returns home, he is justified in slaughtering in the most horrific way, all those who wanted her for her palace and land. Odysseus does not even spare his female servants; all are killed in a terrible revenge.

An appropriate start to working on this play would be to study the differences between my story and the original, and ask what the changes mean. Firstly, the son Telemachus becomes the main character - this is a story about a boy growing up. What kind of man will he be? His Mother, Penelope is not the all-faithful, all-forgiving wife, and Odysseus his father has been degraded by war rather than ennobled. In essence these characters are not ancient but modern and the challenge facing Telemachus is the same challenge facing any young person today; to know oneself and to overcome the obstacles the world throws in the path of this most perilous journey.

Charles Way

The Search For Odysseus

by Charles Way

Nominated as Best Play for Young People by the Writers Guild ('95)
First produced by *Made in Wales* Theatre Company at the Sherman
Theatre, Cardiff in 1994, it will be premiered in Dresden, Germany
in March 1998.
Directed by Jamie Garven.
Assisted by Gilly Adams.
Designed by Jane Linz Roberts.
Music by John Harding.

Telemachus	Robert Harper
Athene	Linda Quinn
Penelope	Janys Chambers
Eurymachus	Simon Walters
Odysseus	Simon Armstrong
Eurycleia	Louisa Eyo
Alcinous	
Laodomus	
Cyclops	
Achilles	
Calypso	
Arete	
Nausicaa	
Messenger	

Cast / Chorus / Calypso's helpers

(The play can be performed by 6 actors doubling)

ACT ONE

Music. Athene, Daughter of Zeus, enters dressed as a beggar.

ATHENE   Once upon a time in the land of Greece,
                    On an island called Ithaca
                    there lived a man named ...

CAST   Odysseus.

Enter Odysseus.

ATHENE   Odysseus was the King of Ithaca,
                    a brave man, a good man
                    and when his country called him to war
                    he put on his bronze armour
                    picked up his sharpened spear
                    and led his men down
                    to the long black ships
                    which lay in wait on the cold tide
                    and his wife wept to see him go.

A light rises on Penelope who holds a baby in her arms.

PENELOPE   My husband.

ODYSSEUS   Penelope.

PENELOPE   Please do not go.

ODYSSEUS   I have no choice.

PENELOPE   Your son, your son.

ODYSSEUS   I'll be home before he's a year old, I promise.

PENELOPE   You promise?   *(silence)*

ODYSSEUS   If I don't come back by the time my son has grown his first beard then consider me as dead and marry again, if you wish, a younger man.

(The cast representing soldiers and people of Ithaca, laugh at this last remark)

PENELOPE   You are my husband. How can you joke at a moment like this?

ODYSSEUS   Because it won't happen. I'll come home to you and to my beloved Ithaca. I shall see the smoke rising from the chimney and my son will run down to the harbour to greet me.

PENELOPE   Not if he's only a year old my husband.

ODYSSEUS *(he smiles)*   Within a year the bell will ring out with news of our victory.

A WOMAN   Look - Odysseus.

Music. Then as if in the sky above the harbour, a small sparrow is chased and crushed in the talons of an eagle. This may be represented through percussive sound.

A SOLDIER   What does it mean Odysseus?

ODYSSEUS   It's a good omen my friends. The sparrow represents our enemy, the Trojans. We the Greeks are the eagle. We will crush the enemy in our mighty talons, win the war and be home for supper.

ALL   Odysseus!

(Odysseus kisses Penelope with love and passion and then he holds up his baby son)

ODYSSEUS   My son, listen for the bell, then I will come home with my arms full of gold, treasures, beyond your wildest dreams - and all for you.

ATHENE   And with these words, brave Odysseus, good Odysseus, set sail for a distant land far across the wine dark sea.

CAST   Odysseus - Odysseus.

Exit Odysseus. Penelope stands looking out to sea.

ATHENE   And his son saw him go but did not understand the meaning of the horizon.

PENELOPE   Hush, hush little one, your father will be home soon, home soon, home soon.

(The music continues low and foreboding containing a sense of the war far away)

ATHENE   But the war did not last a year or even two, or three, or four, or five, or six or seven or eight or nine and all the long years Penelope waited. And her son grew tall, and his name was, Telemachus.

CAST   Telemachus.

Enter Telemachus as a ten year old boy. He comes on brandishing a sword fighting an invisible enemy. Eurymachus, his mother's suitor, watches him from the shadows.

TELEMACHUS Odysseus the hero and his friend the angry Achilles are in a tight spot. Back to back they face one hundred Trojans. The Trojans charge. The swords of the heroes never cease - blood and limbs fill the air - the Trojans die horrible deaths. *(this he acts out)* At last there are only two men left standing, Odysseus and Achilles - but then an arrow flies. *(he falls)*
'My heel my heel' the hero cries, and as he dies he calls out. 'Farewell Odysseus, farewell - my friend'.*(as Achilles, he dies. Eurymachus applauds)*

TELEMACHUS What do you want?

EURYMACHUS The other lads are playing in the courtyard, why don't you join them? *(he picks up Telemachus' sword which is wooden)*

TELEMACHUS Give my sword back.

EURYMACHUS A fine sword.

TELEMACHUS Give it back.

EURYMACHUS I came to talk to you - about your mother.

TELEMACHUS One day, my Father will come home and cut your head off.

EURYMACHUS Here, let's play together, you and I. *(he offers Telemachus his sword back)*

TELEMACHUS I don't want to play with you.

EURYMACHUS Don't be rude, Telemachus.

TELEMACHUS It's my house, I'll be rude if I want.

EURYMACHUS Come let's spar together like Father and Son. *(he throws down the sword which Telemachus picks up)* Come attack me. *(he walks towards Telemachus who is very scared)* We're only playing aren't we? *(Telemachus drops his sword. Eurymachus then puts his own sword against his throat)* Understand this Telemachus. I wouldn't let a man live who spoke to me as you have spoken to me. But you are not a man -

TELEMACHUS My father ...

EURYMACHUS Your father is dead.

TELEMACHUS No - no.

EURYMACHUS And I will marry your mother.

TELEMACHUS No! *(Eurymachus removes the sword)* My father is alive. He will come home and sweep you from the house like so many dead leaves.

EURYMACHUS Perhaps it would be better for your mother if he were dead. Have you thought of that? Or are you too young to understand? Love can grow cold you know.

(A bell rings)

TELEMACHUS The bell. There must be some mistake. *(pause)* It still rings.

Penelope enters.

PENELOPE   Telemachus. The war. The war is over. *(she embraces her son)*

TELEMACHUS *(turns to Eurymachus)* Now, now we shall see. My father will have your head.

Enter Eurycleia.

EURYCLEIA My lady. A messenger is at the gate.

PENELOPE   Let him in, let him in - no wait. Give him food and drink. We must not forget ourselves.

EURYCLEIA Yes my lady.

PENELOPE   It doesn't seem possible and yet the bell still rings. Is it really true do you think?

TELEMACHUS   It must be. It has to be. *(they embrace again)*

Enter Eurycleia.

EURYCLEIA The poor man will not eat. He will not drink but begs to see you now.

PENELOPE   Then let him in, no wait - let him bathe and give him clean clothes ...

TELEMACHUS Mother.

PENELOPE   Yes - let him in - let him in.

Eurycleia exits momentarily and she and the Messenger enter.

MESSENGER My lady, I see by your smile the news has younger legs than me.

PENELOPE   It's true then.

MESSENGER As true as I stand here. The war with Troy is over! *(silence)*

PENELOPE   Good. And - did we win?

MESSENGER *(laughs)*   Aye. Troy is no more than dust. Its men are dead, the women and children sold into slavery. *(Penelope nods, unsure how to react)*

TELEMACHUS My father?

MESSENGER Your father is safe and well. I saw him set sail for home in his own ship with twenty trusted men.

TELEMACHUS *(punching the air)* Yes! Yes!

MESSENGER Brave Odysseus. We all rejoice to speak his name. Not a single Greek would be home yet but for him. Your husband's wits have saved us all.

TELEMACHUS How? Tell me everything in every detail? Mother?

PENELOPE   Yes - go on.

MESSENGER Odysseus of the nimble wits is what we call him now for he devised a plan so clever, so full of cunning. Under his orders we made it seem as if the war had broken all our hearts. For ten years we had camped outside the city walls of Troy and won nothing but wounds and grey hairs. Great warriors like Achilles had been killed, so our giving up was not hard for the Trojans to believe. One morning as they awoke they found the field of battle empty, our camp fires out, our ships gone. They cried out in joy, 'The Greeks have fled, we have defeated them!', not knowing that all our soldiers armed and ready to kill were hiding on an island just a few miles away. The Trojans came out of the city and danced in and out of our empty tents. 'Here camped the merciless Achilles, there the clever Odysseus'. Now gone it seemed, all gone except an offering that we had made to the Gods and left behind.

TELEMACHUS What kind of offering?

MESSENGER A horse. A huge wooden horse. It was made from sawn firwood, and its belly was a cavernous womb large enough to hold twenty soldiers armed to the teeth. Your father was among them.

TELEMACHUS Inside the belly of the wooden horse.

MESSENGER The Trojans in their joy pushed the horse through the gates of their mighty city and for the first time in ten years, after all the wasted blood of the battlefield, by one trick we too were inside. All night the Trojans drank and danced and when at last they fell asleep your father, your husband, glad to be free, led out his men with stealth. He slew the sentry with one silent blow.

TELEMACHUS Yes!

MESSENGER Opened the gates of Troy from the inside and the whole of our army, bristling with knives and swords poured in under cover of darkness.

TELEMACHUS And then?...

MESSENGER *(pause)* And then the moon hid her eyes. No tongue can describe the terrible slaughter of that night.

TELEMACHUS How many did my father kill?

PENELOPE Telemachus!

TELEMACHUS My father is a soldier, and a hero amongst men. They should call him a God.

MESSENGER Aye many of the common soldiers do for he has brought us home and we are glad.

PENELOPE Messenger. Thank you. Where is the fleet that brings my husband home?

MESSENGER There was a storm just a few miles from the coast of Troy which scattered the fleet, so each ship will make its way alone. Your husband's ship was among the fastest. The first mast on the horizon should belong to him and you.

PENELOPE Eurycleia, bring the Messenger some food now. He will stay with us tonight.

MESSENGER My lady, I will resist. I have a son who was just a few days old when the war began. I haven't seen him for ten years, and I've another day's walk to my farm, before I do.

PENELOPE May the Gods bless you.

MESSENGER And your house.

Exit Messenger.

PENELOPE Ten years? Why not ten months, ten days, ten minutes?... *(Eurymachus goes to comfort her)*

TELEMACHUS Leave her alone.

PENELOPE Telemachus, go and prepare to meet your father. Go on.

Exit Telemachus.

EURYMACHUS I'm glad the war's over Penelope.

PENELOPE Yes. Perhaps you should leave before my husband comes home.

EURYMACHUS Are you ashamed?

PENELOPE No.

EURYMACHUS Then I'll stay and greet him.

Music. A fanfare.
Telemachus enters wearing a fine robe.
Eurycleia enters and gives Penelope a fine robe also.

TELEMACHUS Mother! There are ships on the horizon. Can you see them?

PENELOPE *(gently)* Yes, I see them.

ATHENE One by one the ships sailed home from war returning swiftly on the welcoming tide. Husbands and wives, fathers and sons were reunited. Each day another boat came home.

TELEMACHUS Sailor, have you seen my father's ship?

SAILOR   No master, but he should be close behind.

TELEMACHUS He will come home now won't he mother? Now the war's over.

ATHENE   Each day mother and son gazed out to sea until all those who had escaped sheer destruction, either by land or sea came home, all but one man alone.

CAST   Odysseus.

TELEMACHUS Father! Father! Where is he? What could keep him?

PENELOPE   The sea.

TELEMACHUS No! *(he calls out again)* Father! *(silence)*

Exit Telemachus. Penelope goes to a large spinning wheel. She begins to spin and to sing.

PENELOPE   Many years I have waited
     On this cold, lonely shore
     Many tears I have wasted
     for a man and his war.
     Now my eye has forgotten
     the shape of his face
     The sea has devoured him
     and left me no trace.

(She continues to spin indicating that she has become withdrawn and introspective. Eurymachus watches her)

ATHENE   Again the years passed by, and at fourteen years old, Telemachus showed the first signs of his first beard.

Telemachus enters, once again he fights invisible enemies.
Eurymachus enters.

EURYMACHUS Come on Telemachus - we're only playing aren't we? *(Telemachus drops his sword and Eurymachus smiles)* It's past your bedtime - Telemachus. Go on. *(Telemachus picks up his sword and goes to his bed. He plays with a wooden horse from which soldiers descend)*

EURYMACHUS *(goes to Penelope)* Penelope? *(silence)* Penelope.

PENELOPE   Yes?

EURYMACHUS Have you spoken to your son yet?

PENELOPE   What about?

EURYMACHUS About the matter we discussed.

PENELOPE   I've been busy.

EURYMACHUS So I see. *(pause)* What are you making?

PENELOPE   I'm not sure. It will turn into something eventually.

EURYMACHUS Why don't you speak to him tonight? *(silence)* Penelope?

PENELOPE   Mmm?

EURYMACHUS We must move forward, with our lives together. If we wait any longer I fear ...

PENELOPE   *(sharply)* For what? For whom?

EURYMACHUS For you. Every day you sit and spin not knowing what you make. Each day your mind travels to some dreamland where I cannot follow. *(pause)* Penelope, do not waste your life. The time has come for you and your son to accept that Odysseus is dead. Drowned at sea.

PENELOPE   I have not heard that.

EURYMACHUS How would one hear it? Unless the sea spoke. He is drowned and all his men too.

PENELOPE   But still, we don't know that for sure, do we?

EURYMACHUS Penelope, I am a man, alive. I am here. I have been here through all your loneliness.

PENELOPE   Yes, you've been here, Eurymachus, eating his oxen, drinking his wine, sitting in his chair. *(pause)* I'm sorry ... I ...

EURYMACHUS If by any chance your husband still lives, he has deserted you and your son. *(he grabs her arm)* All that I have waited for is mine. *(he lets her go realising he has said too much. Penelope starts to unravel her work)* What are you doing? Stop. Stop. *(pause)* Are you sick?

PENELOPE   So many died in that long war, Eurymachus. So many.

EURYMACHUS But your work is all undone.

PENELOPE *(she smiles)* I can make it again, it's easy.

He backs away. Then sees Eurycleia has been watching. He exits. Eurycleia takes a small chain from around her neck. On it is a small bottle which she now gives to Penelope. Telemachus throughout this scene has been playing in his bedroom. Telemachus stands on the bed, sword in hand.

TELEMACHUS   Odysseus the hero and his friend the angry Achilles are in a tight spot. Back to back they face one hundred Trojans ... *(he then sits dejected)* Odysseus and Achilles. *(he lies back on the bed)*

Suddenly there is a crack of thunder. A change of lighting produces a dark stage. A savage wind blows. Telemachus screams and retreats to the top of his bed holding a pillow in front of him. Two masked soldiers enter - in dance - and then face each other.

TELEMACHUS *(in hope)*   Odysseus and Achilles ...
(another crack of thunder, then the two masked soldiers begin to fight)
No! No!
(Spears and shields clash violently against each other then suddenly Odysseus falls. Achilles stands over him spear raised for the kill - silence. Telemachus lifts the pillow over his head. While he is thus hidden the dream vanishes. It is his bedroom again. He lowers the pillow. Breathing heavily he lifts himself from the side of the bed. An arm shoots out and grabs his ankle. He screams)

ATHENE   Nasty dream that one.

TELEMACHUS Get away from me.

ATHENE   You were crying out in your sleep - but you're awake now.

TELEMACHUS Get out. Get out.

ATHENE *(emerges from under the bed. She is disguised as a beggar, a boy, about the same age as Telemachus)*   Ssh - you'll wake the whole house.

TELEMACHUS Who are you? What are you doing in my bedroom? What are you doing under my bed? Mother!

ATHENE *(pounces on him and puts her hand across his mouth)* No! Be a good boy now - *(she pulls out a dagger and lets him go)*

TELEMACHUS What do you want?

ATHENE   Food. I haven't eaten for three days.

TELEMACHUS Why not?

ATHENE   Because I've had no food stupid.

TELEMACHUS Don't call me stupid. I'm not stupid. How did you get in here?

ATHENE   The window.

TELEMACHUS Are you a murderer?

ATHENE   No.

TELEMACHUS A thief?

ATHENE   No.

TELEMACHUS A beggar?

ATHENE   Yes - now get me some food. I beg you.

TELEMACHUS Beggars don't beg with knives - you're a liar, and a thief. Mother!

ATHENE *(knocks him down)* Cry out once more and I'll think you're scared of me.

TELEMACHUS I'm not scared of anything.

ATHENE   Not even dreams?

TELEMACHUS Dreams are different.

ATHENE   To what?

TELEMACHUS Get out! Get out! Get out! *(pushes Athene away)*

ATHENE   I thought the son of Odysseus would have a little more heart, but perhaps I was under the wrong bed. Perhaps you're not his son at all. Let me see - no - you don't remind me of Odysseus one little bit.

TELEMACHUS   Who are you? *(silence)* You've seen my father? Where?

ATHENE   Food first. I'm not used to hunger you see, and it's driving me crazy.

TELEMACHUS Alright. Wait.

ATHENE   Don't ring the bell - raid the kitchen.

TELEMACHUS I don't have to raid the kitchen. This is my house.
(he rings a small bell - Athene gets under bed again)

Enter Eurycleia.

EURYCLEIA Yes Master?

TELEMACHUS Eurycleia. I feel hungry, I'd like some bread. And cheese.

EURYCLEIA Yes Master. *(she turns away)*

ATHENE   And pickle.

TELEMACHUS And - pickle.

EURYCLEIA Pickle? You don't like pickle.

TELEMACHUS Well - I'll be adventurous.

EURYCLEIA You? You alright Master?

TELEMACHUS Yes I'm fine.

EURYCLEIA Only you're not very adventurous as a rule.

TELEMACHUS Please ...

EURYCLEIA A picky little eater ...

TELEMACHUS And hurry.

EURYCLEIA Very well master. *(she turns to go)*

ATHENE   And some olives.

EURYCLEIA Pardon?

TELEMACHUS Olives.

EURYCLEIA *(suspicious now)* Anything else?

TELEMACHUS No - thank you.

ATHENE *(comes out from under the bed)* So you're a picky little
    eater?

TELEMACHUS How do you know my father?

ATHENE   Unadventurous as a rule. *(he grabs Athene)*

TELEMACHUS Answer me.

ATHENE   Let go. *(he lets go)*
    I lent him something once, on the field of battle.

TELEMACHUS You were at Troy?

ATHENE   Yes. I lent him something and he didn't give it back.

TELEMACHUS What? What did you lend him?

ATHENE   After the city of Troy fell, its men killed and all the women and children sold into slavery, I stowed away on board your father's ship, thinking I would get my ... things back.

TELEMACHUS What things?

ATHENE   A few miles from the coast of Troy, there was a storm. Plank separated from plank and ditched us all into the sea.

TELEMACHUS What happened to my father?

EURYCLEIA *(off)* Master, yer cheese and pickle.
(Athene hides under the bed)

TELEMACHUS Come in.

Enter Eurycleia.

EURYCLEIA Are you alright Master? I thought I heard voices.

TELEMACHUS You should see a doctor about that. They can do wonders nowadays.

EURYCLEIA Don't be cheeky.

TELEMACHUS I'm sorry.

EURYCLEIA I'm not in the mood. I'm all nerves. What with yer mother an'all.

TELEMACHUS What's wrong with her?

EURYCLEIA And pickles? Not like you at all. And cheese you know will give you bad dreams. *(he takes the plate and puts it on the floor. Athene's hand shoots out and the plate vanishes)*

TELEMACHUS Well - I - um have had bad dreams. Even tonight I dreamt I saw my father and his friend Achilles - but they began to fight each other. It was terrible and Achilles was about to kill my father when the vision disappeared and I awoke. What do you think it means?

EURYCLEIA Nothing. Dreams? Load of rubbish.
(The plate has reappeared empty)
You shouldn't eat so fast. Give ee stomach ache.

TELEMACHUS I was hungry.
(She turns to go and then turns back with an anxious look)

EURYCLEIA Oh master - I'm worried for your mother. All day she sits and spins and all night she unravels every inch. Her mind's disordered and I'm not sure what to do. But you're too young.

TELEMACHUS Too young? For what?

EURYCLEIA This house gives me a bad feeling of a sudden, like something dark is about to happen. So be ready Telemachus.

TELEMACHUS Ready for what?

EURYCLEIA I feel sure that good times will visit this house again - one day. One day. *(Athene belches from under the bed)*

TELEMACHUS Pickles.

Exit Eurycleia. Athene comes out from under the bed and flops on to it groaning.

ATHENE   Oh - Oh that hurts most wonderfully.

TELEMACHUS Get up, get up. What else about my father? Are you telling me you saw him drowned?

ATHENE   No - I saw him floating away on a casque of wine. Clutching my things and grinning like a cat. You must follow him, follow and find him.

TELEMACHUS Follow where? I can't. I'm ...

ATHENE   Too scared?

PENELOPE *(off)* Telemachus. Telemachus.

TELEMACHUS My mother. *(Athene gets back under the bed)*

Penelope enters.

PENELOPE   Eurycleia tells me you've been having bad dreams again.

TELEMACHUS Yes. I'm alright now.

Eurymachus enters but stands in the shadows unseen. We also are aware of Eurycleia watching.

PENELOPE   Would you like me to tell you a story? Jack the giant killer? The witch in the woods?

TELEMACHUS I'm too old for those stories.

PENELOPE   Too old? *(pause)* My son, I need to talk to you about Eurymachus.

TELEMACHUS I don't want to talk about him.

PENELOPE   We must.

TELEMACHUS Just get rid of him, throw him out.

PENELOPE   I can't, I can't.

TELEMACHUS Why? *(silence)* Do you love him?

PENELOPE   No - I fear him, and you must fear him too.

TELEMACHUS Why did you ever let him stay then? Why did you let him step foot in our house?

PENELOPE   I needed someone. He was there, that's all. Don't think badly of me.

TELEMACHUS But it's father you love - isn't it? *(silence)*

PENELOPE   How can I answer? He's been gone, fourteen years.

TELEMACHUS But you love him don't you. Don't you?

PENELOPE   Telemachus. We must face the truth now. Either your father is dead ...

TELEMACHUS No. No. He's alive. I know it. Don't believe anything else, and you'll wait for him won't you? As long as it takes, for my sake. Won't you? Won't you?

PENELOPE   Listen to me. Eurymachus wants to be the King of Ithaca. To be that he must marry me. He has waited and grown sour and mean in waiting. He will wait no longer. If I don't agree to marry him, he will kill you. I know it, I can see it in his eyes. *(silence)*

TELEMACHUS If you marry him - I will never speak to you again.

PENELOPE Telemachus.

TELEMACHUS Go away. Or promise me, you won't marry him. Promise me! Promise me! Promise me!

PENELOPE I promise.

Enter Eurymachus with his sword drawn.

EURYMACHUS You're a little viper aren't you?

PENELOPE Eurymachus! Please.

TELEMACHUS Get out of my room.

EURYMACHUS I will marry your mother. I will have the palace and the vineyards that once belonged to your father. I will be King of Ithaca. *(he holds the sword to Telemachus' throat and stares at Penelope)* Marry me!

TELEMACHUS You promised. *(Penelope drinks from the small bottle given to her by Eurycleia)* Mother? *(she falls)*

EURYMACHUS Penelope? Penelope? No - I - wake up. Wake up, I beg you. *(he turns back to Telemachus who is too shocked to move)* This is your fault. You have kept her from her happiness! *(he advances on the boy)*

Enter Eurycleia.

EURYCLEIA I have seen. I have heard everything.

Eurymachus exits.

TELEMACHUS Mother? Mother?

EURYCLEIA Ssh now. It's alright. It's alright.

TELEMACHUS Is she dead?

EURYCLEIA No. She sleeps that's all. A sleep that looks like death.

TELEMACHUS How? Why?

EURYCLEIA To save you and herself from Eurymachus. This potion I prepared for her myself - we knew this day would come.

TELEMACHUS Mother?

EURYCLEIA She will not wake until I give her the opposing medicine.

TELEMACHUS Then give it to her now.

EURYCLEIA No. Eurymachus thinks her dead. Now he will seize the house by force - no one will oppose him. You must escape. Escape.

ATHENE *(has now come out from under the bed and is watching the scene)* Escape. Find your father, and bring him home. He'll know what to do with Eurymachus.

EURYCLEIA Who's this?

ATHENE   A friend.

EURYCLEIA Find your father Telemachus. Go in search of him.

TELEMACHUS I can't - how?

EURYCLEIA If you stay, Eurymachus will kill you when my back is turned.

ATHENE   There's a boat in the harbour that sails on the morning tide - we'll stow away.

EURYCLEIA I'll look after your mother - now go - go.

TELEMACHUS But - I - I've never been more than a mile from shore.

EURYCLEIA Have courage - go with your friend - whoever he is. *(he hugs Eurycleia)* And come safely, with your father. Good luck Telemachus son of Odysseus and Penelope. Good luck.

Exit Telemachus and Athene.

ACT TWO

It's dark. Telemachus sleeps. As Athene raises the sails she sings.
Note: the song should have a wistful air.

ATHENE   Unfurl the sails for the wine dark sea
Unfurl the sails and set me free
tomorrow I sail
tomorrow I'll be
under the stars
on the wine dark sea.
No cross gales, no rocks
No current I fear
If the Gods sail with me
I'll come home my dear
back to the land
of my birth one day
to kiss and make up
in the time-honoured way.

All exit leaving Telemachus asleep. Athene on watch. We hear the
wind. Dawn breaks.

ATHENE   Telemachus. Wake up now. It's nearly day.

TELEMACHUS *(half wakes)* I heard singing - singing ...

ATHENE   Wake up Telemachus.
(She throws some water over him. He stands shocked)

TELEMACHUS Why's the floor moving? Where am I?

ATHENE   You're at sea. On board a ship.
(Telemachus stares out at the sea)

TELEMACHUS The sea? It's a dream - it's a dream ship!

ATHENE   It's no dream.

TELEMACHUS No? Then where are the sailors? Where's the steersman? Where's the Captain? Ha!

ATHENE   They got off.

TELEMACHUS Got off?

ATHENE   They went ashore, got drunk and didn't come back. Rather than miss the tide I - I cast off.

TELEMACHUS You mean ...

ATHENE   We drifted out of the harbour, a stiff breeze came by - I unfurled the sails and - away ... On the open sea, the wind in our hair. The salt on our skin. Hungry? *(he looks in disdain at the food)* People on adventures have to eat what they can find. One of the sailors must have left it behind.

TELEMACHUS *(he won't eat)* This is - awful - this is - we could get killed - drowned.

ATHENE   You can drown in the bath Telemachus.

TELEMACHUS I don't want to drown, anywhere. I want to go home. Where are we going? Who sets our course?

ATHENE   Your father.

TELEMACHUS Why? How? What do you mean?

ATHENE   On the night before the storm which wrecked your father's ship I overheard him talking to his men. He asked them if they would follow him on a great adventure.

TELEMACHUS Follow him? Where?

ATHENE   West and west again to the edge of the world. 'West and west again,' - those were his words.

TELEMACHUS But I don't understand, surely he was on his way home?
(Silence)
What are you called?

ATHENE   Mentor. At your service master!

TELEMACHUS You said you gave my father something on the battlefield at Troy.

ATHENE No, I lent him something. It was a loan.

TELEMACHUS What kind of a loan?

ATHENE The kind you give back.

TELEMACHUS Why didn't he?

ATHENE That I hope to find out.

TELEMACHUS With my help?

ATHENE Two heads are better than one, ask any monster. (*she dances. He stares out to sea open-mouthed*)

TELEMACHUS Mentor. Mentor!

ATHENE Where did that come from?

TELEMACHUS I - it just came out of the water ...

ATHENE A whole island?

TELEMACHUS We're heading straight for it.

ATHENE We are - at a rate of knots. Do you know how to change course?

TELEMACHUS Yes but I - I can't do it on my own - it's a combination of sails and oars - there isn't time. (*they take down the sails*)

ATHENE It just came up - out of the water?

TELEMACHUS Yes. Yes I told you - we're going to hit it. We're going to hit it smack on.

ATHENE Maybe we'll hit a beach.

TELEMACHUS Maybe we'll hit a rock.

ATHENE Then I suggest we jump overboard and swim for shore. What do you think?

TELEMACHUS I think I can't swim.

ATHENE You don't have to swim - just relax, let the waves take you ashore.

TELEMACHUS Waves? What waves?

ATHENE   Are you ready?

TELEMACHUS Wait. Wait.

ATHENE   What?

TELEMACHUS If I should drown, tell my mother.. I - I ...

ATHENE   Tell her what? What?

TELEMACHUS That I - I can't think.

ATHENE   You can't think? You can't swim. What are you - a pebble?

TELEMACHUS Tell her I love her and - and I - wish that ...

ATHENE   I understand - are you ready to jump?

TELEMACHUS Yes.

ATHENE   Steady ...

TELEMACHUS Wait - wait.

ATHENE   For what? We're going to hit the rocks.

TELEMACHUS Tell my father ... if you find him.

ATHENE   What - tell him what? For God's sake.

TELEMACHUS Tell him I ... I ... I'm sorry.

ATHENE   Sorry for what?

TELEMACHUS I don't know - just tell him.

ATHENE   Tell him yourself - are you ready?

TELEMACHUS No.

ATHENE   Good - Jump! Jump!

*There is a climax of sound as they jump into the water. Blackout.
The sound of waves gradually takes the place of the sound of the
ship hitting the rocks. This becomes a gentle sound, a soft lull of
waves and eerie music. When the lights rise again the scene is a
plush green tropical island, very mysterious and in total contrast to
the colours of Ithaca. Telemachus and Athene lie prostrate as if*

washed up on the beach. Calypso the Goddess of the Island watches them unseen.

ATHENE   Telemachus? Telemachus?

TELEMACHUS Am I drowned?

ATHENE   Possibly.

TELEMACHUS The ship?

ATHENE   Gone. *(sits up)*

TELEMACHUS My clothes, they're dry.

ATHENE   Mine too.

TELEMACHUS Perhaps then we are drowned. Oh Gods. Are we dead Mentor?

ATHENE   Do you feel dead?

TELEMACHUS No - but then, what place is this if not heaven?

ATHENE *(to audience)* All about a deep wood grew
with summer leaves, alder and black poplar and
pungent cypress.
Ornate birds here and there
rested their stretched wings.
The scent of thyme and cedar smoke
hung heavy in the air.
Four springs of clearest water
shallow and clear
took channels through lovely beds
of violets and tender parsley.
Even a God who found this place
would gaze and feel her heart
beat with delight.

TELEMACHUS Unless - of course - this is a supernatural place - a place of magic. Hark. Someone is singing? Did you hear? They've stopped now. *(he picks up a stick to defend himself)* Mentor, someone approaches.

ATHENE   I hear them.

VOICE OF CALYPSO Who are you? Why have you come to my Island?

ATHENE   Say something.

TELEMACHUS I am Telemachus, son of the Godlike Hero Odysseus, for whom I search.   *(silence)*   Where are you? Show yourself. One name deserves another.

ATHENE   Well said master.

TELEMACHUS Show yourself.

A wolf enters and its growl is full and threatening.

TELEMACHUS Mentor!

ATHENE   I see it. I see it.

TELEMACHUS What shall I do?

ATHENE   Ignore it.

TELEMACHUS What?

ATHENE   Ignore it - it's not there.

TELEMACHUS But it is there - look - look!

ATHENE   Don't look at it. Don't! It'll take your look as a challenge. Look away. Act superior, feign indifference. It's not a threat. It's nothing. Has it gone yet?

TELEMACHUS I don't know I'm not looking. *(it growls)* It's still there. Shall we run?

ATHENE   No! Speak to the voice.

TELEMACHUS Voice. Is this your creature?

VOICE   Yes. Yes. Yes.

TELEMACHUS I will kill it with my bare hands if I have to *(pause)* and ... and this stick! *(he looks at Mentor and grimaces. She throws him her knife)* I mean this knife.

CALYPSO *(laughs)* Oh Telemachus. I am this creature.
(he looks at the wolf, which then stands and becomes Calypso the Goddess of the Isle. A mature woman)
Welcome Telemachus. Son of Odysseus. And who is this - little one - with the grey eyes?

ATHENE   I am one to be scared of.

CALYPSO   Really. *(a net falls onto Athene)*

ATHENE   Let me go. *(she struggles in vain)*

TELEMACHUS Let him go. Let him go - or you'll live to regret it.

CALYPSO   Indeed - one who lives forever as I do lives to regret everything.

TELEMACHUS Let him go!

CALYPSO   Him? I see no him. I see a her. Tush, tush, have you been keeping secrets little one?

TELEMACHUS What?

ATHENE   I'm a girl - what difference does it make?

CALYPSO   All the difference in the world my dear.

TELEMACHUS A girl?

CALYPSO   So upsetting isn't it, when things aren't what they seem? Never fear - I am exactly what I seem.

ATHENE   Exactly.

TELEMACHUS Who are you?

CALYPSO   I am Calypso, the Goddess of the Isle, which is called Ogygia. How did you come here?

TELEMACHUS By ship.

CALYPSO   Where is your ship?

TELEMACHUS On the rocks.

CALYPSO   Oh no - so you're stranded. Tush, tush - What have you done Telemachus - to anger Poseidon the great God of the Sea, that he should try to drown you?

TELEMACHUS Nothing.

CALYPSO   Something. You must be thirsty - after all that salt he threw at you.

ATHENE   Don't touch the drink.

CALYPSO   And hungry too.

ATHENE   Or the food.

CALYPSO   Do you like pork?

TELEMACHUS Yes - I -

(Calypso points towards Athene in the net who is transformed into a pig)

TELEMACHUS No - No - Mentor. Mentor.

CALYPSO   She understands you. Her flesh is that of a pig but her brain is her own. To be all pig would be no torture at all.

TELEMACHUS Fiend - demon - witch!

CALYPSO   Your father called me sweeter names by far.

TELEMACHUS My father? You've seen him?

CALYPSO   Yes. He was here weeping like a child on this very sand. But sand has a way with tears.

TELEMACHUS When was this?

CALYPSO   Yesterday perhaps, or the year before. I can't remember.

TELEMACHUS Where did he go? Where is he now?

CALYPSO   Come share my table and I will speak of him.

A table magically appears with food.

TELEMACHUS Return my servant to his - to her own form and I'll sit with you.

CALYPSO   *Sit! (he sits)* Why do you seek your father?

TELEMACHUS I ... My mother needs him.

CALYPSO   Ah sweet Penelope. He often talked of her. So feminine, so doting, domestic and sacrificial. No wonder he didn't want to go home.

TELEMACHUS *(stands)* My mother is worth a thousand of you - whoever, whatever you are.

CALYPSO   Forgive me. I forget how high emotions can run in a child. Have something to eat you'll grow more quickly.

TELEMACHUS I'm not hungry.

CALYPSO   Telemachus. Let us be friends - yes?

TELEMACHUS My servant.

CALYPSO   Can wait.

TELEMACHUS How long was my father here?

CALYPSO   Long enough to tire of me, but it wasn't thoughts of home that took him away. It was something else altogether.

TELEMACHUS What could keep him from our home? Tell me.

CALYPSO   He has a craving to see over the next hill. A restless itch to rove and rummage through the world. A common fault in mortal beings but understandable since mortal beings never know when life will end. I who am immortal have no desire to look over the next hill at all. Perhaps I'm just lazy. Still I enjoyed his stay, and I think he did too.

TELEMACHUS Why don't you just say it. You and he were...

CALYPSO   Were?

TELEMACHUS Close.

CALYPSO   As the folded wings of a butterfly. Don't judge him too harshly. He suffered a long hard war, and after all a man alone on an island with an irresistible Goddess ... Tea?

(He takes some drink)

CALYPSO   Oh Telemachus. I'm so glad you came to visit. I lost a man and found a child.

TELEMACHUS I'm not a child.

CALYPSO *(smiles)* I've often wondered what it would be like to be a mother. Is it tremendously hard work do you think?

TELEMACHUS I don't know.

CALYPSO   No? Still - it would provide one with a purpose I suppose - drink up. *(he drinks more. The drink is lovely)* Why do you search for your father Telemachus?

TELEMACHUS I - I told you -

CALYPSO   Do you wish to be like him?

TELEMACHUS Yes, I think so.

CALYPSO   Then let me be your Tutor, stay with me a little while. The woods will be your playground. The creatures will call you by your name and the streams will flow at your command. *(he is quite drugged by now and she has begun to crawl wolf-like up the table towards him)* I will give you knowledge you cannot dream of. Stay with me Telemachus and you will never grow old.

TELEMACHUS *(dreamily)* But I want to grow old - no, no, I want to grow up.

CALYPSO   Up? Up is very overrated. Oh Telemachus it would be such fun to have a child around the place.

TELEMACHUS I'm not a child.

CALYPSO   A boy, a youth.

TELEMACHUS What have you done?

CALYPSO   Ssh. *(she strokes him - he is drugged)* Why do you search for your father?

TELEMACHUS I - I told you -

CALYPSO   Tush, tush - tell me the truth.

TELEMACHUS Where are you?

CALYPSO   I'm here - inside your dreams. Telemachus.

HELPERS   Telemachus.

TELEMACHUS Mother? Is that you?

CALYPSO   My son - don't leave me.

TELEMACHUS I must - I

CALYPSO   Please don't leave me here, all alone.

TELEMACHUS But I have to go.

CALYPSO   Your father has gone to the edge of the world.

HELPERS   Too far - too far.

TELEMACHUS I'll bring him home, I promised.

CALYPSO   You're so scared, so frightened.

TELEMACHUS Yes.

CALYPSO   Don't leave me then - stay.

TELEMACHUS No.

CALYPSO   Tush tush - don't you love me Telemachus?

TELEMACHUS Yes. Yes.

CALYPSO   If you love me, stay with me. Don't desert me as
your father did. You're not like him, are you? Stay and be my son
- for ever.

TELEMACHUS *Mentor!*

CALYPSO   Ssh. I will comfort you as I did when you were a
child.

CAST   Give up your search.

CALYPSO   My son.

CALYPSO/HELPERS The woods will be your playground. The
creatures will call you by name. The streams will flow at your
command.

CALYPSO   My son.

TELEMACHUS Yes. Yes. Yes.

CALYPSO   Yes - Oh Telemachus - welcome - it will be so nice
to have your company. *(a momentous hush. The Helpers gaze on
expectantly)* One kiss from my lips and you will be young -
forever. *(she bends to kiss him. He stabs her. She howls.
Telemachus slumps to his knees. We hear whispered voices
saying:'My son, my son' - and he faints)*

*Lights fade to darkness as the beautiful music of the island returns.
The lights slowly rise as if the dawn is breaking. The dense suffoc-
ation of the previous dark scene is now beautifully contrasted.
Telemachus and Athene, no longer a pig, lie sleeping. Telemachus
wakes clutching his head.*

TELEMACHUS Oh - I'll never drink again - Mentor?

ATHENE *(wakes with a start)*   Ah! What am I?

TELEMACHUS Yourself.

ATHENE   God of Gods - I thank you. Where is she?

TELEMACHUS I don't know.

ATHENE *(shudders)*To be human is bad enough, but to be a human
inside a pig is - disgusting. What happened?

TELEMACHUS I'm not sure - I had a terrifying dream.

ATHENE   I told you not to drink that stuff.

TELEMACHUS I remember now - I think - I killed her. *(he hears
the Voice of Calypso laughing)* Where are you?

*After a moment Calypso enters carrying some gifts of food and
drink.*

CALYPSO   Good morning.

TELEMACHUS What do you want?

CALYPSO   To say goodbye.

TELEMACHUS We can go?

CALYPSO   Of course. You made your decision last night. *(she
brings out a magnificent golden sword)* It seems I cannot keep
you here, anymore than your father. Heaven knows I tried. This
was his sword. It's yours now.

TELEMACHUS My father's?

CALYPSO   Yes.

TELEMACHUS *(he does not take the sword)* He left it here.

CALYPSO All the gentlemen who come here leave their swords, so that I may remember them. I've quite a collection, all shapes and sizes.

TELEMACHUS My father is a soldier. He wouldn't leave his sword. You've killed him haven't you, with your magic, like you tried to kill me?

CALYPSO Take the sword.

TELEMACHUS No.

CALYPSO Please, do not upset me.

ATHENE Take the sword Telemachus.

TELEMACHUS She tried to kill me.

ATHENE *(pulls him to one side)* If she wanted to kill you - you'd be dead. Take the sword. *(he pulls away)* You cannot refuse the gift of a Goddess.

TELEMACHUS My father -

ATHENE Your father lives, and that's his sword. Believe me - I know. This was the sword he used in the final battle at Troy. I saw him. Take it or I will take it.

TELEMACHUS *(takes his sword)* How will you remember my father?

CALYPSO *(laughs)* Oh you're so young. Here's some food for your journey and the raft is yours.

TELEMACHUS It hardly looks safe.

CALYPSO It's like the one your father left in. He built his own.

TELEMACHUS I can build a raft as well as he.

CALYPSO Beware of Poseidon - if the God of the Sea is angry with you - he will ditch you into the deep no matter what craft you sail in.

TELEMACHUS We're safe then, because I have done nothing to anger the God of the Sea.

CALYPSO   Not you perhaps - but your father? I have prepared
this for you. If you are thrown into the sea, drink it - it will give
you the strength to reach land.

TELEMACHUS Thank you.

CALYPSO   Oh Telemachus - you have turned your back on a
long and luxurious life. For what? To follow the wake of your
father's ship? Be careful where it leads.
(Athene and Telemachus get on the raft)
Farewell Telemachus, Son of Odysseus and Penelope.

Music and lights change. The raft is at sea.

ATHENE   The Goddess conjured a warm land breeze to blow
and with joy Telemachus shook out the sail
glad to be on his way. He leant on the oar
steering night after night, unsleeping,
watching the stars.
He drank a dusky wine
which the beautiful Calypso had given him
and for seventeen days and nights he sailed
away from the island of Ogygia,
West and West again -
following his father
To the Edge of the World.

Music - Telemachus and Athene both sleep.

CAST *(sing)*   Telemachus, Telemachus
On the wine dark sea
Sailing westward,
Ever westward.
To the Edge of the World.
Telemachus, Telemachus ...

Telemachus dreams: Odysseus and Achilles enter as in Act One, and repeat their fight sequence. Telemachus turns in his sleep, murmurs 'Stop-stop'. As before the fight reaches a climax where Odysseus falls and Achilles raises the spear for the kill.

TELEMACHUS No! *(wakes)*

ATHENE *(wakes)* Ah!

The dream/vision fades. She jumps up with a start nearly falls in the sea. He catches her, stands for a second holding her, then lets go.

ATHENE Another dream? *(Telemachus nods)* As before?

TELEMACHUS Yes, but it makes no sense.

ATHENE It's a dream. That's all -

TELEMACHUS But my father and Achilles were great friends. Why should they fight?

ATHENE *(hands him some food)* Here. Eat more, dream less.

TELEMACHUS I'm not hungry.

ATHENE As far as I've observed, half the joy of being human is in the eating. *(she eats merrily, while Telemachus stares out to sea with a fixed expression)* What now?

TELEMACHUS You should have told me.

ATHENE Why does it bother you? Half the world is female you know.

TELEMACHUS Friends should be honest with one another that's all.

ATHENE Are we friends?

TELEMACHUS What could you - a girl - have given my father on the battlefield of Troy? What were you doing there in the first place? What are you doing here on a raft on the open sea - with me?

ATHENE   You really are a picky eater.

TELEMACHUS Tell me the truth! Who are you?

ATHENE   Mentis is the female version of Mentor.

TELEMACHUS Mentis?

ATHENE   Call me Mentis.

TELEMACHUS Why can't you tell me your real name? Why are you so secretive?

ATHENE   When you find your father, I will get my real name back - along with the rest of my things. Until then my real name is lost to me - and to you.

TELEMACHUS Why do you need me to get your things back? Why didn't you just go off and find my father on your own?

ATHENE   I have a father too you know, and he told me to find you and urge you on your journey and for me to go with you. It's my punishment.

TELEMACHUS Being with me is your punishment?

ATHENE   In a way.

TELEMACHUS For what?

ATHENE   The things I lent your father on the battlefield of Troy were originally a gift from my father to me.

TELEMACHUS And he was angry when you gave -

ATHENE   Lent.

TELEMACHUS When you lent these things to my father. *(Athene nods)* So then. Who is *your* father?

ATHENE   Before you can open the gate Telemachus, you have to walk down the path -

TELEMACHUS You are infuriating.

ATHENE   I know. I know. You really should eat something.

TELEMACHUS I'm not hungry. *(silence)*

ATHENE   Telemachus?

TELEMACHUS What?

ATHENE   Have you ever kissed a girl? *(he looks at his feet)*
I said ...

TELEMACHUS I know.

ATHENE   Well?

TELEMACHUS It's none of your business. *(she stands)*
(As this is going on, an image of Poseidon appears, large and dominating, as if rising out of the water behind them - they continue oblivious)
What are you doing?

ATHENE   You don't have to kiss me if you don't want to. Do you want to?

TELEMACHUS *(shakes his head)* Yes.

ATHENE   Are you sure?

TELEMACHUS It's just that - I wasn't expecting this - on a raft.

ATHENE   It's alright - no-one's looking. *(by this time the image of Poseidon looms over them. As they are about to kiss, he lets out a thunderous roar. They turn, see him and scream)*

ATHENE   Poseidon!

The raft is split in two - and Athene and Telemachus drift apart. Thunder and lightning.

ATHENE   The potion, drink the potion - she gave you.

TELEMACHUS I can't find it.

ATHENE *(it's on her side of the raft)* I've got it - I've got it.

TELEMACHUS You drink it - it'll give you the strength to reach land.

ATHENE   No - you drink it. *(she throws it across the sea to him. He drinks it)*

The stage goes dark. Mentis has gone. The sound reaches its climax.

TELEMACHUS Mentis - Mentis - Mentis ... *(his voice trails away)*

Blackout.

ACT THREE

Nausicaa.
Lights rise. The stage is empty but for a bush behind which Tele-machus hides, because he's naked. He had been washed ashore on the Island of Phaecia where Alcinous is King and Arete his wife, Queen. Their daughter Nausicaa now enters with her brother Laodomus.

LAODOMUS We ought to be getting back.

NAUSICAA   Why? - it's the best part of the day. Here catch. *(she throws a ball to her brother)*

LAODOMUS Nausicaa.

NAUSICAA   Well come on - throw it back.

LAODOMUS We're not children anymore. *(he puts the ball down)*

NAUSICAA   No.

LAODOMUS Let's make a move.

NAUSICAA   What's the matter, are you bored?

LAODOMUS I don't like coming here - and you know why.

NAUSICAA   Well I do.

LAODOMUS Forget him Sister.

NAUSICAA   Have you forgotten him?

LAODOMUS I'm going home.

NAUSICAA   Perhaps if I sit here for a while the sea breeze will blow him from my mind.

LAODOMUS Nausicaa. Look what I've found. *(he picks up Telemachus' trousers which have been washed ashore)* And here's something else. *(Telemachus' shirt)* You shouldn't stay here on your own.

NAUSICAA Don't worry so much - they're just rags. You go back Laodomus. I'll follow in a little while.

LAODOMUS It's getting cold. *(he leaves her his cloak)*

NAUSICAA You're such a gentleman these days. Whatever happened to my horrid brother?

LAODOMUS *(throws the trousers and shirt at her)* He's still here. *(laughs)* Don't be long.

He exits.

NAUSICAA *(sings)* As I was out walking one morning in May
I saw a young sailor and this he did say
Come to me now and be my dear wife
an' I'll love you truly, all of my life.

TELEMACHUS *(as she finishes the song, he looks up from behind the bush)* Excuse me.

NAUSICAA Laodomus, Laodomus.

TELEMACHUS Please - don't be frightened, I mean you no harm.

NAUSICAA Who are you? Why are you spying on me?

TELEMACHUS I'm not, I'm not.

NAUSICAA Then why are you hiding behind that bush?

TELEMACHUS This isn't what it looks like.

NAUSICAA No?

TELEMACHUS I'm not spying on you. I've been shipwrecked.

NAUSICAA There are no signs here of a shipwreck.

TELEMACHUS It was a small craft - broken in two by the great God of the Sea. It's probably been washed up on another part of the island. Is this an island?

NAUSICAA   What are you hiding behind there?

TELEMACHUS Nothing - whatsoever.

NAUSICAA   Then come out - with your hands up.

TELEMACHUS Um ... *(he raises one hand)* Wait one moment. *(he breaks off a branch and then emerges with the branch strategically placed)* I - I wasn't spying - honestly.

NAUSICAA   What happened to your clothes?

TELEMACHUS I - I took them off when I fell into the sea, fearing that they would drag me under. I swam for many hours - and thought I would drown but then I saw the outline of these hills. By the time I reached the safety of this sand I was exhausted and lay down to sleep. I awoke when I heard you singing. I need help.

Enter Athene carrying his sword.

ATHENE   Telemachus. You're alive - and - naked. *(she sees Nausicaa)* Ah.

NAUSICAA   And this is?

TELEMACHUS My servant - Mentis?

NAUSICAA   I am Nausicaa. My father is the King of this land, which is called Phaecia. The Gods deal out fortune to good and bad men as they please. They have sent you hardship and you must bear it, but now that you have taken refuge here you shall not lack clothing or any other comfort due to a poor man in distress. Yours? *(she gives him his trousers and shirt, turns away as he dresses)*

TELEMACHUS What do you think?

ATHENE   Of what?

TELEMACHUS The princess. She's a Princess.

ATHENE *(sarcastic)* How are you Mentis? I'm so glad to see you alive. I feared you were drowned, and I wept all night but when I discovered you were still alive my heart danced with joy!

TELEMACHUS She's beautiful don't you think? Mentis?

ATHENE   You look ridiculous. *(Nausicaa turns and laughs)*

TELEMACHUS My name is Telemachus.

NAUSICAA   You may present your petition to my father.

Music. A fanfare. Enter Alcinous, King of the Phaecians and his Queen Arete, and their son Laodomus. The palace.

THE KING   Rise stranger. Tell us how you came to my kingdom and how I may help you. We are a generous people.

TELEMACHUS My name is Telemachus. I arrived here by the hand of the great Earthshaker Poseidon - who - you see I was given this raft.

ATHENE   Stick to the point.

TELEMACHUS By the Goddess Calypso, who's a wolf actually, on the Island of Ogygia, and she gave me this sword too.

ATHENE   Don't waffle.

TELEMACHUS Poseidon snapped our raft in two like you would a biscuit and I swam ashore as did my servant, who's a girl, actually. *(the King and Queen exchange glances)* And there I met your daughter, Nausicaa - who *(pause)* you see I'm searching for my father.

THE KING   Ah!

TELEMACHUS He's been missing many years and I must find him because an evil man called Eurymachus has taken control of his house, lands and wealth, and I was too young to stop him.

THE KING   What is your father's name?

TELEMACHUS Proudly may I say it and proud I am to be his son for he is a hero of the Trojan War, the Godlike Odysseus.

(the King's expression darkens, he rises)

LAODOMUS Odysseus! *(the King draws a sword and approaches Telemachus. He puts his sword to the boy's throat)*

ARETE   No.

NAUSICAA   No.

ATHENE   No.

THE KING   I would kill you now but for the sound of women's voices, son of Odysseus.

TELEMACHUS *(much to everyone's surprise, he beats back the King's sword with his own)* Your daughter led me to believe you were a civilised people.

ARETE   We are. *(firmly to her husband)* We are! *(he returns to her side)* No sword will leave its scabbard in this chamber. *(silence)* When did you last see your father Telemachus?

TELEMACHUS I've never seen him, except in my dreams. He left for the war when I was an infant.

ARETE   How do you know then, that he is a hero?

TELEMACHUS By reputation, who has not heard how he fought back to back with the great Achilles against a hundred Trojan Warriors? Who has not heard the story of the Wooden Horse?

LAODOMUS   We heard it - many times - from his own lips.

TELEMACHUS He is a soldier beyond compare.

ARETE   We are a sea-faring people Telemachus. Our ships are blessed by the Gods. We love the sports, singing, dancing and the pleasures of our beds. We do not honour soldiers, as other Kingdoms do. War brings out the beast in men, it makes them liars and cheats. In the case of your father it made him a very good one. He lied to us. He cheated us.

TELEMACHUS It is not so. It is not so. *(silence)*

THE KING Your father was shipwrecked on our shore. My daughter found him as she found you, naked and lonely and afraid, although he would not show it. He was older, mature and handsome. A man of the world who spoke sweetly and with confidence. He swiftly saw the admiration in her eyes. He did not say at first who he was or that he was married. Instead he let her fall in love with him, a girl, who's heart was open, tender and easy to abuse. We fed and clothed him, gave him a royal bed to sleep in. I gave him my own golden cup to drink from, and a ship that could sail the sea sightless, with no need of a steersman, a ship blessed by the Gods which always came home to harbour. These things I gave because I thought, as my daughter thought, that at last the sea had brought our royal house a worthy husband. But in his heart he had no love for her and no intention of staying. When he had procured from us all his needs he told her he was married, with a son. We did not expect to meet you Telemachus. My daughter loved him, and kept his departure secret from us. He sailed away under cover of night, like a thief, taking with him twenty of our sailors whom he had bribed with honey-tongued tales of glory and adventure. *(pause)* He sailed West, leaving behind him grief and bitterness and a young girl's broken heart. *(Telemachus weeps)* Tears become a man Telemachus, but we trust them less today then yesterday. Your father was a copious weeper. We will provide you with shelter and food, and I will decide your fate in the morning.

Exit all but Athene and Telemachus.

ATHENE Telemachus.

TELEMACHUS Leave me alone.

ATHENE Yes Master.

TELEMACHUS How could he behave like that? He couldn't have, he just wouldn't.

ATHENE But he did.

TELEMACHUS Why?

Enter Nausicaa.

Nausicaa.

ATHENE Send her away. If her father finds her here, he will kill you.

NAUSICAA My father is asleep.

ATHENE Telemachus ...

TELEMACHUS Be still Mentis, you'll wake the whole house. Keep watch a while.

ATHENE No. The answer is no.

TELEMACHUS If her father finds her here, he will probably kill both of us, so for your own sake, keep the watch - please.

ATHENE This is against my better judgement. Not that it matters - I'm just a servant. *(she keeps watch)*

TELEMACHUS Is it true what they said about my father?

NAUSICAA Yes.

TELEMACHUS I'm sorry.

NAUSICAA Why should you be sorry? You've done nothing wrong.

TELEMACHUS Why did you come?

NAUSICAA To give you this. *(she gives him a shield of gold, Athene sees this - it is her shield)* Your father gave it me, as a present. He said he won it on the battlefield of Troy. It's yours.

TELEMACHUS But he gave it to you.

NAUSICAA I don't want it. I don't need it -

TELEMACHUS It's solid gold.

NAUSICAA *(smiles)* My 'young heart' isn't as fragile as my father thinks. Please don't think too badly of my father. He's upset, as you could see. *(laughs)* He feels he was made a fool of. His pride was hurt. My mother will talk to him and by the morning he'll be calmer. *(silence)* You're very young to undertake a voyage such as yours.

TELEMACHUS I had no choice.

NAUSICAA Your father told me he came from an island called Ithaca.

TELEMACHUS Yes.

NAUSICAA When he spoke of it he wept.

TELEMACHUS Then why doesn't he come home? *(silence)*

NAUSICAA Tell me about this 'Ithaca'.

TELEMACHUS Ithaca? It's dryer than here, dusty, rocky, but it has - a sparse beauty and if you know where to look there are small lush valleys with silver streams. There are thousands of olive trees and all kinds of places in which to - to play.

NAUSICAA And you live in a large house?

TELEMACHUS A palace, with great oak doors which my father carved with his own hands before I was born. It seems so far away now - like a dream.

NAUSICAA I've never been anywhere. I'm not allowed to leave the island. *(silence)* And your father was so 'travelled'. I have no regrets Telemachus, none, and as for my father, his anger is his own.

TELEMACHUS Nausicaa, when my father left the island did he say where he was going?

NAUSICAA West, and west again.

TELEMACHUS And what lies to the West of here?

NAUSICAA The land of the Cyclops - but do not go near them. They are a race of Giants who if our sailors are to be believed are cruel beyond imagination. I must go. Good luck Telemachus.

TELEMACHUS Nausicaa -

She has gone. He picks up the shield. He matches it up with the sword, then rests.

ATHENE   Night fell over the palace and Telemachus
watchful and full of feeling
gazed on its beauty.
Four spacious orchards surrounded the court,
with trees in bloom
or weighted down for picking.
Luscious figs and olives ripe and dark.
Fruit never failed upon their boughs.
The breathing west wind ripened all in turn.
This was the gift from heaven
to Arete and Alcinous.
But through these pleasant grounds
stalked a prince with murder in his heart
for Telemachus.

Master, Master. Wake up. Someone's coming, stealthily.

TELEMACHUS Who?

ATHENE   The brother of your girlfriend.

Enter Laodomus armed.

TELEMACHUS Laodomus. Why have you come?

LAODOMUS   Pick up your sword. *(silence)* If you refuse my challenge I will run you through for cowardice. Pick up your sword.

TELEMACHUS Why do you wish to fight me?

LAODOMUS   You are your father's son.

TELEMACHUS But not him. I am not him.

LAODOMUS   How quick you are to disclaim him now. Now fight.
(he lunges at Telemachus who jumps aside)

ATHENE   Pick up the sword. Pick it up. *(Telemachus does so)*

LAODOMUS Your father was a great fighter - or so he told me. *(he attacks Telemachus who defends himself but does not fight back)*

TELEMACHUS I urge you to follow your father's example and stay your sword before one of us is killed. *(Laodomus attacks hir* *again)*

ATHENE   Fight back you fool - fight back.

(Laodomus attacks him again and still Telemachus parries and retreats)

TELEMACHUS Then think of your sister. How will she feel, kneeling at the side of your grave?

LAODOMUS *(attacks him more strongly now and pins Telemachus down)* My sister? I saw her come here. Did you think to make fools of us a second time? *(raises his sword to kill Telemachus but Athene cries out)*

ATHENE   No! *(leaps on his back. He throws her down and brings his sword upon her. His sword is about to strike her when Telemachus blocks it with his own)*

TELEMACHUS Once again. Lay down your sword.

LAODOMUS *(now full of rage, he beats Telemachus back again, knocking the sword from his hand)* Whose grave do you see now, Telemachus?

ATHENE   Murder! Murder! Ring the alarm. Murder.

A bell rings. Telemachus uses the shield to ward off the blows. King Alcinous and Queen Arete enter as Laodomus is about to strike the final blow.

THE KING   Hold - Hold Laodomus!

ARETE   Laodomus, lay down your sword.

THE KING   Lay it down.

LAODOMUS But father ...

THE KING   Get out. Get out - out!

Enter Nausicaa.

NAUSICAA   Who rang the bell? Laodomus?
(exit Laodomus)
Telemachus. He's bleeding.

THE KING   Stay away from him.

NAUSICAA   But father ...

THE KING   Will no-one do as I say?

ARETE   Nausicaa. Stand by me.

THE KING   Are you badly hurt?

TELEMACHUS No.

THE KING   The dawn is almost here, there's no need now to delay. You're free to leave my Kingdom. Your craft has been washed ashore. My shipwrights will repair it.

NAUSICAA   Will you give him a proper ship?

THE KING   I will give him his life.

NAUSICAA   He'll perish on the sea, or the current will draw him to the land of the Cyclops. Is that how merciful you are? *(silence)*

THE KING   Of all our sailors bribed by Odysseus only one has returned, one. He says that Odysseus visited the land of the Cyclops, for what reason I cannot tell, only the result, all those men, who were my subjects are dead. *(pause)* If you wish to find your father, go to the land of the Cyclops.

ARETE   Telemachus - forgive my son. On many firelit nights your father filled his head with Tales of Troy, great battles and deeds of blood. How easily the seeds of war are sown in a young man, despite all our care. He promised to take Laodomus with him on his adventures, but when the day came he left him behind, and my son's heart hardened against him. But I am grateful - for if my son had gone ... Farewell Telemachus. May the Gods be kind to you.

TELEMACHUS And to your house.

Exit Queen Arete.

NAUSICAA   I beg you - give up your search. Go home Telemachus.

TELEMACHUS I've come too far.

NAUSICAA   Then avoid the Cyclops.

TELEMACHUS But my father.

NAUSICAA   If your father went there he is dead, and a Cyclops is gnawing on his bones.

TELEMACHUS What do you mean?

NAUSICAA   The Giants of the land, feed on people. Go home Telemachus. Go home.

TELEMACHUS Tell your father not to be too hard on Laodomus. Farewell Nausicaa.

NAUSICAA   Farewell stranger. In your land, if you ever see it again, remember me who found you and offered you the hospitality of my home - and heart.

TELEMACHUS *(kneels)* Daughter of the Great Alcinous and Arete, Nausicaa. May Zeus the Lord of Thunder grant me daybreak in my own country and all my days until I die I will invoke you as I would a Goddess - Princess, to whom I owe my life.

Exit Nausicaa.

ATHENE   Spoken like a man.

TELEMACHUS Laodomus could have killed me - why did you leave it so long - why didn't you ring the bell?...

ATHENE	I'm sorry - I simply assumed that you were the hero of this adventure.

TELEMACHUS Very funny.
(A light rises on the raft)

ATHENE	See, our old friend is here again.

MENTIS	The King is true to his word. Come, lend me a hand.

They pull the craft downstage. As they do the lights change. We hear the sound of the seas, and in the distance we see Nausicaa waving farewell.

TELEMACHUS Farewell Nausicaa.

ACT FOUR

Telemachus and Athene alone on the raft far out at sea heading west.

CAST *(sing)*	Telemachus, Telemachus
	Will you see your home again
	The land you love the best
	Is no more than a dream
	ITHACA

ATHENE *(speaks over the music)* Oh Zeus God of Gods. Look down upon this boy as he sails ever westward to the edge of the world.

ATHENE	Why do you cry Telemachus? *(pause)* You have to admit your father is a resourceful man, like yourself.

TELEMACHUS I'm not like him and don't ever say it again. I should never have left home.

ATHENE	Eurymachus would have killed you.

TELEMACHUS This trip will kill me.

ATHENE   It hasn't yet.

TELEMACHUS Have you no fear Mentis?

ATHENE   Fear? Yes, but I've discovered that fear is nothing to be afraid of. It protects you, stops you making foolish errors. Fear is a friend.

TELEMACHUS Not to me. All my life I've been afraid. Afraid of other children, afraid of Eurymachus, afraid my mother would forget my father, afraid he would never come back. Right now I'm more afraid then ever. All those fears are nothing in comparison to this.

ATHENE   You're scared of the Giant.

TELEMACHUS Of course I'm scared of the Giant. He eats people. I'm a boy. This is ridiculous, the whole thing's got out of hand. How may I defend myself - against such an Ogre?

ATHENE   You have your sword, your shield.

TELEMACHUS A great help. I couldn't even defeat Laodomus, a boy my own age. *(silence)* And if I ever found my father, what then? Does he want me to find him? I don't think so. I want to go home Mentis.

ATHENE   Me too. I have a lovely home, high in the mountains, where the air is thin and clear. You can see the whole world from up there. I'd turn the boat around and head east if I could. But I can't - until I find ...

TELEMACHUS Don't talk to me about your things. I don't care a jot about your mysterious "things" if you won't tell me what they are, they don't exist. *(silence)* I used to lie on my bed and dream of the day I would leave home. I imagined a life at sea, but not like this. The sea seems drier and more desolate than my own Ithaca. If I close my eyes I can see the colours of the Isle. I can smell the thyme on the mountainside. I can hear the grasshoppers singing in the evening and the bells of the goats ringing in the morning as they move down the slopes through the olive groves.

CAST *(sing)* ITHACA

ATHENE   Westward we sailed towards the setting sun.
On the evening of the third day we arrived
at the Kingdom of the Cyclops
and high in cliffs we saw the mouth
of his cave. It was a blackhole from out
of which drifted a vile, foreboding stench.

*(They leave the raft and are outside the cave of the Cyclops. We hear
the sound of hammer on anvil. It gets louder then stops)*

TELEMACHUS What sounds are these?

ATHENE   Where are you going? *(pulls him back)*

TELEMACHUS Are you afraid?

ATHENE   Of course I'm afraid. He eats people.

TELEMACHUS What happened to your curiosity? Your love of
adventure?

ATHENE   Perhaps we should hide, survey the creature from a
distance.

TELEMACHUS If I hide, I'll have time to think. If I have time to
think I'll be overcome with dread. Come let's speak with him and
be gone.

ATHENE   Wait! Wait! Why this sudden impetuousness. Speak
with him by all means, but try not to be so ...

TELEMACHUS So?

ATHENE   Honest. Don't be so ready to tell him who you really
are - it gets us into trouble.

TELEMACHUS   I'm not a good liar.

ATHENE   Poor liars make good meals.

*Lights now reveal the back of the cave and we see the giant as a
huge blacksmith. His one eye is now sightless. He fumbles round his
cave for his tools. He curses under his breath. He then stops and
smells the scent of Telemachus.*

CYCLOPS Who's there? I will find you wherever you are. I can smell the sweat on your skin, the sea in your hair, the food on your breath. Speak to me. *(he picks up one of his blacksmiths' tools which becomes a weapon)* Who's there?

TELEMACHUS A friend.

CYCLOPS I have no friends. What friends I had - I had for dinner. *(he takes a lunge for Telemachus who leaps aside)*

TELEMACHUS I mean you no harm Cyclops.

CYCLOPS *(throws back his head and laughs a huge resounding laugh)* What harm can you do me? Your throat is no wider than a reed pipe, your voice no deeper than a song bird.
(Telemachus turns to Athene and she shakes her head and puts her finger to her lips)

TELEMACHUS *(mouths)* He's blind.

CYCLOPS Are you alone - little one? *(silence)* Since I lost my sight my sense of smell has increased tenfold - but yet though I sense another, I smell only one.

TELEMACHUS I'm not alone. I have a whole crew of sailors waiting on the beach, who will come and slay you if I don't return by nightfall.

CYCLOPS Poor little songbird, you cannot even lie with conviction.*(makes another grab for Telemachus. Telemachus drops his sword - the giant picks it up)* What do you want of Polyphemus? Have you come to kill me? Tell me the truth.

TELEMACHUS I'm looking for someone.

CYCLOPS You are fortunate to have eyes - I am not so lucky. *(he makes another grab for Telemachus who again avoids him)* Whom do you seek?

TELEMACHUS Odysseus. The Hero of Troy.

CYCLOPS Odysseus. What is he - to you?

TELEMACHUS My - my enemy.

CYCLOPS Why do you seek him?

TELEMACHUS To kill him. *(the giant suddenly loses his temper and roars 'Odysseus!' He picks up a sack and turns it upside down and out falls a pile of bloody bones. He picks up a bone and still raging he swipes at the air till he rests)*

TELEMACHUS *(gently)* Odysseus. Has he been here? Are his bones among these?

CYCLOPS Give me your name.

TELEMACHUS I am ... My name is ...

CYCLOPS Tell me the truth. *(Athene shakes her head)*

TELEMACHUS I am Telemachus. The son of Odysseus.

CYCLOPS *(laughs again)* His son. His son. Ah the Gods are kind to me. They weep for the lost eye of Polyphemus. You are their gift to me, and I give thanks.

TELEMACHUS Where is my father?

CYCLOPS Gone! *(silence)* Why did he come here Telemachus? What was I to him? A curiosity - nothing more. These are the bones of his men. Nineteen Phaecian sailors - whom he brought with him. I ate them all but one, who escaped with your father.

TELEMACHUS He lives then.

CYCLOPS He lives, he speaks, he hears, he *sees. (he makes another grab for Telemachus who again avoids him - just)* If he were here, I would make him suffer as he made me suffer, as I will make you, suffer. I will catch you Telemachus, and with burning spikes I will gouge out your eyes and your screams will be music to my soul!

TELEMACHUS He, did that to you?

CYCLOPS He blinded me. He burnt out my eye. My screams reached the heavens, and Poseidon, my uncle, heard me, and has brought you to me - for my sweet revenge. *(he takes another lunge for Telemachus and catches him)* Now Telemachus, what say you?

TELEMACHUS Let me go Polyphemus, and I will find my father and kill him - will that not be revenge enough?

CYCLOPS   You are a trickster too - just like your father.

TELEMACHUS It's the truth - I hate my father.

CYCLOPS   It's a lie - you do not hate your father enough to kill him.

TELEMACHUS I do - I do.

CYCLOPS   Say it then. Say it.. Say it!

TELEMACHUS I hate my father, I hate my father.

CYCLOPS Oh. *(sadly)* There is such sad conviction now in your voice Telemachus. But you do not hate as I hate. I hate him with all the strength of all the armies of the world. I hate him with all the burning power of my pain - my eye. He has taken from me all the pretty things - all the flowers that I loved to see each season. Now the natural world is as dark as my smithy. For what. Why? Why?

TELEMACHUS You destroyed the lives of his crew, you devoured their flesh.

CYCLOPS   But that, my boy, is my nature. All who come here, know this. It doesn't mean I'm bad. I did not deserve this dark world Telemachus. I am innocent, as you are. But innocence does not save us. It will not save you. *(he opens his jaws)*

TELEMACHUS Mentis. *(Mentis gives him his sword - he plunges it into the giant who roars and falls back clutching his heart)*

CYCLOPS   Who? Who gave you the blade?

TELEMACHUS My servant.

CYCLOPS   Servant? I could smell no-one. *(he breathes heavily)* You have killed me. Telemachus. You have killed me. You are kinder than your father.

TELEMACHUS Where is he? Where did he go?

CYCLOPS   West to the edge of the world, beyond which there is nothing, only, only the halls of the dead, where I am bound - where you have sent me - Telemachus, Son of Odysseus. *(he dies)*

ATHENE   Come. Come. We must go.

They retreat back into the light. The cave darkens and disappears from view.

ATHENE   Come on Telemachus.

TELEMACHUS I never meant to kill him.

ATHENE   What choice did he give you? You have to hurry. Your father isn't far ahead. *(she pushes him towards the raft)*

TELEMACHUS What? What are you doing?

ATHENE   Your father has gone to the halls of the dead.

TELEMACHUS I don't care. I do not care.

ATHENE   To get there it seems -

TELEMACHUS I no longer wish to find my father. Therefore I have no reason to continue this journey. *(silence)*

ATHENE   What about me?

TELEMACHUS You. Ha. *(to her face)* Ha!

ATHENE   But don't you care about me?

TELEMACHUS I wish I were dead! *(silence)*

ATHENE   I beg you. Continue the search for your father.

TELEMACHUS Tell me who you are. Why couldn't the Cyclops smell you?

ATHENE   I will tell you everything soon ...

TELEMACHUS Hah!

ATHENE   And I will reward you.

TELEMACHUS You, oh nice! What could you give me that I would possibly want?

ATHENE   Friendship. Self-belief ... Some rope.

TELEMACHUS Do you realise where we are?

ATHENE   I believe, we've reached the edge of the world.

TELEMACHUS The edge of the world?

ATHENE If your father survived it, so can you.

TELEMACHUS Don't - just don't.

ATHENE I'm sorry.

TELEMACHUS Just tell me - what the rope is for?

ATHENE The rope?

TELEMACHUS The rope Mentis!

ATHENE I've heard stories about - a whirlpool.

TELEMACHUS A what?

ATHENE A large amount of water moving in a circle.

TELEMACHUS I know what a whirlpool is Mentis.

ATHENE Which may - if the stories are true - hurl us down to the Halls of Eternal Rest.

TELEMACHUS Oh Gods! Is there no end to this adventure? *(silence)* Giving up is a perfectly intelligent response to this situation.

ATHENE Perfectly. It's just the wrong thing to do.

TELEMACHUS Tie me to the mast.

ATHENE *(kisses him)* Thank you. *(she ties him to the mast)*

TELEMACHUS What about you?

ATHENE Don't worry about me.

TELEMACHUS Well I do - actually.

ATHENE I will hold on for dear life.

Music - lights change. They are at sea.

TELEMACHUS Mentis?

ATHENE Yes?

TELEMACHUS What if the stories aren't true? What if we simply reach the edge of the world - and fall off - into space.

ATHENE   In that case - we should say goodbye.

TELEMACHUS Goodbye Mentis.

ATHENE   Master ...

The raft spins and the sound of the whirlpool gets louder and louder.
They cry out. Blackout. The Halls of the Dead. Lights rise.
Telemachus is slumped unconscious and still tied to the mast. Mentis
has vanished around Telemachus. Lights flicker, which represent the
strange shape of the spirits who walk in the Halls of the Dead.
Behind Telemachus a shadowy figure in rags approaches.

TELEMACHUS *(wakes)* Who's there? Mentis? Is that you? *(he*
  sees Odysseus) Who are you? Stay where you are. *(Odysseus*
  approaches and takes Telemachus' sword. He looks at it for a
  moment and then cuts the boy free and puts the sword down.)
  Are you, one of the dead?

ODYSSEUS   Sometimes I think so.

TELEMACHUS What is your name? *(There is a low moan from the*
  spirits) What was that?

ODYSSEUS   The moans of the dead. The unhappy ones can kick
  up a terrible din sometimes.

TELEMACHUS There are so many.

ODYSSEUS   They are without number.

TELEMACHUS But you. You're not one of them. Are you?

ODYSSEUS   Not yet - I - I work here.

TELEMACHUS Ah!

ODYSSEUS   Though it has to be said there's not much work to be
  done. In fact, I've been waiting for someone to visit. Is there
  some long-departed soul you wished to talk to?

TELEMACHUS I'm looking for my father.

ODYSSEUS   His name?

TELEMACHUS Odysseus.

ODYSSEUS Odysseus isn't here. He isn't dead, though he might wish it so.

TELEMACHUS I must find him.

ODYSSEUS And you are?

TELEMACHUS His son, Telemachus.

ODYSSEUS He didn't tell me he had a son. Strange, for he was here and we talked at length.

TELEMACHUS Why would he come to this cold and lonely place?

ODYSSEUS Curiosity, and to talk to a few old friends.
(Telemachus breaks down and weeps) Why do you weep so?

TELEMACHUS Because I hate him. I hate him.

ODYSSEUS Why do you search for him then? *(silence)*

TELEMACHUS Do you know where he was going? Did he say?

ODYSSEUS No. He had no plans for the future. Please, stay and speak with me. I am no-one but I am someone.

TELEMACHUS I haven't time. I must follow him.

ODYSSEUS You have all the time - time does not pass here. It has ceased to be. You can't waste it or spend it wisely. Besides you need to rest. You're very tired.

TELEMACHUS You said my father spoke to someone, one of the dead.

ODYSSEUS Achilles. The Hero of the Greeks. Who died at Troy. Do you wish to speak to him?

TELEMACHUS Achilles?

ODYSSEUS See there he is ...
(A light rises on a vision of Achilles)
Still covered in blood and bitter wounds as on the day he died.
(Telemachus turns away from him)
Come I'm sure you'd like to speak to him. He's every boy's Hero, but you must offer him this bowl of blood to drink and then he may speak again as he did in life, otherwise he will remain the

voiceless shadow that you see. *(Telemachus takes the bowl and gives it to Achilles, who drinks)*

ACHILLES   Who are you?

TELEMACHUS Telemachus, son of Odysseus and Penelope.

ACHILLES   Telemachus? Why have you come?

TELEMACHUS I'm searching for my father. He was here.

ACHILLES   Yes, the old trickster, master of landways and seaways. *(he smiles)*

TELEMACHUS Why? Why did he come here?

ACHILLES   Since he had no friends left in the world above, he came to make peace with those in the world below. In life, we were friends, but we argued and became enemies.

TELEMACHUS But why? Over what?

ACHILLES   It's strange - I - I can't remember. Thus all anger fades. *(pause)* Why are you searching Telemachus?

TELEMACHUS I don't know anymore. I've looked for him so long, come so far, and now I no longer know the reason. He abandoned me and my mother, to fight a war he said would make us rich. When it was over instead of coming home, as he had promised, he went off on a - cruise - an adventure. He lived life to the full, for pleasure. Those who helped him, he cheated - those who loved him, he abused, and the men who trusted him and sailed with him, they all died. He sacrificed them all so that he might see the world, and what has he seen? Witches, giants, ghosts. And he never came home as he promised, or made any effort to come home and my mother was driven half-mad with anxiety, loneliness and fear, why do I want to find him? I don't.

ACHILLES   Telemachus, let me speak to you as if you were my own son. Hear my words and let them remain with you all the days of your life. Here am I, the greatest soldier of a great army. These are my wounds. Behind me are many others whom I have killed with these hands. I - like your father, was in love with death - but now I would rather be a poor man ploughing a poor field than King of the lifeless dead. Do not lead the life we led,

Telemachus. But go - find your father, for he lives, but be swift for death pursues him like a winged dog and snaps at his heels. Do not give up the search, for the search is life, and for all its sorrows life is good.

(The image of Achilles fades, Odysseus steps forward, having heard all of this)

TELEMACHUS I believed in him. I loved the idea of him, and he never came home.

ODYSSEUS It was a long war Telemachus - at Troy. It wasn't what we thought it would be. It destroyed us, it made demons of us or adventurers or beggars. For ten years we knew nothing but death. We dreamed so hard for home, and love and life that in the end they became dreams, and war alone was real. Every day we watched our friends die, like brave Achilles and every day a little bit of ourselves slipped away until we were no longer men but the shells of men, capable of any cruelty. Finally we defeated the Trojans with a trick. My clever trick for which I am renowned. A wooden horse, pregnant with death, which the Trojans pulled inside their city walls. My 'trick' that led to victory, and to the murder of a thousand men, women and children. I became an empty space Telemachus, where victory had no meaning. I could not fill that space, wherever I went, whatever wonders I beheld and I have seen all the wonders of our world - I could not then fill the empty space inside me. Don't you know me Telemachus? My son.

TELEMACHUS You are not my father.

ODYSSEUS Perhaps I'm not what you expected, but I am your father. For that I apologise.

TELEMACHUS You cannot be. You cannot be.

ODYSSEUS And yet I am.

TELEMACHUS No.

ODYSSEUS No? These hands built the house in which you were born. I laid the lintel of oak across the door myself - at that door I trust my foolish dog still sits waiting for me. His name is Argos.

TELEMACHUS No! *(he attacks Odysseus, who barely tries to defend himself)*

ODYSSEUS *(flatly)* Kill me then. Kill me. I welcome it. For I hate myself more than you will ever hate me. *(Telemachus turns away)* My son?

TELEMACHUS Don't call me that! Ever.

ODYSSEUS You should not have come here. *(silence)* How did you pass the whirlpool?

TELEMACHUS I tied myself to the mast.

ODYSSEUS The Cyclops?

TELEMACHUS I killed him - with this. *(he holds up the Golden Sword)* Which was given to me by the Goddess of Ogygia, who is called Calypso. Remember? And this *(the shield)* was given me by a girl - not much older than I. *(he spits in his father's face)*. These are not the questions you should be asking me, father. Ask me of Ithaca. Ask me about your wife - Penelope.

ODYSSEUS Penelope?

TELEMACHUS Is dead. *(pause)* And her death belongs to you. She's here among these cold shadows. Why don't you summon her and tell her why you never came home. *(silence)*

ODYSSEUS How did she die?

TELEMACHUS A man named Eurymachus has taken your house, land and wealth. He would have taken your wife too, but she stopped him.

ODYSSEUS She killed herself?

TELEMACHUS What? Aren't you sad, no tears?

ODYSSEUS Go home Telemachus.

TELEMACHUS Home?

ODYSSEUS I don't deserve the risks you've taken to find me. I'm not worthy of you, or her.

TELEMACHUS But you must be, you must, you promised.

ODYSSEUS   Leave me. This is where I belong for I am dead in all but name. *(he sinks to his knees)*

TELEMACHUS No. *(he pulls his father up)* You will come home and do what you should have done a long time ago.

ODYSSEUS   I can't. I can't. *(he pulls away from Telemachus)* You do not know how easy it is to lose the way. Telemachus?

Enter Athene at speed. She tries to pull from Odysseus a bag which he has around his neck. He grabs her.

TELEMACHUS Mentis.

ODYSSEUS   What's this?

ATHENE   Villain, robber, liar, thief.

ODYSSEUS   So I am. And you?

ATHENE   I am one to be scared of. *(Odysseus laughs)*

TELEMACHUS This is my servant Mentis. Let her go.

ATHENE   You heard him. *(he drops her. But she has the bag)* Ah!

ODYSSEUS   Those are my things. Give them back - Give them back!

ATHENE   Correction - these are my things. How dare you steal from the Gods, Odysseus, son of Laertes.*(she holds up a pair of golden shoes with small wings upon them)*

ODYSSEUS   Athene?

TELEMACHUS Mentis?

ODYSSEUS   This is no servant - this is Athene, Immortal Goddess, daughter of Zeus, God of Gods.

TELEMACHUS Don't be daft.

ATHENE *(she now lifts her arms. Thunder and lightning strike. Odysseus kneels before her)* So Odysseus, old knife, master of landways and seaways, you have caused me a deal of discomfort. You stole my shoes.

ODYSSEUS   I was merely keeping them safe until ...

ATHENE   My sword you gave to a witch. My shield you gave to a pubescent princess.*(she recovers these items)*

ODYSSEUS   But your shoes ...

ATHENE   Because of you I have been turned into a pig, tossed into the sea, I have felt cold, hot, frightened, jealous and very very hungry. Me a Goddess. What excuse can you give me?

ODYSSEUS   I did what I did to survive. Now that you've been human, if only for a little while, perhaps you'll understand what it's like to know there is an end to life, that time runs against you. *(silence)*

ATHENE   You - why did I ever choose to champion such a smooth-talking Greek?

TELEMACHUS This is ridiculous. *(she points to him and Telemachus feels as if he's been stabbed and cries out)*

ATHENE   I am very annoyed.

ODYSSEUS   Great Athene, thank you for the loan of your golden armour, they were my protection on a perilous voyage. I praise your generosity and am your obedient servant.

ATHENE   Then go home, with your Son, to Ithaca.

CHORUS *(sing)* ITHACA

ATHENE   My father Zeus, Master of Gods and Men, grant me once again my Godlike powers, for I have found the golden gifts that were only yours to give. Know then that I am your daughter Athene, Goddess of the grey eyes.

(Low rumble of thunder. Lightning strikes. Athene receives her full powers)

ATHENE   Now over rock and sea we fly where the young dawn comes bright in the east. Even now she spreads her fingertips of rose upon the Isle of Ithaca.

CHORUS *(sing)* ITHACA - HOME.

ACT FIVE

Ithaca.
Odysseus and Telemachus are back in Ithaca. Athene has vanished.
Enter Eurycleia.

EURYCLEIA Master. Oh it's true then, you have come home.

TELEMACHUS Good Eurycleia.

EURYCLEIA Safe an' well. *(she embraces him several times)* An' still alive.

TELEMACHUS Only just. Now be swift and tell me how things stand here in Ithaca.

EURYCLEIA Your father?

TELEMACHUS I couldn't find him.

EURYCLEIA Heaven preserve us then - what are we to do?

TELEMACHUS *(takes her to one side)* How is my mother?

EURYCLEIA As the day you left her, caught in a sleep that looks like death. This potion will wake her.

TELEMACHUS Then go and do so.

EURYCLEIA But Master?

TELEMACHUS Do as I command.

EURYCLEIA Command? I will not - for all your impudence. Eurymachus thinks her dead and buried. If she wakes heaven alone knows what he might do. He's taken control of Ithaca. No-one calls him King but he is King right enough and rules most coldly. He allows no repairs to the house, the fields are left to weeds, the vineyards be all collapsed. It's as if he willed his own destruction. Oh if only you had found your father. Who is this?

TELEMACHUS No-one. A beggar, I picked up on my travels.

EURYCLEIA Can he be trusted?

TELEMACHUS Who can tell? Go and wake my mother.

EURYCLEIA But I have told you how things stand with Eurymachus. You must leave again for he will come straight here to murder you the moment he hears of your arrival.

TELEMACHUS I'll take my chance with Eurymachus. I have survived ordeals that make a man of his stature shrink to a very common size of foe. Please Eurycleia, wake my mother.

EURYCLEIA Yes master.

TELEMACHUS Be quick - Eurymachus approaches.

Exit Eurycleia. Enter Eurymachus.

EURYMACHUS Telemachus, welcome. You have some nerve, to come back here. I'm impressed, but there must be a reason for such foolishness.

TELEMACHUS To banish you from my house.

EURYMACHUS You don't have a house Telemachus. This is my house. But for old times sake I will allow you to be buried here. Next to your mother? *(Telemachus turns and picks up the two spears which have been used throughout in the dream fights)*

EURYMACHUS Ah - you came to fight. Brave boy.

TELEMACHUS No - your fight is not with me Eurymachus but with my father.

EURYMACHUS *(turns and sees Odysseus who now steps out of the shadows)* This - rag?...

TELEMACHUS Is my father.

EURYMACHUS *(laughs)* I know your father well and I swear by all the gods this is not he. You've been tricked.

TELEMACHUS Believe me Eurymachus this is my father. *(he gives Odysseus a spear)* He will fight you and kill you or if he has no reason to live and loves not himself or his son or the memory of his wife, then you may kill him.

ODYSSEUS Telemachus - please.

TELEMACHUS Don't you love me father? *(silence)* Then fight for yourself. Fight for your own life.

ODYSSEUS Would you have me shed more blood for something which has no meaning?

TELEMACHUS Then fight for your house, your crops your vineyards, your many servants who need you. *(silence)*

EURYMACHUS As I said, this is not your father.

TELEMACHUS I need you, mother needs you.

ODYSSEUS But she's dead, and I'm responsible.

TELEMACHUS No, no, she isn't dead, she lives, she lives.

Music. Enter Penelope on Eurycleia's arm. She can barely stand.

EURYMACHUS What magic is this? What drug have you fed me that I see ghosts?

ODYSSEUS Penelope?

EURYMACHUS This is some deadly vision. She is dead.

TELEMACHUS No. You see father. She is alive. She is alive.

EURYMACHUS It cannot be so. Did I grieve for nothing? If she be not dead, as once she was, she shall be once again.*(he raises his spear against Penelope. Eurycleia stands in his way)* I will not be tricked. I am King of Ithaca. *(he attacks Odysseus. Odysseus, overwhelms him and puts his spear to his throat)*

ODYSSEUS   I am Odysseus, King of Ithaca, Lord of my lands and house, to which my son has so bravely brought me, with more love and tenderness than a father such as I deserve. In his name and in the name of my wife, Penelope, whom I have treated with great disdain, I give you your life.

TELEMACHUS Father?

ODYSSEUS   Shall I deny this man the gift you have given me? Go Eurymachus, and though you be banished from this island, believe me it is small, and the world is large and there is much to see and you may find hope in the strangest of places.
(Eurymachus stretches out his hands to Penelope. She turns away)

He exits.

ODYSSEUS   My wife.

PENELOPE *(looks at him, then walks past him to Telemachus)* Telemachus - you seem - so changed.

EURYCLEIA Be careful my lady. *(she hugs her son)*

ODYSSEUS   Penelope.

PENELOPE *(turns and slaps the face of Odysseus. He kneels)* Do not kneel to me. *(he stands)* Nor stand, nor sit nor anything. *(silence)* But come to my chambers tomorrow when I have had some hours to gather in the storm which rages in me against you. *(she falls and Eurycleia is about to help her up but Odysseus offers his arm. After a moment she takes it)*

ODYSSEUS   Let me help you.

Exit Odysseus and Penelope.

EURYCLEIA What did he expect, a meal on the table? *(Telemachus breathes a sigh of relief)* I suppose you are hungry then, after all your adventures?

TELEMACHUS Yes I am - I am.

EURYCLEIA Brave boy.

TELEMACHUS You knew it was my father all along. Didn't you?

EURYCLEIA They say a person's eyes are a mirror of their soul, but that's rubbish, he had a scar on his forehead which I recognised immediately. All I saw in his eyes, was pain, an' a good portion of it.

TELEMACHUS What do you think will happen between them?

EURYCLEIA Who knows, but I do know it's not in your hands. You are not responsible for their happiness. Understood. Some food then - it'll have to be simple - I'm all of a flutter.

TELEMACHUS Some bread, some cheese.

ATHENE *(from under the bed)* And pickle.

EURYCLEIA *(turns back)* You don't like pickle.

TELEMACHUS Well I am more adventurous than I used to be - and some wine.

EURYCLEIA Oh I say, some 'wine'. We have grown up. I'm glad to have you home, master. There's work to be done here, to make this house well again - but I am optimistic, that's my nature - tis very foolish, but there tis. *(she goes to leave and turns back)* By the way, whatever happened to that boy you left with? That friend of yours, who came out of nowhere?

TELEMACHUS Ah - well the boy turned into a girl, and the girl turned into a goddess.

EURYCLEIA I see. *(aside)* Anyone would think I was born yesterday.

She exits. Enter Athene.

ATHENE   Telemachus - the old sea dog.

TELEMACHUS Mentis.*(they embrace, as the best of friends, but then Telemachus backs away)* Athene.

ATHENE   I came to thank you.

TELEMACHUS Me?

ATHENE   And to give you this. *(she gives him a golden sword)*

TELEMACHUS But your father ...

ATHENE   Has agreed - you deserve to keep the sword.

TELEMACHUS Thank you.

ATHENE   Use it wisely or it will turn against you. So, what are you going to do now?

TELEMACHUS I don't know. I thought I might pick up a boat headed east. I'll go east and east again. See a few sights.

ATHENE   You only just got home.

TELEMACHUS I can always come back.

ATHENE   Not always, things happen. Your father had no way back until you found him.

TELEMACHUS He and I are - strangers, and whatever he says I can't forgive him. I can't.

ATHENE   You owe him nothing it's true, but give him a little time to prove himself. Do this for me, after all I am his foolish Champion. Goodbye Telemachus. I shall never forget our journey and what it felt like to be - so utterly lost. The Gods bless you, and your house, and the Isle of Ithaca.

CHORUS *(sing)* ITHACA

Exit Athene.

TELEMACHUS Athene! *(silence)*

Enter Odysseus.

ODYSSEUS Telemachus?

TELEMACHUS Yes father?

They remain standing, with some distance between them as the lights fade to blackout.

End.

Charles Way

Born in Devon in 1955, most of his artistic life has been spent in Wales. He trained as an actor at the Rose Bruford College in London then joined Leeds Theatre in Education team and wrote his first professional play in 1978. He then became resident writer at Theatre Centre and has since written over thirty plays, many for young people. Nominated 3 years in a row for Best Children's Play by The Writers Guild, **Sleeping Beauty** (94) **The Search for Odysseus**, (95) and **A spell of cold weather**, (96) which eventually won. His plays include **The Flood**, (Collins) **Dead Man's Hat** and **In The Bleak Mid-winter**, (Seren) which was nominated for a Manchester Evening News Theatre Award.

Radio and T.V.: Most recently, a half-hour play for teenagers, **A Figure Of Eight** and a forty minute film poem, **No Borders,** narrated by Bob Peck.

Best known in Wales for his work with Hijinx Theatre: **Ill Met By Moonlight** and **The Dove Maiden** and for his Adaption of **On The Black Hill** for Made In Wales TC. Currently Writer in Residence at BBC Radio Wales and the Sherman Theatre, Cardiff.

Darker the Berry

by J.B. Rose

Darker the Berry - Is how it come?

Darker the Berry was originally commissioned by Second Wave Centre For Youth Arts at the Albany Theatre in Deptford, South London. I came fresh to writing through my experience of performing, song-writing and singing. My work with Second Wave as a drama tutor, bringing young people's ideas to performance, provided me with an invaluable foundation.

The idea for the play came from a variety of sources. Firstly, my mother's personal experience of growing up as an illegitimate child in Jamaica where she had to fight to get educated, and where her struggle to leave her home eventually led her to England where she became a qualified nurse. Secondly, many themes came from my work with young people at Second Wave; parental expectation, rebellion, making one's own way in life, and not belonging. The feeling of being part of a different social class, was important too. Although many young people are of second / third generation Caribbean descent, colour prejudice - the lightness and darkness of skin colour (conscious or unconscious) still has its grip on the black community. Because of this - and because of my own experiences on my first visit to Jamaica - the themes of **Darker the Berry** evolved.

Darker the Berry is a true to life comedy, love story, about a close knit community tenaciously coping with being poor and all that poverty brings with it, a group of people working through some of the old habits and ways that colonialism has left behind. Ultimately it is a Caribbean Cinderella, but unlike the fairytale, Norma finds the courage and strength to make a better life - by striking out for herself.

J.B. Rose

Dedicated to Mrs L.V. Rose and Ann Considine - my inspirations.

Darker the Berry

by J.B. Rose

Originally commissioned and first performed by Second Wave
Youth Theatre at the Albany Theatre, Deptford, South London in
1995.
Directed by Ann Considine.

Miss Faith	Lisa Phillip
Esther	Angela Smith
Norma	Jacy Stewart
Hector	Delroy Mclean
Toto	Stephen Simmons
Eddie	Daniel Robinson
Miss Sophie	Orlessa Edwards
Ruby	Claudia Hamilton
Joseph	Daniel Robinson
Winston	Damien Best
Ezra	Anna Aidoo

ACT ONE
SCENE 1

*Jamaica. Evening. People are gathering, relaxing and gossiping.
Hector and Eddie are playing dominoes. Toto and Winston are
hanging out by Miss Faith's fence chatting. Miss Sophie is sitting
under a tree watching the two children (Ezra and Ruby) playing
jacks (pick up stones).*

HECTOR *(to Eddie)* What's the story?

WINSTON *(to Toto)* And how it go?

EDDIE *(to Hector)* Make we tell you

TOTO *(to Winston)* ... and tell you good.

ALL BOYS   Earth, Water, Flame and Fire.

ALL GIRLS   Earth, Water, Flame and Fire.

MISS SOPHIE *(to Ezra and Ruby)* Two sisters.

RUBY *(to Ezra)* One earth.

EZRA *(to Ruby)* One fire.

Norma enters running from inside the house - secretly carrying Esther's fairytale book. She looks up front and calls Esther to play with her.

NORMA   Esther?

EDDIE *(to Hector)* See that one there.

HECTOR   Eh huh! *(Hector and Eddie exit)*

Esther enters from Spur Tree Hill. She is absorbed in a game wearing her dressing- up clothes. She calls Norma.

ESTHER *(absent-mindedly)* Norma?

TOTO *(to Winston)* See the next one there.

WINSTON   Ee hee! *(Winston and Toto exit)*

RUBY *(to Ezra)* You know the story?

MISS SOPHIE *(to Ezra and Ruby)* This is how it go.

She exits stage right.
Ezra and Ruby remain. Ruby and Ezra run off - stage right following Miss Sophie.

SCENE 2

We see Esther and Norma at the age of eight and nine playing outside the yard. Norma is trying to get hold of a book. Esther won't let her have it.

NORMA   Give me it no? Let me have it?

ESTHER   No it was a present.

NORMA   Well then read it ... read it again!
(Esther carefully opens the book)

ESTHER   Many years ago, in a land where it was always hot ... there was a beautiful princess ...*(Norma acts out the story as if she is the princess)* Now this princess have a birthmark - a mark she was born with - a mark that no-one else had ... except the king and queen of course!
(Norma shows the imaginary birthmark on her arm)

NORMA   Of course ... *(she invents the rest of the story, playing the servant girl)* ... One hot day, a palace servant girl was sweeping ...

ESTHER   Is who book this? Sweep no!

NORMA *(she continues)* ... and you know what ... this servant girl have the same mark as the princess!

ESTHER   What's this? Say the princess You a try mock me?

NORMA *(acting frightened)* No your majesty!

ESTHER   Let me take off that mark! *(starts roughing up Norma)*

NORMA *(proudly)* But it couldn't come off!

ESTHER   When the queen find out about this, she'll tear out your gizzard and feed you to the snakes!

NORMA   Now the queen was wicked and bad minded ... and everybody 'fraid of her.

ESTHER   Quick, quick put me crown on ...
(They gather bits of costume, and put a crown on Esther's head)

NORMA   Then the queen *(pointing at Norma and acting out*
      the Queen)

ESTHER   raise herself to her feet till she big and shout out till
      everbody ear drums bust ... Girl ... who is your real family? Talk
      up quick!

NORMA   I have no father or no mother.

ESTHER   A lie you a tell! Me a go beat you for that! *(she*
      chases Norma as if she is going to beat her) Get out of my
      kingdom, come out ... and if I catch you next time I going chop
      off you head. *(Norma interrupts the story)*

NORMA   Come make we play again ... I'll be the princess.

ESTHER   The story no finish yet!

NORMA   I want to be rich and beautiful. *(she spins round)*

NORMA   See me gown? *(She walks up and down in her make-*
      believe gown)

ESTHER   What gown?

NORMA   Look and see! Where is your imagination? *(picks up*
      the book)

ESTHER   Come me will read.

NORMA   Esther?

ESTHER   Yes?

NORMA   You think your mummy will send me a school to
      read like you one day?

ESTHER   ... don't know. *(pause)* Try now no - gwan!

NORMA   Once upon a time

ESTHER   In a land far away ...

NORMA   There was a *beautiful* princess ...

They hear a loud crashing and banging noise from the house.

SCENE 3

As Esther and Norma are playing, they hear noises - an argument
between their mother and father. They sit on the verandah listening.

FAITH   Adulterer!

JOSEPH   We no join to the hip.

FAITH   I'm your wife!

JOSEPH   Me is a young man, it not healty to stay with the
same woman for so long. Same food, same voice, same titty.

FAITH   You just don't know how to be faithful ... love
woman too much. Have no conscience.

JOSEPH   Me mind slip.

FAITH   You mind slip and forget you vows? You must think
me stupid. Only cause me soft and I couldn't take the neighbours
gossip why me bring in you bastard pickney.

JOSEPH   Just leave me pickney! All you concerned with is
church, that white woman Miss Armatage you work for, an
Esther.

FAITH   Me not to look after the pickney?

JOSEPH   Before you busy yourself with serving you man, you
a shine bacra floor. And run behind Esther like she no have hand.
What happen to Norma?

FAITH   So what? Esther our child no nothing? She not your
pickney?

JOSEPH   Cork up you mouth. Wha' you in a them areas fa?

FAITH   Where Norma mother? Where is you cheap woman?

JOSEPH   Norma mother did know how to treat me. Treat me
like king!

FAITH   Then why you don't go to her?

JOSEPH   You no think if I could I would.

FAITH   Bastard! I should just throw you and you charcoal pickney on the street where you belong.

JOSEPH   You know I tired of your voice. Man should live in peace, enjoy God's fruits.

FAITH   Disease going drop off them fruit one day.

JOSEPH   Me no have to stand for this. I can get better woman, woman who know how to treat their man like lion inside the bed and out.
(He puts on his hat and then starts to look for Faith's savings)

FAITH   Where you going?

JOSEPH   To pick fresh fruit.

FAITH   What about you family, what about me?

JOSEPH   You should have thought about that before you run up you mouth, can't take the hen pecking.

FAITH   Joseph?

JOSEPH   I need peace, not nengay nengay!

FAITH   It's just a little quarrel man, we can sort it out ... don't make things get out a hand.
(Joseph ignores her still looking through Faith's things)

JOSEPH   Mind! *(he pushes her out of the way)*

FAITH   Joseph please, at least think about Esther, we plans to send her to high school.

JOSEPH   Me not staying man ...

FAITH   What you doing?

JOSEPH   Mind youself woman.

FAITH   You can't do this to me!

JOSEPH   Move woman! You should be looking after me not running down strangers.

FAITH   If I don't work how ends meet? *(he finds the money)*

JOSEPH   Is this me want!

FAITH   Me savings Joseph!

JOSEPH	Chu! Me gone.
FAITH	Joseph don't go.
JOSEPH	Out a me way.
FAITH	Joseph! Joseph!

Joseph leaves, Faith watches him. Faith realises the children have been watching. She composes herself and calls Esther.

FAITH	Esther, Esther come here. *(Esther comes over)*
ESTHER	Yes mama.
FAITH	Esther, I'm going to have to send you away.
ESTHER	No mama.
FAITH	You father gawn. *(pause)*
ESTHER	No.
FAITH	... take all me savings. Me no have nothing except the land and me little job. I go have to work extra hard round here. *(pause)* You have to go.
ESTHER	No mama.
FAITH	Yes.
ESTHER	I can help. Work the yard! Get a job.
FAITH	If you were boy pickney, it would be easier. You gots to go.
ESTHER	No mama.
FAITH	I'm sending you to Miss Pea in Kingston. You can concentrate on you schooling.
NORMA	What about me?

(Faith ignores Norma as she wipes tears from her eyes)

NORMA	Me going Miss Pea as well? *(pause)* Learn to read. *(pause)* You no want me around?
FAITH	Norma, go chop some wood for the fire.

NORMA   Me a go with Esther to study?

FAITH   You come in like curse ...

NORMA   You throwing me out?

FAITH   Esther is in a different class. She a go become
something. You, you have to earn your way.

NORMA   Daddy did want me to have an education too.

FAITH   If that coarse head man did want you, him would a
take you marga backside with him. *(pause)* Go do what me say
before me throw you out yes.
(Norma is hesitant)
Wha me say! Get out a me sight! Favour Dopey!

Norma runs out.

SCENE 4

*Ezra and Winston enter playing. Miss Sophie and Ruby also come in
- they fold sheets.*

EZRA   Esther a go sleep in a strange bed.

WINSTON   Norma stopping at home.

SOPHIE   Is tradition! If mother can't take care of the pickney.
Grandmother, auntie or good friend will do the same.

RUBY   A so we stay ...

SOPHIE   ... look out for we one another.

RUBY   Your pickney ...

SOPHIE   ... a my pickney.

EZRA   But Esther no happy ...

WINSTON   ... she a go school.

SOPHIE   She naa form fool.

EZRA   But the heart is sad.

WINSTON   Hurting bad.

EZRA	Watch out for the fire.
WINSTON	Poor Esther.
SOPHIE	Esther what?
RUBY	What about Norma.
SOPHIE	Time will reveal.
RUBY	See how the story grow ...
SOPHIE	Two sisters.
RUBY	Different roads.

EZRA/WINSTON Fire!

They exit.

SCENE 5

Norma is chopping wood for the fire. Toto - an eleven year old orphan boy comes along.

TOTO   Norma! *(notices Norma's sadness)* Trouble?

NORMA   Always trouble, just like you.

TOTO   Me? *(he laughs)* ... me alright man. *(proud of himself)* I find next place to live.

NORMA   Eee hee!

TOTO   Down by the post office. Them have one unused shack. It warm a night time. And I can play with the dogs ... share the scraps.

NORMA   I sorry for you man.

TOTO   Me have health, strength, me no thief, I have a good life . You know, before mamma dead, she give me special instruction not to tell lies, and not to steal. *(he imitates his mother)* Don't take what you never put down. She was a good woman. I going make sure I never let her down. *Ever! (pause)* I miss her still.

NORMA   You ever know you daddy?

TOTO   Never meet him. I hear say he kill himself in a accident.

NORMA   How that go?

TOTO   Him beg a lift off a one truck driver, and fall off the back as them turn a corner. *(he notices Norma's silence)*

NORMA   Me daddy gone.

TOTO   That's why you face long so?

NORMA   Me not going to learn to read. Work in a bank, count money ... write.

TOTO   You no want to bother with office work. Coop up with managers an supervisionaries on you back. Have to be free like the birds, fly in the wind.

NORMA   Free? Not like Esther.

TOTO   In town them say you should be glad you have a roof over you head. Them say you should be grateful, Miss Faith take you in. Offering her good naturedly, charity. Check it, you not really her blood. *(she collects her wood and starts to leave)*

NORMA   A true. I luckier than most. Look on you. Maybe when Esther come back it will be my turn to study.

TOTO   Cheer up man. *(pause)* I go past round tomorrow and show you me new friend.

NORMA   I thought I was your friend?

TOTO   Yes ma', we is - and I don't want to loose you. Is just Jessy - a mouse me find in the shed. But if you don't want Jessy to be me friend I will tell him to go?

NORMA   No man, he's you company.

TOTO   Jessy bring me tings to eat ... spiders ... red ants... I promise to make him a cage so he can come with me. I looking the wood now. Building for the future.

NORMA   I got to go.

TOTO   You going come visit again?

NORMA   Maybe. Take care Toto. Miss Faith must be tearing out her hair looking for me.

TOTO   She will beat you?
          (She starts to leave)

NORMA   Dinner time and me have to put on the food. Last thing she say, if me late she a go beat me till me raw.

TOTO   Walk good.

She exits.

SCENE 6

Norma moves centre stage.

NORMA   Things change when daddy gone. Miss Faith was like a mad woman, if she look on me I get beating. If I look on her she beat me. She ask me to sweep the yard ...

Enter Miss Faith.

MISS FAITH Jesus have his mercy. You too slow man, how you lazy so?

NORMA   She beat me. If I look her in the face when she talking ...

MISS FAITH You a turn big woman?

NORMA   Beating. If I keep me head down.

MISS FAITH What you have to hide - look at me when me talking.

NORMA   She just beating me, beating me. I buck up courage one day and ask Miss Faith if she would school me. Miss Faith,

I'm twelve years old an can't read me name, you would send me to the school down the road?'

MISS FAITH What you say?

NORMA   I will help with the fees, sell in the market, ratcut, fruits, sorrel anyting. *(pause)* Miss Faith laugh.

MISS FAITH *(laughs)* If you did have any money me would a take it for you board and keep. Me look like charity to you?

Enter Esther. She goes over proudly to her mother.

NORMA   Every Christmas, Easter and Summer Esther come home for holiday. She doing really well, top of the class. Teachers say she have a lot of protention.
(Miss Faith takes out a report card and reads it)
A very talented student. When the report card come Miss Faith show it to the whole congregation at church. She proud, proud, of Esther.
(Esther is smiling and lapping up the attention)

MISS FAITH Esther pass! Get distinction. I knew she would go far.

Esther and Faith leave.

NORMA   Christmas come and go and I thought daddy would write, send for me, but he never. After *(she counts on her fingers)* two, three, four, five Christmas pass, I stop looking for daddy. Stop getting me hopes up when postman come. *(pause)* One hot morning, Miss Faith was extra mad, come like she have demons in her.

MISS FAITH Gal! Me head a hurt me. If me have to call you name today - me a go serve you a sauce.

NORMA   A man pass, him have a message for Miss Faith bout daddy. Me heart beat fast an I hide behind a bush. I couldn't hear them talk so me crane me neck out as far as I can. The man say daddy gone to America. Him say daddy got a new wife. I couldn't hear everyting ca' the chickens a mek mek. The man give him message an gone. Daddy never even ask bout me. Naa go send for me. Daddy lef me gone. Gone out of the land. *(pause)* But my turn will come, my turn will come soon.

SCENE 7

Market women come on stage. Ruby and Miss Sophie are gossiping. They are organising fruit and vegetables. Toto, Eddie, and Hector come on stage. Eddie and Toto are selling nuts, cigarettes, odds and ends. Ruby smiles at Eddie.

MISS SOPHIE Ruby.

RUBY   Mama?

MISS SOPHIE Keep you mind on the Calaloo.

(Eddie shouts across the market)

EDDIE   Alright sweetness!
(Ruby smiles at them. Miss Sophie gets annoyed. Eddie eggs on Hector to go over to the woman. Toto does not want to have anything to do with it)

MISS SOPHIE *(disapproving)* Hmm!

HECTOR   How much for the orange?

EDDIE *(shouts across)* Yes! What's you price?

RUBY   Twenty cents.

HECTOR   I tell you what, me a go test it first see if it worth the money. *(steals the orange and runs off)*

RUBY   Thief!
(Hector runs back to his friends laughing, smells the orange)

HECTOR   It juicy Ruby.

EDDIE   Juicy and nice.

MISS SOPHIE Come, come see about you pickney.

HECTOR   Ruby lie.

EDDIE   A lie she a tell yes, *(to Hector)* ... is jacket she a put
on you.

HECTOR   See the father there! *(points at Toto - Toto is
petrified)*

TOTO   No, no!

HECTOR   ... See - him quick to deny it. *(the boys laugh)*

MISS SOPHIE If me find out say a you get me daughter pregnant,
me a go chop off you fingers. *(Hector laughs)*

HECTOR *(mocking - making chicken sounds)* Cluck, cluck, cluck!

EDDIE   Chirpy, chirp, chirp!

Toto, Eddie and Hector exit.

MISS SOPHIE Mouth favour!

RUBY   Leave them mamma.

MISS SOPHIE *(angry)* Leave what? Is that same slackness get you
in trouble. An me not supporting you and you dry head pikney.
Me get anybody pregnant? *(pause)* I still want to know who the
father is? *(Sophie fixes up the stall)* Don't make me see you
talking to those boys again. You shame me already, I don't want
people to think you don't have any brought-upsy.

Faith and Norma come on stage with shopping bags.

MISS FAITH *(calling)* Sophie.

MISS SOPHIE Morning Miss Faith.

MISS FAITH Morning. *(to Ruby)* Beg you how much you selling
the sour sap? I want to make me special recipe.

RUBY   Sixty cents.

MISS FAITH *(to Ruby)* How the baby? *(Faith gets out her money)*

RUBY ... have cholic.

MISS SOPHIE Me husband looking after it.

MISS FAITH *(sympathetic)* Things no easy.

RUBY You still happy to be Godmother? The christening in two months?

MISS FAITH Yes love. *(confidentially)* Don't mind people talk. You can come back to church after the christening. *(she whispers)* I had a word with the Pastor. Of course he is very disappointed - you used to be such a conscientious church girl. Mind you, you could do yourself a big favour by naming de father. *(she waits for an answer)*

MISS SOPHIE She a protect the man.

MISS FAITH In you own time darling. I told Pastor me a go be God-mother and he was very happy to hear that the baby would have someone who'll give the child a firm moral grounding.

RUBY *(sarcastic)* You very good to me Miss Faith. *(Miss Sophie is getting annoyed)*

MISS FAITH At least me lucky not to have to cope with teenage pregnancy. *(to Sophie)* God bless you Sophie. You must be very strong. But you know what them say, everybody pickney can't turn out the same. *(still looking at fruit)* My Esther doing really well you know. She coming home.

RUBY Oh, so you a go kill the fatted calf?

MISS FAITH Esther is coming back for good. A the one daughter me have, and God bless her she pass her scholarship.

MISS SOPHIE She heading for big things?

MISS FAITH Well ... I teach her right from wrong. So she too sensible to get herself in trouble.

RUBY We invited to the celebrations?

MISS FAITH I don't want to trouble you or you mam. I know you have you hands full with the baby ... an no man to support you. *(pause)* Oh dear look on me a chat. Me a make Esther's favourite dinner. I better go home and get on with it.

MISS SOPHIE Tell Esther welcome an she's to pass round come see me.

MISS FAITH She'll be very busy you know - have so much to organise ... university, planning her career ... intellectual ...

MISS SOPHIE Well that is well an good, but you still cleaning for Miss Armatage?

MISS FAITH *(ignores Sophie)* I might suggest to Esther to take over the sunday school - each one teach one.

MISS SOPHIE Faith, how is the domestic work going?

MISS FAITH Miss Armatage likes to think of me as the house supervisor. I'm a valuable employee. Anyhow see you. The devil finds work for idle hands.

She leaves beckoning to Norma to follow. The women start to pack up.

MISS SOPHIE Who the hell she think she is. Eee? Going on like she don't mash ants. Look me in the eye an criticise me. Chat me business to me face. Esther this, Esther that, Esther get the cream from the cat.

RUBY　　　　Oh mamma she don't mean anything.

MISS SOPHIE If you did keep you legs closed an go a school when me did send you - she couldn't tell me that. *(referring to Faith)* *Firm moral grounding.* She stay there. Me hear say Hector - Esther's oldtime playmate want to rekindle the fire.

RUBY *(very interested)* How you know?

MISS SOPHIE *(suspicious)* What's it to you?

RUBY　　　　Just asking.

MISS SOPHIE Kingston girl come home. Let's see how long miss high and mighty can boast about her scholarship daughter.

RUBY　　　　Miss Faith think Esther a creme.

MISS SOPHIE A pity I can't said the same about you. Up to now you no tell me the pickney father name? Esther would never do that to her mother. *(pause)* Come, pack up the things. Me blood pressure gone up, and I tink I'm getting the sugar. See how your slackness make me ill!

SCENE 8

Early evening. Esther is returning home after seven years. Faith is excited and is preparing a meal in the kitchen. Norma is sweeping.

MISS FAITH The mutton taste fresh. Pass the salt. *(Norma stops what she is doing and gets the salt. Faith snatches it. Norma gets back to what she was doing)* I want when Esther come, the place spotless. You hear - *spotless!* You tidy her room?
(Norma is in a world of her own, Faith gets the spoon and whacks it over Norma's head)

NORMA   Owch!

MISS FAITH Pay attention! Esther is coming home. Home for good, everything must be right.
(Norma kisses her teeth)
Don't make me hear you a try start fight with her today. She's a scholarship girl now, educated, going to college.

NORMA   She better kibber her mouth, she too facety.

MISS FAITH A jealous you jealous.

NORMA   Hmmm!

MISS FAITH Esther come every holiday and you always want to start confusion with her. Before you h'admire her achievements.

NORMA Chu! she think she better than me.

MISS FAITH But see'ar she better than you yes! You ugly as sin, you can just about read you name, you real mother don't want you ... *(she pauses to look at her sweeping the floor)* Norma! You call that floor sweep? ... couldn't even employ you as a domestic. What you good for?

(Pause. Faith continues cooking. She gets irritated with Norma because she's so slow.)

MISS FAITH   You too slow man. She soon come. Sweep round here... *(Miss Faith gestures Norma to sweep)* ... just take off the talking and leave the whispering.

Esther enters carrying baggage.

ESTHER: Mamma!

MISS FAITH   Me baby, me baby ... *(she hugs Esther - Esther pulls away)* ... come home for good. Make me look on you. Lord you rosie. Miss Pea take good care a you.

ESTHER   A nothing.

MISS FAITH   A something yes. Turn round make me see you, *(pause)* ...eee hee, you backland spread out, and what's this? Breast? You turning big woman on me.

ESTHER   I haven't changed.

MISS FAITH   You here for good now. *(she looks at the baggage)* Norma! Why the bags still in the doorway? *(pause)* Put them in the bedroom, unpack them while you there. Stupid! *(She pulls Esther to sit down)* You make me so proud. My daughter h'educated. You hungry? Come sit down.

ESTHER   I going to me room.

MISS FAITH   Plenty time for that man, I have plans for you now you home. Come and eat.

ESTHER   No thanks.

MISS FAITH   Miss Armatage is well. I thought you might visit her.

ESTHER   Me a go lie down.

MISS FAITH   You sick ... not feeling too good? The mutton will be bring up you strength. I don't want when people see you looking fenky fenky. *(pause)* Esther? Why you no wear you hair out long? It suit you better, make people see say you have good quality hair.

ESTHER   Mum!

MISS FAITH That old lady must be what ... seventy-three? These white people no live long in Jamaica hot sun. So if you good to her, maybe when she dead she might leave you something nice. *(pause)* Esther - What happen?

ESTHER   I want to be alone.

MISS FAITH I was looking forward to a chat. Catch up.

ESTHER *(under her breath)* If you never send me away, there would be nothing to catch up on.

MISS FAITH *(furious)* If I never send you a town you would be a backward, country gal. *(pause)* ... wi no prospects.

ESTHER   I weary from the travel.

MISS FAITH *(regains control)* Rest now me will call you later.

Esther goes into her bedroom. Norma is inside Esther's room - reading one of her books.

ESTHER   Come outta me things.

NORMA   Is this what mamma send you a town to learn?

ESTHER   ... you dunce as bat.

NORMA   Given the chance. I could show mamma I could do better than you. Look how the book easy.

ESTHER   Go 'bout you business!

NORMA   You vex? *(Esther starts to unpack)* What for?

ESTHER   Leave me no?

NORMA   She been looking forward to you coming home ... look ... *(she shows her the spot where she got hit earlier)* ... me suffer because of you. See the bump there!
(Esther doesn't respond)

You lucky, get the chance to live with a rich old lady. No chickens to feed, goats to tend to, house to clean. Me would a swap with you anyday.

ESTHER　　Miss Pea never born me. I should have been here.

NORMA　　Poor you. And what say me, living here in you shadow like unpaid slave and you ever see me complain?

ESTHER　　I'm not as docile as you.

NORMA　　So what you saying?

ESTHER　　After being away so long, I don't know.

NORMA　　You looking for something?

ESTHER　　Me know no. But whatever it is, I don't think it's here.

MISS FAITH *(shouts from outside)* Norma! You no hear the gal say she tired!

NORMA　　I coming. *(Faith makes a noise in the kitchen)*

MISS FAITH　Kiss me neck! You put salt in the mutton?

NORMA　　No ma!

MISS FAITH　How it taste so salt?

NORMA　　You put it in.

MISS FAITH　You no tink me would remember?

NORMA　　... just before Esther come you put salt in the food.

MISS FAITH　You a lie on me?

NORMA　　Just before you conk me in the head. Before Esther come.

MISS FAITH　Come here gal!
(Norma shakes her head in disbelief)
Me say come here!
(Norma tentatively goes to Miss Faith)
Fetch the switch. *(pause)* I going to cure your giddyhead.
(Norma goes for the switch)
You tink you smart ... but nobody smarter dan me!

Lights down.

SCENE 9

Morning. Norma is making breakfast - cornmeal porridge. Esther comes out of her bedroom. Stretches and languishes on a chair in the yard. Norma dishes out the porridge and puts it on the table.

ESTHER   What this? *(Norma takes her time to answer)*

NORMA   You forget how cornmeal porridge stay?

ESTHER   How the bowl chip up so? You must tink you feeding the dog. Take it back you here. Pauper food!
(Norma washes plates. Esther gets herself a banana - she starts to peel and eat it)

NORMA   Mamma say to clean the lamp.

ESTHER   I never go a Kingston, get scholarship to do your dirty work.

NORMA   Me just the messenger.

ESTHER   Then me never get the message.

NORMA   You hand join church? Too posh for lickle cleaning.

ESTHER   We did have helper. Claris them call her. One idiot gal with a lisp. Miss Pea did have to knock sense in a her 'nough time. We did have posh side board with silver, crystal and a lovely bedspread she get from England. The gal no burn up the spread one day ... *(Norma pours Esther some juice)* ... iron go straight through. Is bad mind, she was bad mind - so Miss Pea lick her. Lick her yes! She was too covetous. She should learn to respect her betters. *(pause)* A so me a go live one day. Live good.
(Norma starts sweeping the yard)
The house nice, man, electric lamp, cooker with gas   bottle - never have to fool round no lamp ... or bus' me neck a night time fe ketch water, an pee pee a bush with cricket and lizard looking on.

NORMA   This is not the city.

ESTHER   You train up for this work? *(she gets up and*
stretches) Chu I gone to beautify meself.
(Norma cleans the lamp)

NORMA   Hector asking after to you. Want to know when you
coming back.

ESTHER   You see him?

NORMA   All the time.

ESTHER   What him say?

NORMA   Nothing more than so.

ESTHER   Oh!

NORMA   Talking 'bout Spur Tree Hill, how you used to play
together down the stream, ketching fish, picking almonds off the
tree.

ESTHER *(reminiscing)* Him still remember that?

NORMA   Still go there him say. A look fe you.

ESTHER   After all this time. *(pause)* Him going college?

NORMA   Is the same Hector we talking? Him naa do nothing -
just one useless yabba youth hanging on street.
(Esther changes course, puts on her shoes and starts going out)

ESTHER   I soon come.

NORMA   Where you gone? What happen to the lamp?

ESTHER   Do it no?

NORMA   What me fe tell you mama?

ESTHER   Miss Armatage did ask after me. Tell her is there me
is.

NORMA   If is Hector you going, remember how people stay.
By this afternoon it shout 'pon tree top.

ESTHER   Them too fast!

She exits leaving Norma.

NORMA *(under her breath)* Church girl, fooling round with thief. *(to Esther)* ... a who fast? You carry on. Miss high an mighty, my time soon come.

SCENE 10

Early next morning. Esther is carrying washing from Miss Armatage. She is being heckled by some boys.

TOTO	Mad them Dora!
EDDIE	Scholarship gal! You think you better than we?

Where Hector there? *(she ignores them and carries on)*

TOTO	You coming to dance?
EDDIE	To the shubein? Hector get lucky. You give it up

yet?

ESTHER	Huh! Go long!
EDDIE	Think you nice. A gwan like toponarter.
TOTO	Brown skin girl.
EDDIE	Mek me swap my gal for you no?
ESTHER	Go mind foul an n'yam them feaces.
EDDIE	Eah ... eah she facety.
ESTHER	Unoo no stay like me - so beg you stop call me

name.

EDDIE You give Hector de goodness yet?
(Esther kisses her teeth) Time is the master. Fruit ripe, time to pick. *(pause)* Come here nice browning. *(she reacts as Eddie comes closer)*

ESTHER *(threatened)* Touch me, and me a go let police lock up you clothes basket!

EDDIE	A joke we a joke.
TOTO	He's only teasing Miss Esther.
ESTHER	You surprise me Toto. *(Toto hangs his head)*

EDDIE   Nice girl ... come talk to us.
(Eddie moves closer and tries to touch her. The clothes drop on the ground)

ESTHER *(angry)* Take you nasty thiefing hand from me. You must think me desperate. *(she picks up a stick to hit Eddie)* Come ... come make me lick you! *(the boys run back)*

TOTO   Him never mean no harm.

EDDIE   Just play we a play.

TOTO   Cus cus never bore hole in skin.

Esther leaves, they start to exit.

EDDIE *(conspiratorially)* She up to something.

TOTO   Up to no good.

EDDIE   Come make we find her sister.

TOTO   Norma?

EDDIE   Yes, Norma beat up one gal a street.

TOTO   My friend.

EDDIE   When them black, so what you expect?

TOTO   What goes around comes around.

TOTO   Esther up to something.

EDDIE   Up to no good.

Ruby and Ezra are walking on the way to market. They are carrying oranges for selling.

EDDIE   What you a sell gal?

RUBY   Who you a call gal?

EDDIE   Give me some of what you got.

RUBY   Darling, you can't afford it.

EDDIE   Maybe I already try it.

RUBY   Did it sweet you? *(playing with the oranges)*

EDDIE   Nice man! Nice.

RUBY   You afraid to try it again? Take it on proper.

EDDIE   Me soon ready.

RUBY   You soft! Job too big?

EDDIE   Me is a man you know?

RUBY   Then prove it.

She laughs with Ezra and leaves. Eddie watches them. Toto is looking at Ruby as well.

TOTO   Hey Eddie ... I tink Ruby desire me. You no see how she looks at me. Y'eyeball to y'eyeball - Lustful and concupiscience.

EDDIE   You dreaming fool.

TOTO   No, no, I tink she aching to have me body. Thirsty to drink from my cup of love and bewitchment.

EDDIE   You been smoking?

TOTO *(indignant)* I am a man of righteousness. I will not dishonor that magnificent flower. She have it hard already with no man to protect her. I will look out for she. *(pause)* After a while, I will court Ruby Simith in a proper and mannersable fashion.

EDDIE *(jealous)* You finish you stupidness? Come make me make you a tonic. Fix you head.

SCENE 11

Hector is by the stream throwing stones. Esther comes in.

ESTHER   Hector? *(Hector turns round startled.)*

HECTOR   Esther! ...You come back for true. Since when?

ESTHER   Just yesterday.

HECTOR   Bwoy long time you know. Long time since them send you way.

ESTHER   I just passing.

HECTOR   Not looking fe me?

ESTHER   Mamma say to pop up the hill and say howdy.

HECTOR   She still a try to con Miss Armatage to put you in her will? *(she ignores him)* From we was small, your mother a boast off 'pon my mother say Miss Armatage a go help you out.

ESTHER   Chu you a joker. *(Hector gets intimate)*

HECTOR   You mamma never know me was stealing your kisses behind the bushes ee? ... under the tree - round Spur Tree Hill.

ESTHER   We was little then. *(she pushes him away)*

HECTOR   You pretty when you get embarrassed. *(pause)* That's why me like you.

ESTHER   Stop it man! *(he teases her)*

HECTOR   Miss Faith know is me you dream 'bout at night? She know is me you really want?

ESTHER   Stop fooling.

HECTOR   Make me look on you.

ESTHER *(she turns)* Like what you see?

HECTOR   Yes sa, skin clear an brown, fresh and ready. School do you good.

ESTHER   School alright.

HECTOR   Top of the class?

ESTHER   Of course.

HECTOR   A so me like my ladies sophisticated, educated, someone I can converse with. *(Hector changes the subject)* So, you back fe good?

ESTHER   Maybe, I not too sure of me plans - thinking of going university.

HECTOR   Lawd! You speaky spokey ee ... *(pause)* What about here?

ESTHER   Life too hard round here.

HECTOR   You taste de high life an you wan' go back?

ESTHER   Could be.

HECTOR   Looking fe someting?

ESTHER   I don't know what I want, but I know it not here.

HECTOR   Be careful, one day you just might get it.
(she starts to leave) Wait ... wait man. Me no finish wid you. Make me look on you proper.
(She stops, he walks around her and appraises her)
You look good. Grow nice. Everything in the right place man - would a tek set fe you ... looking so nice ...

ESTHER   How you know dem never try?

HECTOR   You have s'maddy?

ESTHER   Guess no ...

HECTOR   The way you look, man would a put question to you yes ... but I tink you still my woman ... don't it? *(he moves closer to her)*

ESTHER   I have to go.

HECTOR   Wait no man ... you no answer me.

ESTHER   Work it out fe youself.

Hector pulls her close and kisses her. As they kiss Norma walks by with wood for the fire. They pull away.

NORMA   Morning.

HECTOR   Gal wa you want?

ESTHER   You no wait till you fass wid me?

NORMA   Just picking sticks fe de fire.

ESTHER   How many place you could a go?

NORMA   Make sure you don't take up someting you can't manage.

HECTOR: How can somting so dark an ugly be so fresh?

NORMA   The kettle a call the pot black.

ESTHER   Go 'bout you business. *(they try to run her off)*

HECTOR   Keep out. Gwan! Backward wretch!

ESTHER   Say anything and I tell mama you a keep up with Toto Masters.

HECTOR   She bust you arse.

NORMA   Say what you like.

Hector and Esther leave. Ruby turns up carrying water from the pump. She wipes her brow and sits down.

RUBY   Howdy Norma.

NORMA   Sun hot.

RUBY   You up early?

NORMA   Working ... you know ...

RUBY   ... whole heap a wood you have dere. You baking?

NORMA   Now Esther back, Miss Faith want her to eat right. Me making fresh bread, an bula cake.

RUBY   Everybody know your baking is de best in de district.

NORMA   Eat off of me table, and you lick you ten finger. *(pause)* What you out so early for?

RUBY   Mamma on me back. Giving me a hard time. I decide to keep busy, stay out de way, take her mind off the baby father business.

NORMA   Miss Sophie, Miss Faith all de same, how them come so?

RUBY   How you mean?

NORMA   Miserable.

RUBY *(agrees)* An hypocrite, them both go a church but when them ready fe lash you with them tongue. Jesus!

NORMA *(she mocks)* You wicked an evil?'

RUBY   Then out come the strap.

NORMA   Always de strap.

RUBY   You know Hector was talking to me ...

(Norma kisses her teeth disapprovingly) ... say the slave masters used to keep us under control with the beating. Now that slavery gone we still keep up the tradition.

(Ruby wipes her brow again)

NORMA   You look tired.

RUBY   ... can't sleep, the baby keep me up, an mamma ...

NORMA   Miss Sophie down on you?

RUBY *(mocks Miss Sophie)* Ruby, you too legobeast. Oh mamma I was only having fun. Fun, when I was your age there was no time for fun, I had to milk the goats, feed the chickens, make the breakfast and walk ten miles everday to school an back. There was no time fe fun.

NORMA *(laughing)* Stop that man.

Ruby cocks up her foot on the bucket. Miss Sophie looms up over the hill.

RUBY   It's true man. Everyting me do she have someting to
say. You keep up wid too much man ... always on de street.
Seems you never learn de first time an you want to disgrace me
again. I should get a iron bar and lock up you crutches. Throw
'way the key. If only you was like Esther Lewis. You know, she's
a cantankerous old lady. Sometimes I wish I could lock up her
mouth.
(Norma stops laughing. Ruby realises why Norma has stopped)

MISS SOPHIE *(enters)* Cantankerous eh! Who you a take make
joke? You no have baby fe nurse? When I was your age I never
had time to enjoy life. It was work, hard work and more hard
work. Look at you with you foot cock up.
(Ruby puts her foot down. To Norma)
Would Esther do this? Mock Miss Faith?
(Norma doesn't answer, she goes back to Ruby)
Exodus 20 Verse 12. The scripture say - honor thy mother and
father and all the days will be long on the land the Lord thy God
giveth thee. But you really bent on disgracing me. Making me
look bad. Come see to you pickney. Pick up the water.
(Ruby slowly gets up)
Walk with life mam. Quick! Me a go show you there is only one
woman in a me house. Move you behind!

*Miss Sophie marches Ruby away. Norma chuckles and picks up her
sticks and goes.*

Lights down.

SCENE 12

Eddie is selling tobacco - Toto is sitting on the wall. Enter Hector.

EDDIE   W'happen boss.

HECTOR   Yeah man. Hear say you come into money?

EDDIE   Me grandmother dead. Lef' me the house and a few
dollars.

HECTOR   So me can borrow a money off you?

EDDIE   Me!

HECTOR *(coaxing)* Hey! Wa you a say man?

EDDIE   You ever give me anyting?

HECTOR   How much time me feed you when you come with you hungry belly?

EDDIE   One piece a dry hard dough bread? You a joke!

HECTOR   You spend you' money gone?

EDDIE   Me buy one criss suit fe de dance Saturday and a cart fe sell.

HECTOR   I gwoing try again when you feeling generous.

TOTO   After him drink two drink, you can get the clothes off his back.

EDDIE *(to Hector)* I ready fe you.

HECTOR   W'happen Toto? *(no answer)*

EDDIE   Him a solomise 'bout him predicament.

TOTO   Ruby say the baby is mine.

EDDIE   You ever hear a bigger joke? Them call him name, an him fool, a own it. *(laughs)*

TOTO   I can't do noting. Ruby stuck fe a father an blame me.

EDDIE   Him a feel de pressure. Christening soon come.

HECTOR   You a man or a mouse bwoy? *(they playfully push him around)* If you no do it, then you no do it. Fix up you face!

EDDIE *(teasing)* Bwoy! Hitch up your lip.

HECTOR *(they grab at his trousers)* Where de mouse deh?

EDDIE   De mouse is more a man than you.

HECTOR   Fix you business. Don't let no gal rule you.

EDDIE   Control the situation man. *(they laugh at Toto)*

TOTO *(to Hector)* Is one a you do it .

HECTOR   Wha' you say bwoy?

TOTO   You do it, threaten Ruby not to say nothing. That's why me have to carry the bucket.

EDDIE   Carry de can - Fool!

HECTOR   You have one imagination on you.

EDDIE   Relax man. It will all blow over.

HECTOR   Soon gawn.

EDDIE   Check it - Who no touch Ruby Smith? *(he reminisces)* Bwoy she nice! The back of her calf ...

TOTO *(to Eddie)* A you! You do it!

EDDIE   Relax man. Me no trouble it since last Christmas.

HECTOR   By this weekend, a next sinting come to take up people time.

EDDIE   Chill out man.

HECTOR   Cool breeze. *(they all hang out in the sun)*

EDDIE   Eh Hector! What you a do with that posh gal?

HECTOR   Which gal?

EDDIE   Esther Lewis.

HECTOR   So is what?

EDDIE *(teasing)* You like her init?

HECTOR   Chu! Go way bwoy!

EDDIE *(moving closer)* You like her bad init?

HECTOR   Dress back star.

EDDIE   You want to taste it? ... you want her bad, bad, *bad!*

HECTOR *(threateningly)* You stay there.

EDDIE   Hey, between me an you. You love her?

HECTOR   Wa! *(threateningly)* Your want me fist to brok up your face?

EDDIE *(openly laughing)* Esther Lewis out of your league.

HECTOR   How you mean?

EDDIE   She no Miss Faith's prize possesion?

TOTO   ... best daughter.

EDDIE   She would a kill you!

HECTOR   All the women them want me. Even Miss top notch Esther can't resist it.

TOTO   You want to disrepute the nice girl!

EDDIE   Disrespect.

TOTO   Ooh, oh, oh.

HECTOR   She disrespect I. Me not privileged, speak nice, dress posh - them fancy woman there, treat we like play ting.

EDDIE *(agreeing)* A true - like any toy.

HECTOR   But you know what? Any gal come and try cross me, try use them head on me - naa go leave me with them draws on. Mark my words.

EDDIE   So you no touch it yet fe true?

HECTOR   These things take time. Only white man and bwoy rush it. But I soon sort that out.

EDDIE   ... hope I don't have to rescue you from Miss Faith big dumpling hand.

TOTO   She cus you till you turn dust.

HECTOR   Where you get the cigarette them?

EDDIE   Thief it from the warehouse store

TOTO   You no have money?

HECTOR   W' happen to you inheritance?

EDDIE   Me, fresh an facety. Why buy when you can just walk in a place and just get it!

HECTOR   Beg you a pack cigarette.

EDDIE   One dollar. *(gives Hector some cigarettes. Hector begins to walk off)*

EDDIE   Hey! where the money deh?

HECTOR   You no thief them?

EDDIE   So is what?

HECTOR   Watch this - thief a go thief from thief.

He laughs and exits. Ruby appears with her friend Ezra. Eddie watches as Toto goes over.

RUBY   Toto, come here man.

TOTO   Ruby, how you do this? Everybody pointing them finger at me.

RUBY *(she looks him over)* You look good today. You bathe?

TOTO *(pleased)* I trying me best an thing, you know.

RUBY   Me mam want to see you. Tonight fe talk.

TOTO   What me fe say?

RUBY   Anyting man, just come.

TOTO   I know we is friend, but when we do this? Mek baby? *(still leaning up against the wall watching)*

EDDIE *(still leaning up against the wall watching)* Hear say you sleep walk at night. Bet you never know you enjoy you slumber that much?

RUBY   Seven o'clock. *(she starts to go)*

EDDIE   Toto wishing he was awake when him do ting. What an education.

RUBY *(turns back)* Bring someting nice fe mama. *(flirty)* An get me a present too. Don't be late now.

TOTO   Yes ... yes ... Seven o'clock on de dot. *(showing off)* Sharp as a razor, ... not minor but major ... just like a tiger ...

EDDIE *(mocking)* ... when was you inside her.

RUBY *(to Eddie)* Fool! *(to Toto)* I see you later.

She leaves looking at Eddie as she passes.

TOTO   I tink she like me ... can you see she does. Giving me that look. That special *I like you* look.

EDDIE   You too fool. She just a play with you.

TOTO   If she never like me why she ask me if I did bathe? She want me. She do.

EDDIE *(incredulous)* Bwoy!

TOTO   I tink I need to give you de h'advice about women. You no seems really have what it takes.

EDDIE   You really a fall fe all this nonesense. Idiot!

TOTO   You could do me a favour and lend me the suit you bury you grandmother in. I have to look fabulous, splendiferous an scrumptious fa Miss Sophie and Ruby.

EDDIE   A the one suit me have.

TOTO   Wha' me a go do? Me no have noting.

EDDIE   I'm not you keeper. *(Toto has an idea)*

TOTO   Is alright man. I know. Me will ask pastor fe sort me out. After all him supposed to look after him flock so me is a sheep, baa!

They exit. Lights down.

SCENE 13

Norma is washing clothes and Esther is rinsing them further down stage. Miss Faith is cooking in the kitchen. Enter Toto.

TOTO   Miss Norma ... Miss Norma you have a minute?

NORMA   Toto! What is it?

TOTO   I have a secret, an I mustn't tell.

NORMA   Then don't tell.

TOTO   I want to tell you.

NORMA   Alright I won't say nothing. *(getting annoyed)* What is it?

TOTO   The rumours. Ruby baby. Is not mine. You believe me don't it?

NORMA   Toto ...

TOTO   I wouldn't lie, you believe me?

NORMA   You want me to get in trouble?

TOTO   I just want you to tell me that you understand. Miss Sophie say me must support the child. Pay fe the baby ... the christening. If not, Miss Sophie say she a go slice off me teapot.

Miss Faith comes out.

MISS FAITH What's this? Toto! What you want?

TOTO   Good morning Miss Faith, how are you this lustrious superficious morning?

MISS FAITH *(to Norma)* You finish the clothes?

NORMA   No.

MISS FAITH An you standing here yapping? *(she makes a gesture)* Girl, you living on prayer. Me a go save this beating for later. Now, Toto Masters. What you doing on me property? You no get one girl pregnant already? What? You want to breed up the whole Island?

TOTO   Miss Faith believe me is not true.

MISS FAITH Then who trouble Ruby? *(he looks towards Norma, bewildered)* But wait Norma! Me never done tell you fe finish the washing?

Norma leaves.

MISS FAITH What you want round here?

TOTO   I was humbly hoping that maybe your gracious self, have any job you would want me to do ... the heavy work you know?

MISS FAITH Norma do all that.

TOTO   I thought I could fetch the kerosene bottle ... just fe a few cents.

MISS FAITH I don't want to encourage any undesirable people. Especially around me family.

TOTO   I won't get in anybody way. *(pause)* Please marm? I don't eat fe two days straight?

MISS FAITH Alright, alright, hurry up and get the kerosene and then get off me property, before anybody see you. *(takes out some money and gives it to Toto)*

MISS FAITH Hee!

TOTO   Congratulations Miss Faith. Marvellous. Tanks. Tanks. Fabulous. God will smile on you.

He leaves. Miss Faith shouts at Esther as she goes into the kitchen. Esther is washing clothes in a basin.

MISS FAITH Esther you finish de work yet?
(Esther continues washing)
When the washing done, give them to Norma to rinse down the river. Tell her to rinse them out well.

ESTHER   Me going up a top yard.

MISS FAITH What you say?

Norma enters. She starts to hang up the clothes she'd been rinsing down the stream.

ESTHER   I get little work.

MISS FAITH *(shouts)* Speak up!

ESTHER   She a go pay me.

NORMA   Learn fe dance a yard before you dance abroad.

ESTHER   What!

NORMA   You have things fe do right here so.

ESTHER   Why have a dog and bark youself? Hee, *(she pushes the tub of washing to Norma)* ... the clothes wash. You hear mama, take them go rinse.
(Norma ignores her and carries on with what she's doing)

NORMA   You going to the dance?

ESTHER   Me no know.

NORMA   Me tinking about it. These hips no get a good work out fe a long time.

ESTHER   Plenty man there ... glad fe easy woman like you.

NORMA *(smug)* Hmm ... you want to go?

ESTHER   Why mama no say anything? Cause you don't belong to her.

NORMA *(taunting)* You a dead fe go.

ESTHER   You will see me there. Don't worry.

NORMA   Puss an dog no have the same luck. If you mother catch you, Johncrow a bake bammy fe you.

ESTHER   You only here cos you's me father's child. Mama take pity on you.

NORMA   Like you take pity on that fool, fool half idiot wretch Hector. *(threatening)* Make me tell Miss Faith!

ESTHER   Is none a you business.

NORMA   I thought you had more sense. You and Hector soon go reach mama's ears.

ESTHER   Me soon leave this place. And you, you a go dead a old maid.

NORMA   You running off with you sweetheart?

ESTHER   Hector! That! You mad.

NORMA   You just a play with him?

ESTHER   Hector is a friend.

NORMA   Him too poor don't it? Him too black?

ESTHER   Butt out.

NORMA   Tell me no? What you up to?

ESTHER   You will see.

NORMA   Try me now no?

ESTHER *(pauses to think)* You ever think 'bout the world, and how it big? You ever consider that this little church, farm and school is only a small part of it?

NORMA   Hang you basket where you can reach it.

ESTHER   You will never have nothing.

NORMA   Don't judge a book by its cover.

ESTHER   I have a scheme - if you interested me will rope you in.

NORMA   *Me!* If dopey hate you him give you basket to carry water.

ESTHER   You going to want to know when the money a run. Just remember that.

MISS FAITH *(shouts from the kitchen.)*Esther, you idle?

ESTHER *(jumps)* No mama just ... *(she looks for an excuse)* ... sweeping the yard. *(she picks up the broom. Norma comes back and listens to Faith and Esther.)*

MISS FAITH Humph! *(muttering)* Lazy a kill you backside. Since you come back seem like you 'fraid fe work. Me can find something fe you to do.

ESTHER   Is alright mama ... it's alright.

MISS FAITH Remember, you never too big fe get a lick. Scholarship or none.
(Esther starts to walk down the road)
Esther? *(Esther ignores her)*
Esther!

ESTHER   See you later.

MISS FAITH Esther, what me say?

Esther leaves. Faith comes out to look for Esther. Norma quickly grabs a book and sits reading under a tree.

MISS FAITH ... Esther! *(she sees Norma)* She gone? *(Norma nods)* What you have there?

NORMA   Esther book.

MISS FAITH You can read it?

NORMA   I was hoping if Esther would bring up me reading.

MISS FAITH What! Don't make me hear you a bother her. She have enough on her plate. Waste her time on someone like you?

NORMA   You promised I would go school now Esther back.

MISS FAITH When me promise that? *(Norma shrugs)* Stop the complaining, plenty people have less than you. You be grateful for what you got. *(pause)* Norma?

NORMA   Yes ma.

MISS FAITH Make sure you have the book the right way up next you a try to impress me.

Norma checks the front and realises it's upside down. Faith goes back in the house.

SCENE 14

Esther finishes the work at Miss Armatage's. She counts her money. There are some beggars on the way.

ESTHER   Tanks a again. I come around tomorrow and finish off de rest.

TOTO   Beg you a dollar no?

WINSTON   Gimme that watch!

TOTO   What you have can give? Anything sister. Me will try sell.

WINSTON   Things hard fe de black man.
(Esther ignores them)

TOTO   Money fe de pickney - can't buy a shirt.

WINSTON   Just to get a bite.

TOTO   Me naa beg, me a ask. Have a heart.

WINSTON   Little change me browning.

TOTO   Little squeeze. Beg you a dollar no? How bout shilling?
(As Esther walks down the lane she hears a noise. She puts the money down the front of her dress)

HECTOR *(hiding, pretending to call chickens)* Sch ... sch ... sch ... sch ... sch ...
(Esther stops, looks round, sees no-one and carries on. Hector continues to make the sounds)

ESTHER   A who that? *(she stops again, looks around)* Somebody there? *(she carries on. Hector jumps out)*

HECTOR   Boow! You in the money.

ESTHER *(startled)* Hector!

HECTOR *(laughs)* What you doing? You want to kill me? Me see you a come from top yard.

ESTHER   You calling like me is any chicken.

HECTOR   Just a joke.

ESTHER   Me look like foul to you?

HECTOR   W' happen sexy!

ESTHER   Me not no animal. Me look like like foul or what?

HECTOR   You know say me like chicken. And the leg a the chicken sweet. That's why I call you my sweet sexy, chick, chicken. *(he goes to kiss her and she pushes him away)*

ESTHER   Fool!

HECTOR   You a go spend some a that on me?

ESTHER   Stupid!

HECTOR   Don't do that, call me stupid. Just cause you mother think you is royalty ... don't chat to me like that.

ESTHER   How you temper quick so?

HECTOR   No talk to me like dat. After me no dog.

ESTHER   Chu! You too hot head. *(Esther changes the subject)* I have an idea you know. *(Hector is sulking)*

ESTHER   You interested?

HECTOR   What?

ESTHER   I was thinking of throwing Pardoner, start up little savings. What you say?

HECTOR   Pardoner! That thing always cause war and bad feelings.

ESTHER   But me a go run it right. Everybody put them money in and each month the next person in line draw them hand.

HECTOR   As easy as that?

ESTHER   ... earn a few dollars, amongst me friends and some of the youths round here. *(pause)* I want to afford nice things.

HECTOR   Is that why you a work so hard?

ESTHER   I want to be independent.

HECTOR   You live at home - what money you need? Share de secret no.

ESTHER   You too suspicious Hector. *(pause)* All I need is the first person to start me off, then we gone clear. You a go back me up?

HECTOR   So is that why me hear say you a go church these days. You setting fe God's money.

ESTHER   People mouth big eee!

HECTOR   I remember how them did have to beat you to go a service. *(pause)* You smart you know.

ESTHER   I'm encouraging the youngster to spend a little, save a little. Mama is an elder in de church and I think dem interested but I need the first contribution.

HECTOR   No sa! Find a next guinea pig.
(Esther cuddles up to Hector to try and persuade him)

ESTHER   Oh baby ... sweetheart? You'll get it back, ten, twenty times over. Mmm Cherry pie?

HECTOR *(his mood lightens)* You coming to the dance?

ESTHER   No.

HECTOR   So who me fe dance with?

ESTHER   Keep yourself to yourself!

HECTOR   Come on baby, a long time we no go out.

ESTHER   Mama will take the stick to me.

HECTOR   Come on man. *(silence)* Don't bother go home, stay with me and come straight. *(silence)* Come on baby ... sweet chicken foot? Come tonight an I'll show you how much I care.

ESTHER *(plotting)* Tell mama, Miss Sophie had more work, so I had to stay.

HECTOR   See it there!

ESTHER   Then I can relax.

HECTOR   Eee hee!

ESTHER   But, where me a go stay?

HECTOR   What a silly question.

ESTHER   You must be mad! Me naa stay a your yard!

HECTOR   You safe with me.

ESTHER   That is exactly what Hyacinth Williams' boyfriend say an look she have six pickneny an another one on the way.

HECTOR   Them deh man no know what them a do. It's all about control.

ESTHER   Well me not interested.

HECTOR   Come on man. You want to come to the dance?
(silence) Then concentrate on that no. I will sort the rest.

ESTHER   Alright, but I sneaking home fe clothes first.

HECTOR   Problem solve.

ESTHER   Scheming brute you. *(she smiles)*

HECTOR   So wha' you a say?

ESTHER   Me naa say nothing.

They go off together.

SCENE 15

Norma and Ruby are on thier way to the schubein. Norma has a lamp in her hand.

NORMA   It's a warm night.

RUBY   Full moon.

NORMA   Just right fe dance.

RUBY   How Miss Faith let you come?

NORMA   She ask me to make a cup of coffee with a drop of rum in it. *(whispers)* Me just put in a little extra so she don't wake. Tonight, if the house on fire she would never know.
(They laugh)

RUBY   Bwoy you bad eee!

NORMA   Is who looking after the baby?

RUBY   Me daddy, him like babysitting. Tell me fe go enjoy
meself.

NORMA   Ruby, tell me the honest truth. How come you say Toto the daddy? Everybody know it not his. You a protect the fadha fe true?

RUBY   You think me wrong?

NORMA   It not fe me to say.

RUBY   Me mam was giving me such a hard time. I get one tongue-lashing till one day in the heat of it, I call Toto name.

NORMA   I understand.

RUBY   You is a good person *(pause)* Norma, I think there is something you should know. *(pause)* Miss Armatage send message that she want me to go a Kingston an work fe her. She movin there fe good. Country life don't agree with her. *(confidentially)* A young helper she a look, fe work in her posh new house.

NORMA   She tell Miss Faith she don't want her anymore?

RUBY   I don't think so.

NORMA *(still surprised)* A big thing you a tell me. Mama a go loose her job.

RUBY   I thought you should know. *(silence)* I sorry to bring you this news. I feel bad fe you. But I beg you keep it safe. *(pause)* Norma, you could do me a favour? Run give this message tomorrow morning to Miss Armatage.
(She gives Norma a note)

NORMA   You not taking the job?

RUBY   I don't want to leave me family, not now. An I'm hoping the real father come clean.

NORMA   I think you a still carry feelings fe him.

RUBY   What you take this ting fa, I not that soft.

NORMA   You' eyes tell a different story.
(They laugh and walk on a little more)

RUBY   I always think bout you Norma. How them never school you.

NORMA   I feel shame you know, I can't read or write properly.

RUBY   I tell you what, I teach you.

NORMA   You would?

RUBY   No problem man. Maybe a little more on top.

NORMA   I can come round tomorrow morning?

RUBY   Yeah man. *(pause)* Come, party time. *(she starts to dance)* Let's go to the dance.

NORMA   Show them big mouth bwoys ...

RUBY   Show them how a real woman moves.

NORMA *(laughs)* Bwoy! I can just hear mama when she find out that she a go loose her job.

RUBY   You a go get it?

NORMA   Cus me an tell me how me black.

RUBY   Pay her no mind. Darling, she don't have the understanding ... you know what them always say from long time, de darker de berry ...

NORMA/RUBY ... de sweeter de juice.

They exit laughing.

ACT TWO

SCENE 1

The dance. Music is being played. Toto, Eddie, Ruby, Ezra, Winston and Norma are dancing. Enter Hector and Esther.

HECTOR   Night young. Breeze warm. It hot.

ESTHER   Night young. Breeze warm. It hot.

HECTOR   Me have me woman in me hand. She feel right. Hug me up. Lord it nice!

ESTHER   Place full with 'nough woman and man. Sweet them up. Play things right. Lord money night tonight.

HECTOR   Bass line a reach. Ridim steady and tight.

ESTHER   Ridim steady and tight.

HECTOR   The sensee take me on a journey. An a the same spot me a stop.

ESTHER   Pardoner thing must can work. Me naa go stop till the money drop.

HECTOR   Me bredthren just a rock. Side to side like so.

ESTHER   Me sistren just a rock. Side to side like so.

HECTOR   An the brew, special. Put me in the mood.

ESTHER   The drink turn them fool. So watch me make my move. *(she approaches Eddie and Toto in the club. Ruby and Norma are with them. She tries to persuade them to get involved in the Pardoner)*

EDDIE   I hear say you collect whole heap a money? A true?

ESTHER *(flirting)* Some people have sense. Know when them bread is buttered. I thought you were smart. *(pause)* Seem say I misjudge you.

EDDIE   Pretty girl like you would rip me off?

ESTHER   You no have nothing to worry about.

EDDIE   Me always thought about saving. Maybe this will help me.

ESTHER   An you know you safe with me.

EDDIE   Me have a bad temper, I can really trust you?

ESTHER   But no must.

TOTO   You learn about money at the top school?

ESTHER *(ignores Toto, flirts with Eddie)* I have all the right credentials.

EDDIE *(moves closer)* I believe it.

ESTHER *(moves in)* See it as an investment.

EDDIE   Lord you persuasive ee!

ESTHER   Think about you future.

TOTO   You have all that dead lef' money. Best put away.

EDDIE *(to Toto)* You is me banker?

TOTO Just a little h'advice.

EDDIE Keep you fool, fool, mouth out a me business.

ESTHER Listen, him talking sense fe once.

EDDIE Alright, alright, me will join this Pardoner thing.

TOTO Esther count me in.

ESTHER You have anyting?

TOTO No but ...

EDDIE Give her you mouse.

ESTHER *(snottily)* Keep you small change darling.
(Toto takes out his money. Eddie takes out some money. Norma interrupts and takes Toto aside. Esther writes it in her book)

EDDIE How about a dance to seal the deal? *(they dance)*

ESTHER See Hector deh.

EDDIE No worry bout him.

HECTOR *(annoyed)* W'happen? Her eye a wander. Something on her mind. Then talk to me no baby. Come make me love you up, soothe you' heart and rub you up. Her mouth drop. She look on me like say ... something smell bad under her nose. Tell me say, me no have no ambition. Have no life. All me good fa is making sport, breeding woman ... and theifing people wife ... *(pause)* This is not my woman. Demon possess her mind. Ooo, you can't talk to I in this fashion and no expect no come back. All me did want was to have a good time. Me no want no fight. Me stupid, me fool, me never go a school. And de herbs a turn me fool, fool ... she may have education. She may have style. But common sense and knowing when to talk is mine. She up to something. Things a gwan. But me paitient cos time will reveal and I have 'nough time. But hear what, a me woman and me like her still. Must be the time a the month or sun hot. Make her mouth run way. Cause me no form fool. Look! watcha no, me gawn ... if me stay me will do someting that won't make me proud. So hear me no. Walk good. Me gone.

Hector walks out and passes Norma and Toto who are walking away from the dance.

NORMA   Toto, you really have to watch what you doing. People wiil take advantage.

TOTO   I wanted to save.

NORMA   With what? Shirt buttons? Stay away from Esther. She's trouble.

TOTO   ... prospects. Building fe the future.

NORMA   Ruby is not your look out. Come on walk with me.
(they walk a little)

TOTO   Norma, I want to do sometimg fe the baby, make something ... a cot, a rocking donkey.

NORMA   Toto, you shouldn't be putting you hopes in Ruby - she love another man.

TOTO   I want to make someting nice fe the baby?

NORMA   Gwan an make it.

ESTHER *(she runs out looking for Hector)* Hector! Hector wait man.

TOTO *(referring to Hector)* ... a lovers' sniffle. *(they sit down)* It's a peaceful, contentious night don't it? Love in the air, can't you feel it? I feel it ... moon a shine. Stars sparkle. *(he takes a deep breath)* ... breeze a blow ... See the trees - shadows on the red earth.

NORMA   Toto, have you wanted anything really bad? I mean so bad that you head spin an you eye cross. Me two foot shake when me think bout it. Everynight I wonder, dream. I just sit on the verandah - lie back. Smell the fresh air. The bread me make cooling on the ledge fe breakfast, floor scrub clean, hens clucking and the yard sweep. I wonder, I wonder what people up to in the rest of the world, in all the different houses in all de different lands.

Toto stands up. He helps Norma up and starts to sing as they exit.

TOTO   Mamma I love your daughter, no gestering, I love your daughter, no gestering ...

Lights down.

SCENE 2
Esther chases after Hector

ESTHER   Hector! Hector! *(pause)* Hector, wait man! *(he turns and grabs hold of her)* Hold on.

HECTOR   To raated! Who you think me is?

ESTHER   Don't be like dat.

HECTOR   I don't like the way you treat me. The whole night you a eggs up to all the bwoys in the club. You never even spit pon me.

ESTHER   So you leave me stranded?

HECTOR   If you come out with me, you fe stay with me.

ESTHER   People interested in the pardoner ... Winston, Eddie Simpkins, Mickey Regis. All of them want to join.

HECTOR   My woman no fe hustle, hustle so. You should let me look after to you.

ESTHER   With what? What you got? *(pause)* You make me laugh. You no have two penny to rub together, yet you say you want to look after to me!

HECTOR   I know them man deh ... I know what them after.

ESTHER   Not the same thing you after?

HECTOR   You're not like them, you can't mix up, mix up like that.

ESTHER   You sound like mama. *(she goes to leave)* Make me pass.

HECTOR   No man.

ESTHER   Move out the way Hector. *(he holds her arms, she starts to struggle)* Get off! Let me go! Leave me alone!

HECTOR   Quiet you mouth. You want you mama hear you was with me? *(she goes still, he turns on the charm)* I want when you leave tonight you have a smile on you face. *(Esther kisses her teeth)* Come man, come home, come on ... *(he cuddles her)*

ESTHER   No. *(she breaks away)*

HECTOR *(his mood changes)* So you collect some of this money yet?

ESTHER   Most of it!

HECTOR   And when your time fe draw, what you spending you money on?

ESTHER   I'm not sure yet. Maybe go a foreign.

HECTOR *(laughs)* Foreign!

ESTHER   Hector don't laugh, this is serious.

HECTOR   You intend to get big money from this Pardoner?

ESTHER   Don't you ever get bored of walking the same road everyday? The same places, same people, just getting old. Just living?

HECTOR   It all the same to me.

ESTHER   I have an aunt, you know. Blossom in England. We write now and then. When she talk about England, job, opportunity ... Jamaica come in like a place fe the living dead.

HECTOR   So what?

ESTHER   I would love to just get away.
   (Hector is moving closer to her, playing with her hair)

HECTOR   Hmm ...

ESTHER   You know what I mean Hector?

HECTOR (*playing with her hair*) Yes man.

ESTHER   Me can't do nothing right fe mama. Everyting is always wrong. All she want to say is that I have a high school certificate. And a Degree. You know what I'm saying?

HECTOR   Eee hee.

ESTHER   She keep telling me I'm a disappointment. I can't listen. Me no want to live mama life. I want to live mine. (*pause*) So I'm doing what I want. Hector! What you doing?

HECTOR   You' skin clear an nice like honey. Tonight - the sexiest, prettiest most gorgeous ting in the dance. When it comes to looks all the girls was in the shade. You outshine them all.

ESTHER   If you walking me home then come no. (*she starts to go, he pulls her back*)

HECTOR   Come home with me. You ever seen me stamp collection?

ESTHER   Fool!

HECTOR   You don't believe me? (*coaxing*) Come and see it.

ESTHER   No Hector. I'm in enough hot water already.

HECTOR   Alright. (*pause*) Look. I come round to the idea of this Pardoner thing. I have a little money saved. Me will back you up. Come over now and I'll give you a five dollar. Come no. What! You no trust me? (*pause*) Look, I will give you the money and if you want to go home, then alright. Tonight, I won't do anyting you no want me to do. (*he walks away a little and stretches out his hand*) Come. (*she takes his hand*)

They kiss and walk off.

SCENE 3

The next morning. Toto is in the yard feeding and talking to the animals.

TOTO   Morning mother hen, master goat, missus cow. Me soon come to you. Me have to feed the pigs first, you know how them stay. Greedy, and the noise if I don't feed them first ... *(he tuts and shakes his head)* ... you understand. *(pause - he kneels)* Hey missus hen, stop fighting with you husband. You is man an wife, blood. Be good to you one another.

Enter Norma, coming from Miss Armatage's house.

NORMA   Toto what you doing in me yard this time a morning?

TOTO   Feeding the animals.

NORMA   You know Miss Faith don't want you hanging round here.

TOTO   I was waiting fe you. Where you was?

NORMA   I was up the hill at Miss Armatage. I had to take a message for Ruby.

TOTO   Is Ruby going away too?

NORMA   No, she staying here with the baby.

TOTO   I'm very glad, very happy to hear that. Marvellous, joyous news. I don't mind being a daddy. I think I would be a good daddy. You agree? Look, I practicing on the animals.

NORMA   Toto ...

TOTO   You think the baby would favour me?

NORMA   How you work that out? Toto, you have to start thinking fe yourself. What would it be like if I wasn't around? Who would look after you?

TOTO   Don't know.

NORMA   You would manage?

TOTO   You going somewhere?

NORMA   Miss Armatage ask if I want to go to Kingston, live wid her.

TOTO   You get job?

NORMA   I not sure.

TOTO   Oh.

NORMA   Don't tell no-one, especially mama. It's a secret. I can depend on you to keep it?

TOTO   Yes ma' but I don't like this secret, *(upset)* don't like it at all.

Esther walks in on them.

ESTHER   What's this? Toto Master. Here in the yard this time a morning? Take you rass tail off of me property before I get the machete an chop you up. *(she chases him off)* Come out!

NORMA   Is just now you a come?

ESTHER   Get on with what you doing. *(she begins to go in)*

NORMA   Hector did look vex.

ESTHER   What you know?

NORMA   Dancing too close wid Eddie.

ESTHER   You never pull last night?

NORMA   I leave that to you, mattress always have job.

ESTHER   But old bike easier to ride.

NORMA   You stay there. Every dog have dem four o'clock.

ESTHER   A who you a talk to? You forget say you is just an old rag, maid, the bastard pickney.

NORMA   Sticks an stones ... *(Miss Faith hears all the commotion)*

MISS FAITH Esther! Esther a you that? *(Esther gets scared)*

NORMA   She down here.

MISS FAITH *(enters)*Where you was last night? *(pause)* Esther - me never tell if you stay out at night come back ready fe a fight. Where you was?

ESTHER   I stay with Miss Sophie.

MISS FAITH You was with a boy?

ESTHER   No mama. *(Norma starts to laugh)*

MISS FAITH But wait, Norma. Me never tell you to see 'bout the goats?

NORMA   I was waiting for Esther to help.

MISS FAITH Me call Esther name? Gwan go look about the food. *(Norma does not move)* Me say Gwan!

Norma leaves swiftly but gives Esther a smug look.

MISS FAITH You was with that boy?

ESTHER   No. Miss Sophie.

MISS FAITH Me say, you was with that bad breed, ugly mouth bwoy?

ESTHER   No.

MISS FAITH I'll ask again *(raising her voice)* You was with that broad nose, low down, stink mouth, black, sinting from down younder?

ESTHER   No mama. *(Miss Faith walks around, and takes her time)*

MISS FAITH Miss Sophie pass round first thing this morning. Bring me bammy and nice piece of fish. *(pause)* For the last time.

ESTHER *(defeated)* Yes.

MISS FAITH   You no have no ambition.

ESTHER   What about Norma?

MISS FAITH   Norma can do what she want. You are my daughter. She is not. She can waste her life. Before you do something useful with you time ... you a catch up with bad breed people and keep man. Boy wid tree in a him face.

ESTHER   I never do anything.

MISS FAITH   Him have him way with you?

ESTHER   No mama. We just hung out.

MISS FAITH   Which part a you hang out! Me no want no belly business in me house, especially from that boy.

ESTHER   Nothing happened.

MISS FAITH   Before you do better than me, you a go back to the gutter. Norma can ruin her life, cause she no know better. Hector is not in a fe we class. We have a certain pedigree. A standard. People like Hector, Ruby, even Miss Sophie don't have it. *(posh voice)* Not our type at all.

ESTHER   Mama it's not like that.

MISS FAITH   I work hard fe you for seventeen years. You must can do better than me - a doctor, lawyer, even nurse.

ESTHER   Mama I will.

MISS FAITH   I struggle too much, brock me back on the farm, to see you amount to nothing. People respect me in the church and around the parish. Me and my family must set an example, decent and proper. So you better buck up you ideas otherwise ...

ESTHER   ... otherwise?

MISS FAITH   If is Hector you want, you better leave and don't call me name again. You can shack up with you' dead loss man and turn kitchen slave. *(she exits, calling)* Norma? Norma? A whe' the backside that gal?

SCENE 4

Ruby and Norma are out in the bushes writing on a slate.

RUBY   Trace the letters next to you name. That's right. *(Norma does as she is told)* Now spell it out loud.

NORMA   ... L ... E ... W ... I ... S - Norma Lewis

RUBY   Good, print it again, form the words better this time. Make the M like so. *(she shows her)*

NORMA *(writes)* See it deh.

RUBY   You doing real good Norma, you should be proud.

NORMA   ... think so?

RUBY   Soon noting gwoin stop you. Esther won't be de only one in the family with brains. *(Norma hugs her slate to her)*

NORMA *(proud)* Esther getting suspicious ... don't know where me go everday after breakfast. She would fart if she find out. *(they laugh)*

RUBY   Miss Armatage say anything when you give her my note?

NORMA   ... thank me fa taking the trouble.

RUBY   How Miss Faith going cope when she find out that her valuable employer don't feel the same way? *(they laugh at the situation)*

NORMA *(mocking Miss Faith)* Esther naa go get any legacy money. Lord! Whole heap a bangarang.

RUBY   You think Miss Faith heart will be able to keep up with it?

NORMA   Too much excitement!

RUBY   You better lace her tea with some more of that rum. Soften the blow. *(they laugh some more)*

NORMA   Miss Armatage, ask me to go wid her.

RUBY *(disbelief)* What!

NORMA   Go to Kingston.

RUBY *(shocked)* You going?

NORMA   I can't leave mama?

RUBY   Cat lick me ears! Why not?

NORMA   I never thought I would ever get this type a chance.

RUBY   You chance come - take eee. It might not come
      again.

NORMA   I'll think about it.

RUBY   You want to be a poor thing all you life?

NORMA   No.

RUBY   Then that done.

NORMA   I see Miss Sophie coming out in you everyday.

RUBY   We don't do things like mama or Miss Faith. We do
      things in a fe we way.
      *(Norma takes out the fairytale book Esther and Norma read when
      they were young.)*

NORMA   After, you could teach me to read this?

RUBY   Cinderella.

NORMA   We used to play with it when we was young.

RUBY   You try an stop me. As morning come ... bring the
      book ... can't have you going to Kingston backward.

They laugh together. Lights down.

SCENE 5

A few months later. We see Esther, Norma and Faith getting ready for church. They are putting on sweaters, jackets, and hats. Norma is polishing shoes. Esther is putting on stockings.

MISS FAITH Norma! The shoes polish? *(Norma gives her the shoes)* Do Esther own, and remember to take off dat rag you wearing. *(referring to her apron. Norma cleans the shoes)* Esther!

ESTHER Yes mama. *(Esther does as she is told)*

MISS FAITH Pass me the Bible and bring me me comb.

ESTHER Yes mama.

MISS FAITH Service was lovely this morning, Pastor preach! - uplift me soul I look forward to this evening. *(Norma gives Esther her shoes. Esther puts them on)* Esther! Put on you sweater. It hot now but tonight the breeze cold. *(Esther does as she is told)*

NORMA Judgement day a come. *(Esther ignores Norma)* Those that don't hear will feel. You no think me no see you?

ESTHER You' mad! ... ready fe Bellview.

NORMA Is you want the doctor not me.

ESTHER *(worried)* What you up to?

NORMA Me never know you stay so. *(refers to her belly)* Belly no show yet. *(pause)* Fret not, me naa say nothing.

ESTHER Me no know what you a talk 'bout.

NORMA Ginal! You get ketch! Mama know?

ESTHER Watch me get you in trouble.

Esther kicks over the shoe polish tin. Miss Faith comes out of the house ready to go.

MISS FAITH What's going on?

ESTHER   Norma throw way the polish.

MISS FAITH You have dropsy? Wha' do you?

ESTHER   She did want to get it on me good dress.

MISS FAITH Esther! Come walk beside me, ca' me no want to beat he gal a roadside. *(they all walk a little, Esther stops)*

ESTHER   Mama I left me Bible.

MISS FAITH What!

ESTHER   At home.

MISS FAITH *(annoyed)* Oh Esther!

ESTHER   I'll be quick.

Esther leaves. They reach outside the church. There is a big argument between Toto, Ruby and Miss Sophie. Eddie is also there.

MISS SOPHIE *(to Toto)* How you mean you no have money? Who a go pay fe this?

TOTO   Miss Sophie. I not sure.

MISS SOPHIE You really is a champion fe idiot. *(to Ruby)* You mean to say you really lid down with this? Who a go pay fe the christening? I trust all this money. Me naa foot the bill.

MISS FAITH Sophie you no shame? This is God's house.

MISS SOPHIE I tired of all the lying and soo, soo, soo, soo behind me back. Toto - up till now me no hear you admit that you is really the father of the pickney.

RUBY   Mama drop it. Leave Toto.

MISS SOPHIE *(to Toto)* Me look in a the baby face an it no favour you.

RUBY   Why can't you drop it mama? How can you embarrass me, here, now?

MISS SOPHIE If me throw you on the street, them would say me wicked. If me make you get rid a the baby - me wicked again. I can't win. I don't have the money to feed so much greedy mouth. Mark my words, me a go check out every ugly man in here. Me will find the culprit tonight. *(to Toto)* Look pon him.

RUBY   Just stop it mama, stop it. Give me a chance!

Lights down on Ruby, Miss Sophie, Norma, Eddie, Winston, Ezra and Toto.

SCENE 6

Esther finds Hector on Spur Tree Hill.

ESTHER   I never see me period I tink I'm in trouble. *(pause)* You said you know what you were doing.

HECTOR   You' pregnant?

ESTHER   Me no want it. I can't have it. I need your help. Anything man ... just get rid of it ... anything just take it away.

HECTOR   What you asking?

ESTHER   Norma knows already. If mama find out ... everybody in the parish ... I can't have it.

HECTOR   Kill me pickney?

ESTHER   Me not ready fe baby.

HECTOR   But baby ready fe you!

ESTHER   I trusted you Hector, and look what you do. Find somebody to give me something. I'll go anywhere. Me have the money ... look. (*she takes out the Pardoner money. The book that she used to write people's names in falls out*)

HECTOR   Me naa kill me pickney. Me youth. Me seed.

ESTHER   You don't have to bear it. I never know nothing - you just take advantage. Control!

HECTOR   Esther, you confused, only thinking about yourself. What about us? We can start a life together.

ESTHER   You crazy! I want to go to college!

HECTOR   You really believed you mother. Think you some queen.

ESTHER   I can't face mama like this.

HECTOR   The higher the monkey climb, the more him expose him bottom.

ESTHER   There can be nothing between us. Nothing!

HECTOR   I not good enough fe you, that's why want to kill me baby. If me was red and did have money, live on hill top, things would be different. Me come from yard so me no fit de picture.

ESTHER   What life can we offer a child? *(pause)* You have to help. Take the money Hector. Find somebody who can do this.

HECTOR   No. *(he dashes the money to the ground)* Me naa do it. I can't help you like that. *(she slowly picks up the money)* Is it such a bad thing to have me child? I'll get a job. Esther, we will survive, you me and the youth.

ESTHER   It's easy fe you.

HECTOR   Esther, I can't help you like that. I glad to hear about the baby. Me and you is one now, fe true.

ESTHER   I don't want to just survive ... and that's all you offering - survival!

She exits.

SCENE 7

Outside the Church. Ruby, Miss Faith, Miss Sophie, Toto, Winston, Ezra and Eddie are waiting to go in.

TOTO   We no better go inside?

MISS SOPHIE Ruby, don't mek me have to cus no R, C, B, C, in here tonight.

MISS FAITH *(disapproving)* Sophie!

RUBY   Mama if you give me the chance I will say.

MISS SOPHIE I wait too long now. If I have to get the whole district to take a blood test then so be it.

EDDIE   Stop the commotion man. A me do it.

MISS SOPHIE A you ...

EDDIE   A fe me.

MISS SOPHIE You Eddie Simpkins owning it? A what de ...

EDDIE *(holds up his hand and silences Miss Sophie)* Hol' you mouth. Ruby, come make we talk.

They leave.

TOTO   Him masterful eee?

MISS FAITH *(unimpressed)* What a turn up fe de books.

MISS SOPHIE That rascal a the baby father.

MISS FAITH We is all the same in the sight of God.

MISS SOPHIE Him better pay up now.

MISS FAITH Come now, let's go inside an pray. *(for Sophie's ears)* Let us thank God fe small mercy an ask him to forgive us when we show our true colours in his presence.

They sing a hymn. 'Rock of Ages.'

SCENE 8

We see Esther standing by her suitcase.
The light gradually fades up on her as she stands very still.
Esther is reading a letter.

ESTHER *(reads)* Dear Mama, I know you a go wake up to find me gone ... gone to England. Mama, I have to go. *(pause)* I know was wrong to take everybody savings, the Pardoner money. But when everybody find out I carrying Hector's child ... I know I had to leave, come out of Jamaica. *(pause)* I shame mama ... When I reach England and things work out, I will send you the Pardoner money. Maybe one day you'll forgive me and let me put tings right with you ... *(pause)* your daughter ... Esther.

Esther exits with her suitcase.

SCENE 9

Eddie, Ruby and the baby are hanging out. Toto runs up excited.

TOTO   Everybody. Big news! Catastrophe! Weeping, wailing, Miss Faith bawling. Crying her heart out. Whole heap a bangarang!

RUBY   What is it?

TOTO   Esther gone, leave first thing this morning an gone. Write letter, say she pregnant. I see everyting.

EDDIE   What!

TOTO   She gone!

EDDIE   Me never see her the other day?

TOTO   She jump on the bus to Kingston. Say she a go a foreign.

RUBY   She can't be far.

TOTO   Long gone by now.

EDDIE   I don't believe it.

TOTO   Believe it.

RUBY   She really gone.

TOTO   Pack a grip and take a trip.

EDDIE   Me a get mad now!

RUBY   Calm down Eddie.

EDDIE   I ask her fe me money, she say me a go get it soon. Look now.

RUBY *(to Toto)* She do gone for true?

TOTO   Yes.

EDDIE   When me catch her me a go slap her up.

RUBY   Calm down, here comes mama.

MISS SOPHIE *(enters)* You get it?

EDDIE   Esther have me Pardoner money. Gone with it.

MISS SOPHIE You trying to wriggle out again?

EDDIE   She gone with all me have.

MISS SOPHIE *(to Ruby)* Him telling the truth?

RUBY   Seem so.

EDDIE   ... run way with everything.

Hector enters on his way to see Miss Faith.

EDDIE   That bastard Hector in this too. See him there!

RUBY   Look.

EDDIE   Thief!

EDDIE   Make we catch him and skin him alive.

TOTO   Hector them looking fe Esther.

EDDIE   Hear say she free it up. You finally taste the goods.

TOTO *(to Hector)* You better run! Them after you' balls!

EDDIE   Esther a go have baby.

MISS SOPHIE *(to Hector)* Esther pregnant? You make Esther pregnant? But hear me trial!

HECTOR   Me a go see Miss Faith.

EDDIE   Is that why you thief we money? Pay fe you ugly pickney.

HECTOR   Go to hell!

EDDIE   You woman did go on the same way. And look now. She gone with me money, and get herself in the family way.

MISS SOPHIE Knock me down with a feather! Esther pregnant?

TOTO   She was always up to no good.

MISS SOPHIE *(disbelief)* Esther pregnant.

EDDIE   All the youth them at church out of pocket.

RUBY   What you going to do about Eddie money?

MISS SOPHIE I can't wait to see Miss Faith. Esther pregnant.

EDDIE   Something have to happen.

RUBY   She better pray for her life.

MISS SOPHIE Esther was always the wicked one. When them pretty so, you can't trust them.

HECTOR   Leave Esther out of this.

EDDIE   Lady by day and slaggy by night.

HECTOR   Watch it Eddie. Esther is quality. Make me bust you lip, like how I do you a school.

EDDIE   She owe me money. A my turn fe draw in the Pardoner and the gal run off with everything. Woman or no woman, she a go dead fe that!

HECTOR   Touch her and dog eat your supper.

EDDIE   You was involved with Esther? To embezzzle we?

HECTOR   Eddie, you was fool fe give way you money.

MISS SOPHIE What him say?

EDDIE   You want to dead fe true. Make me shot you a box, teach you not to mess.

TOTO   No. Uno don't fight.

EDDIE   Give him one bitch lick, see how you brave after that.

TOTO   Cool down man, cool down.

EDDIE   You better find you lady and get we money.

MISS SOPHIE Then we coming fe you.

EDDIE   If you pocket empty. You a go pay anyway.

MISS SOPHIE ... deserve one lick.

EDDIE   Beat you side in - make you worse ugly.

MISS SOPHIE Worsera!

EDDIE   Me want what's mine. *(Eddie chases Hector)*

RUBY   No ... no ... stop it.

TOTO *(sees Miss Faith coming)* Look there's Miss Faith.

RUBY   See her there.

TOTO   Let she talk.

MISS SOPHIE Miss Faith will know where Esther is, she will have
to deal with this.

Miss Faith enters as Eddie nearly catches Hector.

MISS FAITH   Bwoy! A you name Hector?

HECTOR   Miss Faith, I was coming roun' by you.

MISS FAITH   Me hear say me daughter thief people money.
Anything to do with you?

HECTOR   No ma.

MISS SOPHIE Lie!

EDDIE   Tear him tongue out fe that.

TOTO   Listen, wait no.

MISS FAITH   Esther is no thief. And I know say the breed a you is
prison bird.

MISS SOPHIE Faith, I was very surprised and disappointed to hear
about your Esther. I thought she would do better than that.

MISS FAITH   What you expect with all this bad company around
her?

MISS SOPHIE Now Miss Faith I have to talk for Ruby an me son-
in-law.

MISS FAITH   Who you a talk 'bout?

MISS SOPHIE Mister Edward Simpkins.

TOTO *(to Ruby)* Is who that?

MISS SOPHIE Ruby is getting married.

EDDIE *(grins)* We getting hitch as soon as we can.

MISS SOPHIE You see, my daughter's financee (FINE-NANCY) was led to believe that he would draw him hand in the Pardoner. But I hear Hector and your Esther do a bad thing. Miss Faith I know you are having a few domestic problems, but someting must be done.

EDDIE   Now!

MISS FAITH Well Sophie, I hope you will be able to cope, with the likes of Eddie Simpkins. Him don't do a honest day work in him life yet. But I'm sure God will guide you.

MISS SOPHIE If you live in a glass house ...

HECTOR   Miss Faith, please tell me if it is true, she really gone? Gone with the money? Is the first I hear 'bout any a this. I will bring her back, reason with her, make she see sense. You know how she hot-headed ... know how she stay. Me will find Esther. Calm her down.

MISS FAITH Me tell her no fe talk to uno mamby, famby, dutty bwoy. Cos bwoy lacka uno no come off a good table.   Teach me daughter to thief and mash up her life with pickney.

MISS SOPHIE Look at how me good to Esther ... the little jobs, a few dollars here and there. See how she repay me.

HECTOR   Is not my doing.

MISS FAITH ... see de culprit deh. *(points at Hector)*

EDDIE   Then make me get him.

TOTO   No, no man.*(he holds him back)*

MISS SOPHIE We must can sort this out in a civilised way.

RUBY *(eggs him on)* Them a take you fe joke!

EDDIE   The whole a them.

HECTOR   I know you upset ... but I intend to stick by her - get married.

MISS FAITH Hmm ... You better come off a dat one darling. What you have? Bwoy like you no have no ambition, you no come from nowhere. Me always tell Esther anything too black no good.
(Silence. They are all shocked)

RUBY   She think she better than we.

MISS FAITH I teach Esther to pick an choose, cos we not like some people, glad fe get any man. *(to Hector)* You better forget 'bout marriage, cos she gone.

HECTOR   Gone where? Please, please, tell me where she is? I'll fix it, make things right.

MISS FAITH People a knock my door fa Pardoner money. You know anything 'bout it?

HECTOR   Esther mention someting but ...

EDDIE   Collaborator!

RUBY   It all coming out now.

MISS SOPHIE If she not here, who a go pay?

MISS FAITH Hold up, wait a minute Miss Sophie. Nobody inform me about any a dis. When everybody was throwing good money after bad, you was quite content to keep me in the dark.

RUBY   We know you.

TOTO   An you go a church.

EDDIE   We did think you know.

MISS FAITH No sa. Me no in a them things deh. No believe in it. It always cause cussing and bad word.

TOTO   Me never think this would a happen.

MISS FAITH You no have mind? Big cow people give them hard earn money to one lilly gal. Uno no stupid? Me have my money an me put it in the bank.

EDDIE *(to Hector)* A him do it ... twist up her head.

HECTOR *(to Miss Faith)* Me tell her I happy 'bout the baby. Say I will stand by her.

MISS FAITH   That is all you have to give people good girl children. Baby. Me tell her fe look fe a better class a man. Somebody uplifting. Raise her colour. You can look after baby? Look 'pon you foot.

HECTOR   Miss Faith you wrong.

MISS FAITH   Me never have nothing. Bad luckid with man, an now bad luckid with the one daughter. You see how you spoil me pickney? If a pin drop, she'd a pick it up come give me. But as she see you, she turn fool. As she look 'pon you, she change. If you did come off a good table this wouldn't happen. Baby, imagine that.

HECTOR   I need to find out where she staying. Miss Faith, please tell me.

EDDIE   So wait - we not get nothing?

MISS FAITH   Chu! *(back to Hector)* The last thing she tell me. *(takes out letter)* See the letter deh. She never wanted to go to Kingston. A top school, and look how she ungrateful. Is me she a try fe punish. *(she starts to cry)*

TOTO   Lord! must be break you heart. *(takes out a handkerchief for Miss Faith, she brings out her own and ignores him)*

MISS FAITH   Anyhow, it could be a blessing in disguise. She naa go mix up, mix up with unoo.

HECTOR   I leave you to cool off. Later we talk.

MISS FAITH   Chu bwoy! Move you face out a me morning. Make me pass and keep your distance.

Miss Faith exits.

RUBY   Miss Faith shame.

MISS SOPHIE You reap what you sow. *(to Hector)* Hey Hector you have to pay.

RUBY *(to Hector)* You not off the hook yet.

TOTO   Settle down now.

EDDIE   Uno go 'long. Is blood me want. *(he chases Hector)*

RUBY   No boys ...no!

MISS SOPHIE *(holds back Ruby)* Leave them ... stand by you man.

Eddie runs after Hector, Toto, Sophie, Ruby follow.

SCENE 10

Lights up on Norma. She is waiting. A rather dishevelled Miss Faith walks in and trips over some bags.

MISS FAITH What the ... Norma?

NORMA   You back.

MISS FAITH Me no live ya?

NORMA   I'm waiting.

MISS FAITH Waiting? I'm not in the mood. Get me slippers. *(Norma does as she is told)* Why the bags them bungle up in the door? *(Miss Faith puts on the slippers and tries to settle down in a comfortable chair)*

NORMA   I'm going.

MISS FAITH Going. Where?

NORMA   Miss Armatage buy a house in Kingston. ... ask me to go.

MISS FAITH Don't try me patience. *(rubbing her feet, she notices Norma's dress)* What you wearing your good church frock for?

NORMA   I'm helping her to pack.

MISS FAITH *(wraps a shawl around her)* Fetch some wood. The night getting cold. *(Norma gets her bags)*

NORMA   I spending the night. We go a Kingston in the morning.

MISS FAITH Stop your lies. Put on you' apron. Clean the stove. I tell you to do it from yesterday an it stay same way. Norma? (*Silence. Norma looks directly at Miss Faith*) Who you a look 'pon. You is not any big woman around here! (*pause*) But wait, you have enough sense to look anybody in de eye so strong?

NORMA   Ruby show me how to read.

MISS FAITH You!

NORMA   ... a few words.

MISS FAITH Don't make me have to lick you till you pee pee!

NORMA   She's waiting.

MISS FAITH If you put one foot out of here, you not coming back. (*pause*) You think me wrong? Don't it? You think I could a do better fe you? You think my Esther should have worked the fields fe you? ... looking at me as if I could have done you better ... Jesus give me strength and have mercy on my soul. I could have thrown you out, and me never. So me not wrong.

NORMA   Toto meeting me down the bottom.

MISS FAITH You're not leaving this house. Is me care you when you mother throw you out. Is me suffer to bring you up. I take you in when nobody want you and is me one will take you out.

NORMA   You never treat me fair.

MISS FAITH What you know about fair? A ugly lickle scrap like you. (*getting angrier*) You father was worthless. Him bring you in, an him leave you. Why should I take me energy an school you? Did he send any money? No. He never care to send a penny fe you, so why should I care? You is not my blood ...

NORMA   You never treat me fair.

MISS FAITH My Esther gawn. My pretty baby gawn. How Esther do this to me? Now I can't even walk the street without the shame of what she do. (*she turns on Norma*) You come in like curse.

NORMA   Take care, walk good.
(*Norma starts to leave. Miss Faith jumps ahead and takes her bags and throws them out*)

MISS FAITH   Get out! Out of me house! Off me property! Don't bring you scrawny tail around here. *(watching her pick up all her bags)* I hope you have all you tings cos you naa come back. Get out! As Jesus is my saviour I rebuke you with your ungrateful ways. You hear me! You hear me! You will never have noting!

Toto is waiting down the bottom of the yard. Norma goes to him. Toto takes the bags. They walk. Miss Faith is still cussing in the house. Norma stops and looks back.

MISS FAITH   Don't come back. Me no want to see you again.

TOTO   Don't mind Miss Faith. *(Norma sighs)* ... a so she stay. *(pause)* Come. When you go a Kingston you a go miss this pretty picture view. The view from the top of Spur Tree Hill ... blossoms in spring?

NORMA   Truly.

TOTO   Don't pay her no mind. Just like spring it's your time to blossom. You only eat a berry from de tree when it ready. Eat it too early an you get belly ache. The berry must be red and ripe. An you know the longer you leave the berry in the sun, the darker an sweeter it taste. Cos you take long in reaching, but when you reach, you reach! Fruit ripe time to pick. *(pause)* Miss Norma, I don't want you to leave.

NORMA   I know.

TOTO   But I overstand. *(they hug)* Gwan man, go 'bout you business.

Norma takes her bags and looks ahead of her, ready for the world. Lights down.

End

J.B. Rose

J.B. started her career in 1983 as a vocalist and actress. Her strong interests in working with young people, moved on to teaching drama and singing, as well as directing and producing plays for various youth groups, theatres and schools. In 1994, she was commissioned to write **Darker the Berry** for Second Wave. Her writing soon progressed to television, with the pilot sitcom **Striking Out** for Chrysalis TV (95) and episodes of **Brothers and Sisters** (UK's first black soap drama) for the BBC.

In the summer of 1997, J.B. once again took on the role of director, where **It's all about Us** was performed at the Brixton Shaw. Throughout her career, she never strayed too far from her first love - singing. Having completed a vocal teaching course at London Music College, she continues coaching singers and is on the verge of completing her debut album, due for release in 1998.

GLOSSARY

b'alt. Wait.

backland. Backside, bottom.

backra. White person/caucasian.

bangarang. Confusion, arguing.

Bellview. A mental home in Jamaica.

boy with tree in a him face. An ugly boy.

brought upsey. Brought up well.

browning. A black person with lighter skin tone.

callaloo. A vegetable, similar to spinach.

cat lick me ears. A surprised exclamation.

champion fe idiot. Stupid person.

criss. Wicked! looks good/nice.

cus cus never bore hole in skin. Names never harmed anyone.

dog eat your supper. You're in trouble.

dopey. Ghost.

dress back. Get out of my face, leave.

every dog have them four a clock. Everybody's chance will come.

facety. Rude, cheeky.

favour. You look like.

fenky fenky. Feeble, weak.

gal. Girl.

ginal. Liar.

gwan. Go on, going on as if ...

hang your basket where you can reach it. Make sure you're being realistic.

if dopey hate, them give you basket to carry water. To be given an impossible task.. Carrying water in a sieve.

jacket. A child brought up by a man who believes he is the father (when he's not)

johncrow a bake bammy for you . You're in trouble (johncrow = vulture)

kibber her mouth. Shut her mouth.

lawd. Lord.

learn fe dance a yard before you dance abroad. Put your house in order before you try to put someone else's house in order.

legobeast. A loose woman.

lick. To hit someone/something.

mad them dora. An encouraging term used when someone is looking sexy.

mamby famby. Weak and feeble/useless.

marga. Skinny.

mek mek. Making noise.

naa form fool. Not messing about.

nengay, nengay. Nagging.

nyam. Eat.

Pardoner. A Caribbean savings scheme.

pickney. Child/children.

puss and dog no have the same luck. Not everybody has good luck.

R.C.B.C. Abbreviated Jamaican swear words.

raated, rass. Alternative for bottom, backside.

ratcut. Loose coffee beans.

s'maddy. Somebody.

sensee. Weed, cannabis, grass.

speaky spokey. Someone who speaks well.

shubein. A dance/party usually all night.

sinting. Something.

soo soo soo. Gossiping behind someone's back.

sorrell. A red fruit drink for festive occasions.

sour sap. A type of fruit.

take off the talking and leave the whispering. Dust over, take away the worst of the mess.

the sugar. Diabetes.

top yard. House on the hill, master's house.

topnarter. A posh person, snob.

yabba youth. A rough boy.

Geraniums
by Sheila Yeger

Geraniums

In 1985, I was commissioned by the R.S.C. to write a play to commemorate the 50th Anniversary of the Battle of Cable Street, due to take place in 1986. Colin Chambers, the Literary Manager had a strong personal interest in the event and encouraged me to be as ambitious as I liked with regard to numbers and scale.

My parents had grown up in the East End of London, the children of Jewish immigrants from Russia and Poland. Both they and my uncle, as well as many of their friends, had been members of the Young Communist League in the 30's and had been involved in Cable Street and the events which led up to it. As I interviewed my parents, my uncle and aunt and others I soon saw how the same event could be interpreted and recalled in many different ways - how memory is fallible and how personal emotions can colour the account given of a past event. This was to become a central theme of the play.

Later I spoke with Professor William Fishman the distinguished academic and chronicler of East End history and with Phil Piratin the former Communist M.P. Their accounts of the event and their evaluation of its political ramifications were enormously informative. I also read extensively: eye witness accounts, newspaper reports and many differing analyses of the occasion itself and its long term repercussions. I was able to compare favourable newspaper coverage with blatantly prejudiced accounts and to see for myself in old Pathé newsreels the charismatic and undeniably glamorous figure of Oswald Mosley.

I began to see clearly that the Jews in the 30's had been subjected to as much racial prejudice as Blacks and Asians in later years. This gave the play a strong contemporary significance. The R.S.C. never produced **Geraniums** and when my son, Ben Yeger was appointed Artistic Director of Le'an Theatre Company in Camden, he asked if he could direct the play with a cast of young people. However, the text as it stood, was over 150 pages long and clearly not suitable for the purpose.

It's never easy for a writer to allow her work to be edited. The painstaking and thoughtful work which Ben has done in editing and reorganising the original text was carried out with immense skill, sensitivity and good humour. Undoubtedly he has improved it beyond recognition. The result is, I believe, a much tighter, more focused play, which still retains the passion and the power of the original, and which is eminently suitable for performance by youth groups. It is therefore a source of much pleasure and very great pride that this very personal piece of work should finally have come to fruition through our joint efforts.

Sheila Yeger

Director's notes:

We performed the play in a promenade performance style. The audience became participants in the Jumble Sale and the YCL Meeting. In The March scene they were given banners and cajoled into joining in the chanting of *'They shall not pass'*. The production toured to youth organisations and colleges, performing to over 1,000 mainly young people. Before seeing the play, few of them had heard of the 'Battle', the BUF, Blackshirts or Oswald Mosley.

During the rehearsal process I was interested to discover whether the young people wanted to change the world. I did endless games and exercises with them and invited several speakers to rehearsals but for the most part they didn't have a strong feeling about unity, community or standing up for what you believe in - things which must have been second nature to young people in the thirties. The choice of style enabled audience and cast alike to engage as active partners in a communal and unifying experience, whilst giving the important issues an immediacy and clarity which might have been lost with a more conventional theatrical style.

Ben Yeger

Geraniums

by Sheila Yeger

First performed by *Le'an?* Jewish Youth Theatre in 1995 at John
Reubens Theatre, M.A.C. West Hampstead and toured nationally in
1996. Directed by Ben Yeger

(In 1936)

Harry Lazarus about 20 yrs old	Gideon Lyons
Zelda Lazarus late teens	Sima Kramer
Phil Levine late teens	Adam Zacks
Danny Cohen late teens	Craig Sherrad
Joe Aronovitch late teens	Daniel Mellins
Rachel Steinberg late teens	Rachel Mercer
Madge Lewis late teens	Kim Anders
Jimmy Harris late teens	Kerrin Gold
Micky Harris about 16	Tammy Braunhold
Speaker at street meeting	Rachel Nyman
Men at meeting	Karen Morris/Keren Cohen
Woman in crowd at meeting	Stacy King
1st Policeman	Karen Morris
2nd Policeman	Keren Cohen
Woman in Bakery	Karen Morris

(In the 1990'S)

Harry Lazarus in his 70's	Gideon Lyons
Zelda Lazarus in her 70's	Natalie Marx
Phil Levine in his 70's	Adam Zacks
Clare - Late teens	Eli Davis

The action in 1936 takes place in and around Whitechapel during
September/October. Many of the places mentioned *did* exist: - e.g.
Andy's Café, the Workers' Circle, Plummers Row, Jane Street, but
Paradise Road is purely fictitious, as is the Paradise Road group of
the Young Communist League. All the incidents shown in the past
are based on *real* events.

ACT ONE

SCENE 1

The 1990's: A modestly comfortable suburban living room. Enter
Zelda, a vivid, lively and robust looking woman in her 70's. Enter
Phil about 2 years older. Zelda picks up a letter lying on top of the
sideboard, holds it up.

ZELDA   Are you going to answer this or not?

PHIL   What's that?

ZELDA   The letter about Cable Street. I told you a million
times. Mr *(scrutinises it)* it looks like Marsh ... no ... it's Marshall
- Mr Marshall of Bexley Heath would be grateful for your mem-
ories of the so-called Battle of Cable Street. He says someone in a
W.E.A. Class passed your name onto him. 'So-called battle' eh?
Well, *are* you going to answer it, or what? *(pause)*

PHIL   I'd rather wear my white shirt, Zelda. The blue one's
too tight.

ZELDA *(waving letter)* I'll put this in the bin then, shall I?

PHIL   No ... perhaps I'll show it to Harry. He'll know what
to say. Tell you the truth, I can't remember nothing much ... not
after all this time.

ZELDA   Do me a favour, Phil. Just go and get yourself
changed.

Phil exits slowly. Zelda watches him, exasperated. Then she puts the
letter back on the sideboard.

ZELDA   Won't. Won't remember. Prefers not to remember.
(She looks out as if remembering something from her past.)

The lights change.

SCENE 2

1936: In the blackout, the voice of a public speaker is heard.

SPEAKER   We live in a period in which politicians are not very popular and believe me, you have my sympathy. Politicians are regarded as people who have learnt to talk but not to act and you demand action and rightly demand it in dealing with unemployment. I don't ask you to judge us by what we say at election time. Anybody can come down and make promises to the unemployed during elections. Anyone can do that, and by heavens they do it. But when they go back to Westminster, when they've got your votes from you, the same story is not told in Parliament.

Lights gradually come up on a street corner, where a small number of people stand listening to a Speaker. He wears a black shirt, is very clean-cut in appearance. He is flanked by police. At the back of the crowd, Harry, Zelda, Phil. Zelda carries a large bag.

SPEAKER   We live in a period in which we can only survive by vigour and by action.

WOMAN *(shouts)* Action? Don't make me laugh! Talk ... that's all you lot can do ... *(general agreement, laughter. She continues)* Anyhow ... that's not Mr Mosley ... he ain't good looking enough. Get off pig-face! We come to hear Mr Mosley. *(general agreement. Some call out)* Yeh, where's Mosley!!? We wants to see Mr Mosley.

Enter Jimmy and Micky. Jimmy immediately takes in the scene and joins in loudly, sending it all up.

JIMMY   We wants to see Mr Mosley ... We walked all the way from Cable Street, me and my brother ... Don't tell me he ain't here.

MICKY *(to Jimmy)* Who the fuck's Mosley?

JIMMY   Dunno. Some bastard politician. How should I know? *(Jimmy spots Zelda through the crowd)* Here, I like that. *(He points her out)*

MICKY *(looking)* Do me a favour, she's a bloody Yid.

JIMMY   How can you tell?

MICKY   By the size of her arse. They all got big arses. Haven't you ever noticed?

JIMMY   Can't say I have. Still ... I'm not prejudiced. Very nice. Very tasty.

SPEAKER   We are the victims of a cancer and a foul disease. That cancer is called communism and the cause of it is standing next to you in this audience. Look around you, my friends ... what do you see ... *foreigners!!* This is England, remember ... *England* ... not Russia, not Poland, not Germany ...

WOMAN *(shouts)* Who are you calling a foreigner? I was born in Wapping.

MICKY *(shouts)* That's foreign ain't it?

SPEAKER   They have the faces of foreigners. They have the habits of foreigners and yet they are occupying our cities. The big Jew puts you out of employment by the million, while the little Jew sweats you in Whitechapel ...

MICKY *(shouts)* He's right ... my last boss was a Jew - he used to drive round in this bloody great car and he never paid me enough to scratch my bloody arse with.

JIMMY *(to Micky)* You got a big mouth all of a sudden.

MICKY   It's right though, ain't it? I mean, let's face it, they're everywhere.

JIMMY   I know. Shocking ain't it?

SPEAKER   Jew landlords with moneybags, Jew employers in the factories ... first your jobs ... then your homes ... while the Jew-boy communists stir up trouble in the streets ...

HARRY   Now ...

ZELDA *(begins to pelt the Speaker with rotten tomatoes, shouting)* Stop Mosley ... stop the fascists.

PHIL   Mosley is the threat. Fight for work - don't fight your fellow workers!

JIMMY *(shouts)* That's right, girl ... you tell em! *(to Micky)* Ooh I love redheads. Specially when they get themselves all worked up!

ZELDA *(shouts)* Stop Mosley ... stop the fascists. Mosley is the threat. Fight for work - don't fight your fellow workers...

HARRY *(shouts)* Ever heard of the three monkeys? Well we've had numbers one and two - Mr Hitler and Mr Mussolini and our friend Mosley's number three. Three monkeys with little black moustaches. See evil, hear evil, and speak evil ... Here it is, brother ... the gospel of hate ... divide the working classes and rule ... We don't want you here, fascist scum ... Join your union ... the union makes us strong ... Fight for workers' unity ... don't fight your fellow workers ...

(The Speaker catches the eye of two men near the platform. They move towards Harry)

HARRY   Stop Mosley here! Stop Franco in Spain! Fight the fascists at home and abroad. *(the men descend on Harry)*

1ST MAN *(to Harry)* You got a big mouth, Mr Cohen.

ZELDA   His name isn't Cohen.

2ND MAN   You're all called Cohen.

1ST MAN   A big nose and a big mouth ... we don't like that, do we Jack?

2ND MAN   No we don't

1ST MAN   Think we'll have to see about it, don't you?

2ND MAN   Definitely ... *(he grabs hold of Harry and holds him while the 1st man systematically punches at his face. Harry offers no resistance. Suddenly the men stop the assault)*

1ST MAN   I think that'll do. For now.

2ND MAN   Yeh ... (*touches Harry's mouth*) Keep it shut in
future. Alright?

*They move off. Pause. Jimmy walks across to Zelda. Micky follows.
Jimmy pretends he did not see the assault.*

JIMMY   What happened?

ZELDA   He tripped over a crack in the pavement.

MICKY   Unlucky.

JIMMY   Where you lot from?

ZELDA   Plummers Row.

JIMMY   Bit off your patch.

ZELDA   No law against it, is there?

MICKY   Not yet there ain't. *(pause)* Looks like you need a
policeman.

HARRY   Don't make me laugh. Please.

JIMMY   Can he walk?

HARRY   Course I can. I'm not a cripple.

JIMMY   Do me a favour ... Don't talk. The inside of your
mouth looks like a plate of raw liver.

HARRY   The day I stop talking I might as well be dead.

MICKY   I thought we was supposed to be going for a pint.
They'll be closed by the time we get there. Bloody good
Samaritan!

ZELDA   We can manage all the same.

JIMMY   Can you hell?...come on ...

*He puts his arm round Harry's shoulder. Zelda holds Harry's other
arm. They start to move off. Phil follows. Micky does not.*

JIMMY *(to Zelda)* I like your hair. Think I'll call you Ginger. *(pause)* Can you dance?

ZELDA No, but I can whistle. *(demonstrates)* There's a saying in Yid ... *(corrects self)* my father always says ... a girl don't whistle ...

JIMMY Not many girls *can* whistle ... not in tune anyhow ...

They exit, supporting Harry. Micky is left. He picks up a rotten tomato from the ground, and after a moment hurls it after them.
The lights change.

SCENE 3

1936: A gymnasium. Joe Aronovitz in shorts, vest and wearing boxing gloves is hitting the punch bag with determination. He looks very fit. Zelda stands watching. She wears a coat.

ZELDA *(after a while)* Don't it hurt?

JOE *(stopping)* Who, me or him?

ZELDA Either.

(Joe resumes hitting the punch-bag. Zelda goes over to him. She hits the punch bag experimentally)

ZELDA Ow! *(Laughs)* It ain't as easy as it looks!

JOE Close your eyes and pretend it's wearing a black shirt. *(Zelda makes an all-out assault on the punch-bag)*

JOE That's it! Give him one for me! Go on ...

ZELDA *(subsides breathless, laughing, examining her hands)* Think I'll stick to skipping.

JOE You could always try a few press-ups. Here ... *(he demonstrates expertly. She watches, then tentatively has a go)* Nah ... do it like this ... it's a bit easier. *(he shows her press-ups from the knee)* Better take your coat off ...

(She does so, then starts to do a few press-ups. Joe watches) Not bad ... specially not for a girl.
(She continues. Joe returns to the punch bag)

ZELDA   I only came in looking for Harry. He said to meet him here after evening class.

JOE   Noo ... where *is* the mumser? Eight o'clock we said. Special training session. I thought we agreed.

ZELDA   He had to go to a Branch meeting after work.

JOE   You don't say.

ZELDA   There's a demo on Thursday. We went to collect some leaflets.

JOE   Meetings. Demos. Meetings *about* demos. Yak, yak yak ... If you ask me, we done enough bloody talking. *(Zelda stands up and goes to pick up the clubs)* Watch out ... they're too heavy for girls.

ZELDA   Harry says you joined JUDA.

JOE   Then Harry's right ... for once.

ZELDA   He said he thought it was a 'potentially dangerous development' ... an underground Jewish defence organisation.

JOE   It ain't the Stepney Jewish Youth Club, that's for sure. *(pause)* What else did he have to say ... your big brother?

ZELDA   Nothing really ... *(pause)* Joe ... what do they actually *do*? JUDA, I mean?

JOE   Well, choochka, they don't play no table tennis ...

ZELDA *(puts the clubs down)* I want to know.

JOE   We prepare ourselves.

ZELDA   What for?

JOE   For anything.

Zelda considers this information. Enter Danny eating a large platzel. He has a soft, flabby appearance. He wears an unflattering hand-knitted sweater.

JOE   Danny ... nice of you to drop in!

DANNY   Not late am I? What's been happening?

JOE   Not much.

DANNY   Thank God for that!
(*He sits down. Zelda goes back to the clubs. Joe goes back to punch bag. Danny watches munching*)

JOE (*calling to Danny*) Like the sweater!

DANNY   My aunty made it. She knows I feel the cold.

JOE   Sehr shan. Take it off.

DANNY   It's freezing!

JOE   Nights are cold in Spain, I hear. Specially in the mountains. (*bellows*) Take it off!
(*Danny struggles out of the sweater. Joe picks up the medicine ball, calling to Danny as he throws it*)

JOE   Catch!
(*Danny misses it. Zelda abandons the clubs, picks up a skipping rope and begins to skip. Joe goes over to Danny, grabs a handful of spare flesh on his arm*)
Look at the state of this!

DANNY   I thought it was hot in Spain.

JOE   Not in the winter, schmendrick! Forty press-ups ... that's what you ought to do. Regular. Ask Zelda, she'll show you. (*He starts to demonstrate. Danny looks on*) Fifty even.

DANNY   What, a month?

JOE   No, pupick a *day. Twice a day.* (*chants*) If we want to fight fascists, we got to get fit.

DANNY   *If* we want to fight fascists ...

Enter Harry carrying a pile of leaflets. He holds himself very straight. He is very serious, rather tense.

HARRY *(to Zelda)* What the hell are you doing here?

ZELDA   Waiting for you.

JOE   I've had her on the old press-ups ... shaping up very nice your sister.

HARRY *(he is not amused. He goes up to Zelda)* Get your coat on.

ZELDA   It's not late. I want to have another go at the clubs ... *(She goes and picks up the clubs. Harry comes and takes them out of her hands)*

HARRY   Get your coat on, I said.
(to Joe) Who said the girls was going to join in?

JOE   Freedom of sport ... freedom of thought ...

Enter Phil carrying an open notebook, quietly spoken with a dreamy air.

PHIL   There's this new graffiti in the gents. It says:- 'If men want to make things better ...'

HARRY   '... they must first understand them as they are.'

DANNY   Sounds a bit familiar.

HARRY   He's pulling your leg, schmerel.

PHIL   The revolution can start anywhere, comrade. Even in a lavatory. You got to be prepared, eh Joe?

JOE   What happened to the group training session? I thought we decided. Top priority: physical fitness, we said.

HARRY   We never voted on it ... in fact, I want to bring this issue up for discussion at ...

JOE   Forget it.

HARRY   No automatic assumptions, Joe. No autonomous decisions. You got to keep the dialogue going. It's all part of the process.

ZELDA   My mother had her windows smashed again last
     night.

JOE   Don't worry, pupick, it's all part of the process!

ZELDA   Why don't she go to the police?

JOE   Don't make me laugh.

ZELDA   That's what they're there for, ain't it?

HARRY   Zelda, we got to go. Tatta will start to worry.

ZELDA   Well, ain't it?

HARRY   I'll tell you all about it on the way home. (*he shep-
     herds her to the door. Danny puts on his sweater and joins them*)

JOE   You staying, Phil? We could have a quick warm-up
     with the ball.

PHIL   Maybe next week.

ZELDA *(to Joe)* I'll practice the press-ups.

JOE   Don't do me no big favours.

He starts to punch doggedly at the punch bag as the others exit.
The lights change.

SCENE 4

The 1990's: A ring at the doorbell. Phil suddenly perks up. He looks
at his watch.

PHIL   Dead on time. Trust Harry.

He exits eagerly. Zelda shakes her head. After a moment, we hear
the voices of Phil and Harry off stage.

PHIL   Noo lundsman ...!!!!

HARRY   Noo ..!!!!

Phil comes back with Harry. Harry Lazarus is in his late 70s, practically crippled . He moves with the utmost difficulty but does everything possible to conceal his disability. He appears to be strong, uncompromising and almost too forceful.

PHIL   A taxi noch ... Nothing but the best!

HARRY *(hobbles over to Zelda, embraces her).* Zelda ...

ZELDA *(kissing him)* Happy Birthday. Still the same old Harry.

HARRY   Birthdays. At my age.

(He struggles across the room. Phil and Zelda watch. They know better than to offer help. He lowers himself into an armchair with difficulty)

ZELDA   Did you hear from the hospital?

HARRY   Not yet.

ZELDA   But it's ... it must be six months.

HARRY   There's a waiting-list as long as your arm.

ZELDA   Freddy said you ought to go private. It's no disgrace. If you're in pain.

HARRY   I told you before ... over my dead body. Private doctors! Over my dead body.

ZELDA   It probably will be.

PHIL   Give Harry a drink.

HARRY   Just a cup of tea.

PHIL   Have a drink. It'll do you good. What've we got Zelda?...brandy, Martini, Sherry ...

HARRY   I told you. I don't want no drink. *(pause)*

ZELDA   Freddy knows a good man ... a specialist.

HARRY   He *would.*

ZELDA *(ignoring this)* Someone he worked with in the Middlesex, I think he said. Look Harry, why don't you at least? ...

HARRY   Privilege Zelda. That's why. Paying for what other people can't afford. If everybody starts forking out for what should be ours by right, we'll end up without a Health Service.

(The doorbell rings)

HARRY   You expecting visitors?

ZELDA   Only you.

HARRY   Might be the police.

ZELDA   These days we don't get too many visits from the police.

(Someone raps on the window)

PHIL *(draws aside the curtain)* It's Clare. Little Clare. *(to Harry)* Freddy's girl.

ZELDA   I'll go. *(she hurries to the door)*

HARRY   She lives round here?

PHIL   She don' live nowhere much. You know youngsters these days!

Zelda comes in with Clare. She is in her teens. She is dressed in a ragged assortment of layers. She wears various badges, among them, Rock against Racism and the Anarchist emblem. She is well-spoken but attempts a kind of classless cockney.

CLARE   No-one told me it was a party or I'd have put on my best frock.

PHIL   You haven't got a frock. *(to Harry)* I've never seen her legs - can you believe that? Never!

HARRY   Her legs are an unknown quantity.

CLARE   Hello Uncle Harry. When's the revolution?

PHIL   It's your uncle's birthday.

CLARE   Happy Birthday!! Any nosh? I'm bloody starving!

PHIL   Always hungry. Don't they feed you where you're living?

CLARE   They? Who's *they? (she goes to the table and helps herself to some crisps or such-like)*

PHIL   Still in the same place?

CLARE   Yeh.

PHIL *(to Harry)* They call it Buckingham Palace. Somewhere in Bristol. You give a girl a nice home, send her to a smart school with Panama hats and holidays in Switzerland and where does she end up? In a Bristol slum. I ask you.

CLARE   St Paul's is not a slum. It's a very interesting area.

PHIL   Interesting? It that what they call it these days?

CLARE   You got any chopped liver?

ZELDA   I thought you were a vegetarian?

CLARE   Jack called it a 'petty bourgeois affectation'.

ZELDA   Who's Jack?

CLARE   A friend.

(Zelda, Phil and Harry exchange glances. Clare looks to the window, distracted)

HARRY   Looking for someone?

CLARE   Not exactly.

ZELDA   Phil, go check on the borscht will you, make sure it's not boiling.

Phil exits, Harry follows him. Zelda goes to Clare, touches her silver cross.

ZELDA   I'm not so sure about this.

CLARE   Jack gave it to me. I never take it off.

ZELDA   Crosses. So what does your father think of this Jack? He has met him I suppose?

CLARE   No. And he's not going to either. I phoned him up the other day and he actually put the phone down. Anyhow, I don't give a toss. *(pause)*

ZELDA   Are you short of money?

CLARE   You ever tried living on the dole, Grandma?

ZELDA   I've lived on far less.

CLARE   And there were six of you in one bed. I know, I know.

ZELDA   Haven't you had any interviews ... for jobs, I mean?

CLARE   Are you crazy? You don't have interviews for jobs anymore, only for Social Security. *(she picks up the letter on the sideboard, starts reading it)* What's this - The Battle of Cable Street? What battle? Where's Cable Street?

ZELDA   It's nothing. History lessons. *(she takes the letter and replaces it on the sideboard)* Is something wrong?

CLARE   No.

ZELDA   Are you sure? *(Clare looks away)* What are you doing in London?

CLARE   I got a lift.

ZELDA   Specially to see me? I'm very flattered.

CLARE   There was this concert actually. Rock against Racism. Jack and I ...

ZELDA   The famous Jack. ...

CLARE *(jumps up)* Can I have a bath? I smell like a pigsty.

ZELDA   I'll put on the immersion.

CLARE   Forget it ... Look, I didn't know it was anyone's birthday ... I shouldn't have ...

ZELDA   It's not exactly a party. Stay for dinner. There's plenty.

CLARE   There's always plenty.
(*They look at each other. Zelda moves towards her. They hug.*
Then separate)

ZELDA   So, was it a good concert? Nice music?

CLARE   Actually it was more of a demo than a concert ... a
demonstration.

ZELDA   I *do* know what a demo is Clare. I hope nobody got
hurt.

CLARE   Hurt? Why should anybody get hurt?

ZELDA   It happens. People get excited. Lose their tempers.

CLARE (*touching the geraniums*) I like these flowers. You've
always had these, haven't you? I remember when I was a kid.
What are they called? They're such an amazing colour. Like
flames or blood.

ZELDA   People out in the street. Things can easily turn nasty.
(*pause*) Geraniums ... they're called geraniums ...

Harry and Phil re-enter with naughty boy grins on their faces.

HARRY   The borscht is lovely, Zelda. Just like mother used
to make. (*pause*)

ZELDA (*to Harry*) Phil got a letter.

PHIL   Harry don't want to be bothered with no letters.

CLARE   Something about a battle. Cable Street? Sounds
exciting.

PHIL   Harry don't know nothing about no battles. (*pause*)

HARRY   What about Cable Street? Don't tell me they're
making another one of them documentaries. Load of rubbish the
last one was. Pack of lies.

ZELDA   This one's writing a book apparently. A 'historical
perspective' ...

HARRY   History, schmistory, eh Phil? History, schmistory ...

PHIL   It's a long time ago, Zelda. More than fifty years. What's the point of digging it all up?

ZELDA   You used to call me Zelly. Everyone did. *(to Harry)* Phil always says he can't remember. He *can* remember. When it suits him ...

HARRY *(suddenly, to Clare)* Schwitzing. We was always schwitzing, your grandpa and me. *(Clare looks blank)* Schwitzing ... sweating. How come you don't know Yiddish?... a nice Jewish girl?

CLARE   I went to a Roman Catholic school. The nuns must have forgotten to put it on the time-table.

PHIL   We used to sit in this little workshop, eh Harry? Wasn't enough room to swing a cat. Six days a week, if we was lucky.

HARRY   Work ... I tell you ... people these days don't know the meaning of the word. We used to schwitz, eh Phil ... how we used to schwitz.

PHIL   Danny Cohen ... all the boys ...

HARRY   Joe Aronowitz. Poor old Joe ... Schwitzing ... schwitzing ...
(Zelda and Clare exchange glances, as Harry and Phil share the memory)

As the lights change, we hear the loud noise of heavy sewing machines, the thump of a heavy gas iron.

SCENE 5

1936: Lights up on the corner of a small clothing factory. Phil and Danny work machines. Joe is pressing by hand. Harry stands by a table. He sews at speed. The noise from the machines makes it necessary to shout to be heard. It is evidently very hot.

HARRY *(looking at seam)* You been drinking, Phil? This pocket looks like you sewed it on with your eyes closed.

DANNY *(singing)* So I smile and say, when a lovely flame dies ... smoke gets in your eyes. *(Joe bangs the iron down heavily)* Go on Joe ... give him one for me!

HARRY	About time we knocked off, ain't it?
PHIL	The governor's sweating on this order.
DANNY	And I'm sweating on my fish and chips.
PHIL	I'm just sweating.
DANNY	I'm bloody starving.

(The power suddenly switches off. Everyone except Joe stops)

DANNY *(goes over to Joe)* Come on Joe. They ain't paying us no overtime.

JOE *(he puts down iron)* I was miles away ... halfway through the fifth round. *(he shadow-boxes rather dreamily)*

PHIL   When's the big fight?

JOE   October third. It's a Saturday.

HARRY   Fighting on Shobbos, eh? Tut Tut.

DANNY   Well, he asked God and he said, 'Joseph, my son ...' *(Joe punches him playfully)* I give in, I give in.

HARRY	So what else is new?
DANNY	You wait.
HARRY	I'm waiting ...
DANNY	Fish and chips anyone? *(general groans)*

Danny exits. The others take out flasks, rolls, etc.

HARRY   If he gets to Spain, I'll eat my boots.

PHIL   It's been done before. The boots, I mean.

JOE   He's not such a bad kid.

HARRY   He's not bad. He's just soft. He's got no ... *(searches for word)* motivation.

PHIL   His mother makes great lokshen pudding.

HARRY   Tell that to Franco.

JOE *(shadow-boxing, very intent)* If I can keep fighting, I might just make it.

HARRY   That goes for all of us.

Danny re-enters with newspaper.

DANNY   You seen this?

PHIL   What?

DANNY   October fourth it says. A march ... A big one.

HARRY   What march! Let's see. *(he tries to take paper)*

DANNY *(holds onto it)* Mosley is planning a mass-uniformed march of the B.U.F. it says ... through the East End on the fourth of October.

HARRY   He should be so lucky. Over my dead body.

PHIL   That's the day of the demo in Trafalgar Square ... Y.C.L. - raise a hundred for Spain ... October fourth.

HARRY   What paper is it in? *(takes paper and looks, reacts with exaggerated disgust)* Surprised you couldn't smell it - 'Blackshirt' *(hands it back)* Better disinfect your hands.

DANNY   I just had my chips out of it.

PHIL   That'll teach you to eat Kosher in future.

(Danny pretends to throw up)

ALL *(together)* Comrades, we got to get organised!!

(The power is suddenly switched-on and drowns their voices)

HARRY *(shouts over it)* I'm telling you, Mr Mosley ... You want a confrontation? Well ... believe me ... you're going to get one!

The noise of the machines intensifies.

Blackout.

SCENE 6
*1936: Jimmy and Micky's house, Cable Street. Micky, wearing work
clothes, is changing into a Blackshirt uniform.*

MICKY   I saw him, you know. The big man, Mr Mosley. Just
the once. But close as this. I could've touched him. Well, nearly.
He was tall - taller than my dad even. Lovely black hair, all shiny
like he'd buffed it up with shoe polish. Natty little black
moustache and the sort of eyes that look right through you. We
was at the Albert Hall. Big turnout. He'd finished his speech and
they was all cheering him like he was Jesus Christ. He was
coming past and suddenly he stopped and looked right at me. I
started to shake like a bloody leaf. I could've touched his arm.
Honest. He was that close. I wanted to say something. Tell him. I
opened my mouth and nothing came out. No words. Because
there wasn't no words for what I wanted to say.

SCENE 7
*The 1990's: Lights up on Zelda. As she mentions the various
characters from the past they appear on stage.*

ZELDA   The fourth of October ... yes. 1936. It was a very hot
day, if I remember rightly. We was all supposed to be going to
Trafalgar Square. Some demo about Spain. Joe was there ... no ...
no, he wasn't. Rachel ... Rachel, Friedburg. No, Freedman ... no
... *Steinberg*, that's it. Steinberg. German girl. Lost all her family
in the camps. *(pause)* There was another girl called Maggie. No
... Madge. Came from Chelsea. Educated type. Was she there? I
forget. *(suddenly)* Jimmy was there too - at Cable Street. I
remember him carrying bricks. I tried to sell him a red scarf once,
but he said it would clash with my hair. Did you know I used to
have red hair?

*As the lights change, the scene of a jumble sale is set up. Cries of
'Arms For Spain' and 'Help Our Boys At War', etc.*

SCENE 8

1936: A jumble sale, much hustle and bustle. A red banner stretched across reads - Arms For Spain. Members of the Y.C.L. are scattered around, as are the crowd. Zelda, selling clothes, is looking at a red scarf. Jimmy comes up; he has already spotted and recognised her. Throughout the scene the dialogue is interspersed with a chorus of sellers in the jumble sale which should actively try to sell to the real audience. This is simply marked - Chorus. The length of their interventions should be judged by the director and company.

CHORUS *(chant and sell)*

JIMMY   Nah ... not red. Red's not my colour. *(holds it up)* Anyhow, it'd only clash with your hair.

ZELDA   Go on ... I reckon it really suits you.

JIMMY *(points to another scarf)* How much is this?

ZELDA   Tuppence?

JIMMY   Daylight robbery!

ZELDA   Every penny goes to Spain.

JIMMY   What's happening in Spain?

ZELDA   There's a war on. Didn't you know?

CHORUS *(chant and sell)*

JIMMY   What do you reckon?

ZELDA *(suddenly realises who Jimmy is)* Brick Lane!

JIMMY   Do what?

ZELDA   The day Harry had his - little accident ... Remember?

JIMMY   How could I forget? I been looking for you ever since.

ZELDA   Liar.

MADGE   Not interrupting anything am I? I mean ... *do* say ... one doesn't like to be a gooseberry.

JIMMY   Oh, one doesn't, doesn't one ...

ZELDA *(reluctantly diverts herself from Jimmy)* I'm dying for a cuppa ... who's on teas?

JIMMY   I'll go and get you one. I like looking after the ladies.

He goes.

CHORUS *(chant and sell)*

JIMMY *(returns)* You lot commies or something?

ZELDA   Of course we are. Ain't you?

JIMMY   Never really thought about it. Always thought they was a bunch of maniacs.

ZELDA   And now?

JIMMY *(touching her hair)* I love girls with red curly hair.

HARRY *(comes over)* How you doing , Zelly?

JIMMY   Zelly, eh ... what kind of name's that?

ZELDA   Short for Zelda.

JIMMY   Nice.

HARRY *(to Jimmy)*What's your name, comrade?

JIMMY   Jimmy ... Jimmy Harris. Brick Lane ... we just worked it out. I live down Cable Street.

HARRY   You working?

JIMMY   Off and on.

HARRY   You mean no.

JIMMY   I mean ... I did a few days last month ... down the Surrey ... sweeping up ... last week I went out cleaning windows. Any more questions ... *comrade?*

ZELDA   It's alright - we're on your side.

JIMMY   Nobody's on my bloody side.

Chorus start packing up jumble sale. Enter Rachel.

RACHEL   How much did we take?

MADGE   Don't know. Harry's been counting up.

RACHEL   Not as much as last time was there?

ZELDA   Nobody's got no money. That's the trouble.

PHIL *(comes over, looks at the money taken)* We sending this lot to Spain?

HARRY   Of course.

MADGE   Harry - are they going to win?

HARRY   They? Who's they? *We* ... there's no 'they'. We are going to win.

MADGE   I suppose the general feeling is that Spain is more important than Mosley. I can see that in a way ...

HARRY   You're talking out of your touchous as usual. It's all the same struggle. If you don't understand that, I've been wasting my time. We've all been wasting our time.

MADGE   You don't think we all might be over-reacting just a bit - I mean , Spain is a war - this is just a march.

HARRY   I told you -this is a war - it's a continuous process - You know your trouble, don't you? You're politically naive - comes of having a high-class education. Roedean - was it?... well, what do you expect?

MADGE *(calls out)* Hey Zelly ... I think your brother's trying to insult me.

JIMMY *(stopping dead)* Brother ... is that your *brother*?

ZELDA   Of course. What did you think? *(goes over to Harry and Madge. To Madge)* You ought to be flattered. Harry only insults the best people. Can't be bothered with the rest, can you, Harrile? *(she tweaks Harry's ear)*

Danny enters eating a large piece of cake.

PHIL   Danny, give us a hand packing up will you? *(pause)*

DANNY   Thing is ... I was just going to get a plate of chopped
herring.

*He exits. Everyone groans. The clearing up continues throughout the
following.*

JIMMY *(to Zelda)* Do you like chopped herring?

ZELDA   Not specially. Do you?

JIMMY   Never tried it.

ZELDA   It makes your breath stink something horrible. *(they
look at one another)*

JIMMY   Which way you going?

ZELDA   Don't know. *(pause)* Harry?

HARRY   I got to finish off here.

JIMMY   You seen the new Chaplin?

ZELDA   I don't see many films. The time I get home from
work ...

JIMMY   We could go up west. Only I can't treat you.

ZELDA   I don't want you to ... *(she appeals to Harry again)*

HARRY   Do what you want Zelly. Don't look at me. *(he
makes himself very busy)*

ZELDA   I've got to iron my blouse ... *(pause)*

JIMMY   I'll see you then. *(he starts to leave)*

ZELDA *(coming after him)* Don't forget your scarf -

JIMMY *(he stops, she puts it round his neck)* I'll see you.

He exits. She goes back to Harry and starts putting things in boxes. Long pause.

ZELDA   Can't stand Chaplin. He gives me the creeps.

HARRY   Know what you mean.

ZELDA   Harry ... I ...

HARRY *(surprisingly sharp)* Forget it, Zelda ... We all got work to do ... Do me a favour ... Just forget it ...

Lights change.

SCENE 9

1936: A basement in Phil's house, Paradise Road. A noisy meeting in progress. Harry, Zelda, Danny, Rachel are present. Zelda is very agitated.

ZELDA   If you ask me, it don't make sense.

HARRY *(pulls her ear)* Who's asking you, pupick?

ZELDA   No-one ... that's the trouble.

DANNY *(brandishing newspaper)* But it's here ... it's in 'The Worker' ... It says -

ZELDA   I don't care if it's in the manifesto. It still don't make sense.

HARRY   Since when are you the big expert?

ZELDA   I live here, don't I? I got eyes.

DANNY *(reading)* The call was sent out by the London District Committee of the Communist Party for workers to go in their thousands to Trafalgar Square and after the demonstration to march through the East End to show hatred to Mosley's support for fascists in Spain ...

ZELDA   What's the point of going to Trafalgar Square? Mosley's in the East End.

PHIL   There's something in that ...

HARRY   There is a large demonstration planned in Trafalgar Square. We go there first and then ...

ZELDA   Mosley and his mob will be laughing themselves sick ... Honestly, Harry, I can't see why? ...

HARRY *(to Zelda)* I thought you was supposed to be taking the minutes. (*he passes her a pad and pen. Zelda is squashed. She angrily jabs the pen into the notepad. Pause*)

Enter Madge. She wears a King's College scarf, looks rather flushed.

MADGE   Sorry I'm late, comrades. I had a five o'clock lecture. Then I couldn't get the bloody car to start. Battery was flat as a ...

DANNY   Five o'clock lecture, eh?

HARRY   Cut it out Danny - you're wasting time.

DANNY   Margaret - we are indeed honoured by your presence. Comes the revolution we may of course have to requisition private vehicles ...

MADGE *(sitting down)* Comes the revolution you may have to use your mouth for something other than eating and abusing people.

HARRY   Who's supposed to be in the Chair?

MADGE   I thought it was Joe.

ZELDA   Joe's not here.

HARRY   I think we can see that. (*pause*) Comrades ... can we get on with some business?... Danny, didn't you?...

DANNY *(holds up a copy of 'The Daily Worker')* There's this whole page article in 'The Worker'. It says: 'All able-bodied persons are called to the front in defence of Madrid. Report for duty this weekend'. Point is ... surely you ain't trying to say that Mosley is more important than Spain? It says here 'Rather we stand than die'.

HARRY *(cutting him off)* Suddenly everyone's a hero! To the barricades, comrades ... It's the romantic dream, innit ? To die on foreign soil. What's it that poet said - *Dulce et decorum est. (he pronounces 'dulce' as 'dulls')*

MADGE *(correcting him)* You say *dulchey*. It's Latin.

HARRY *(shouts)* I know it's Latin. You think I don't know it's Latin? We can't all live in Chelsea.

ZELDA   Phil ... talking of poetry ...

(some groans, protests from Madge and Danny)

PHIL   I think it may be relevant. At least I ...

ZELDA   Let him ...

HARRY   What's the difference? I mean, it's already like Piccadilly Circus here ... *(more kindly)* No ... go on, Phil.

PHIL   Only if you're sure. It's called 'In these streets' I wrote it yesterday.

DANNY   Hot from the press.

(Harry glares at Danny, nods to Phil to read. Phil starts hesitantly, then grows more confident)

PHIL *(reading from a notebook)*
          In these streets
          Blood flows
          It is the blood of my comrades
          In France and Spain
          It is the blood of my fathers
          In Russia and Poland
          It is the blood of my brothers
          In Germany and Italy
          The blood of the oppressed,
          The blood of injustice,
          The blood of suffering.
          Today I walk these streets

A free man
But I tread in their blood.
Yesterday Berlin,
Today Madrid.
Tomorrow London
Brothers, we cannot turn aside.

(Silence, then a burst of applause)

PHIL   I'm not sure about the last line. Perhaps it should read 'must not'... I don't know.

MADGE   It's brilliant. Absolutely brilliant!

HARRY   It's terrific, Phil. Very appropriate.

PHIL   We'd better get on.

MADGE   Who *is* the Chair?

HARRY   Rachel, isn't it?

RACHEL   Oh no, I ... thing is, today I don't feel so good.

HARRY *(puts on feeble voice)* Please Mr Lenin, have the revolution without me. Today I don't feel so good!

MADGE   Harry ...

HARRY   Sometimes you make me weep ... the whole bloody lot of you ... you make me weep ...

He gets up, stalks off. Enter Joe carrying a training bag. His hair is damp. He takes in the atmosphere.

JOE   What's happening?

ZELDA   Everyone's gone mad.

JOE   So what else is new? Did I miss much?

DANNY   Not a lot. They invented the wheel. Course it'll never catch on. Oh - and they finished the pyramids ... sweated labour as usual. Nah - you ain't missed a thing! Why you so late?

JOE   I been talking to my coach.

RACHEL	And?
JOE	Seems if I can win this next bout - he can get me a few fights in America.
RACHEL	Joe, that's really something ... you must be so proud.
JOE	I haven't won yet. What's wrong with Harry?
ZELDA	He's been under a lot of pressure.
JOE	Trouble with Harry - he won't delegate.
DANNY	That's because he don't trust nobody else.
ZELDA	Except the District Committee ...

Re-enter Harry. He carries a tray with mugs. Everyone looks at him.

HARRY	I made tea. *(everyone cheers, the tension broken)* Where've we got to? *(to Zelda)* Got to your item about Jarrow, yet?
ZELDA	No ... we're still considering the five year plan.
HARRY	Didn't know we had one.
RACHEL	Perhaps we should.
PHIL	Is that a serious proposal? Because if it is I'd like to second it.
HARRY	Who's in the Chair?
MADGE	Danny - Rachel deferred to a higher authority.
RACHEL	Did I?
PHIL	Take Zinoviev ...
HARRY	Perhaps if the Chairman would call the meeting to order -
ZELDA	I vote we scrap the agenda and devote the rest of the meeting to discussing a plan of action for October fourth. *(general agreement)*

HARRY   It's not up to us to have no plans of action. We got
to do as we're instructed.

PHIL   That may be a matter of opinion.

HARRY   Are you saying you want to oppose the decision of
the District Committee?

MADGE   No-one's actually *said* it but ...

JOE   It's obvious, in it? It's alright for that lot sitting on
their arses up in Walthamstow or Maida Vale or wherever they
come from ... it's us poor sods what are out on the street every
night of the bloody week, not them. District bloody committee ...
what do they know? Was they out in the Lane that day when the
blighters turned over all the stalls and the women was screaming
and the kids was crying ... nah ... of course not. They was at home
reading 'The Daily Worker'. I tell you, this is direct provocation.
Mosley's got to be stopped ... and I mean stopped ... Here ...
now... and before it's too bloody late. *(pause)*

HARRY   You don't necessarily have to meet force with force,
comrade. You ought to know that.

JOE   Don't you? What's the matter ... afraid people might
not want to join the party if they see dirty boys out fighting on the
street? Got to keep our little hands clean, have we, if we want the
popular vote? The Labour Party always likes to keep itself nice ...
don't like to get mixed up in nothing messy. Even the TUC
wouldn't vote to support our comrades in Spain in case people
might start thinking they're a load of left-wing troublemakers ...
and now it's softly, softly here too. Is that why we joined the
Communist party ... to stay out of trouble?

(An uncomfortable silence)

MADGE   Mr Chairman. Can I draw your attention to an item
in 'The Daily Worker?' It concerns a petition organised by the
Jewish Peoples' Council to the Home Secretary - shall I read it?
(general approval, except from Joe. She reads) We the under-
signed citizens of London view with grave concern the proposed
march ...

JOE	Grave concern, eh?
HARRY	Let her read it, Joe.

MADGE   The proposed march of the British Union of Fascists upon East London. The avowed object of the fascist movement in Great Britain is incitement to malice and hatred ...

HARRY *(impatient)* Yes, yes ...

MADGE   We consider such incitement by a movement which employs flagrant distortion of truth and calumny and vilification ...

DANNY	Someone swallowed a dictionary.
MADGE	As a direct and deliberate provocation.
JOE	Didn't I just say that!
PHIL	That's just what Joe said!

MADGE   Provocation. We therefore make an earnest appeal to his Majesty's Secretary of State to prohibit this march and thus retain peaceful and amicable relations between all sections of East London's population.

JOE   Who are they trying to kid?

RACHEL   Things haven't been so bad. Not lately. I thought it all died down a bit.

JOE   It never dies down - what, with meshuggenehs like Raven Thompson around? Did you hear him speak the other Sunday. I swear to God, if I'd had a gun, I'd have -

HARRY   Joe ... I told you ...

JOE   Yeh, and look what happened. What we need is vigilante groups ... armed, ready to fight ... *They* got weapons ... you know they have ...

(There is a loud knocking at the door. Instant silence)

JOE	Who knocks round here?
RACHEL	Police?
HARRY	It's not illegal to hold a meeting.

ZELDA   Not yet. *(general unease)*

Jimmy comes in. Zelda jumps up.

JIMMY   Nothing on at The Paragon - Andy's is closed. Can't
afford the bus fare up west. So here I am. When's the revolution?
(silence)

HARRY *(he looks furious)* Hello Jimmy.

JIMMY   Harry.

HARRY *(to Zelda)* I suppose *you* told him.

ZELDA   He's very interested in joining the party.

HARRY   He's very interested in something but I don't think
it's that.

ZELDA   Next thing you'll be calling him a Yok.

JIMMY   Tell you what, why don't I take down my trousers
and then you can all see how the other half lives.

HARRY   Get in, sit down, and keep your filthy mouth shut for
a change.

JIMMY   Is this what you call a typical Jewish welcome? *(he
sits)*

HARRY *(stands, holding a piece of paper on which he has written a
few lines)* Comrades - I'd like to make a proposal - I propose that
we, the Paradise Road cell of the Stepney Young Communist
League, make contact with the D.P.C. and express our concern -

PHIL   Dissatisfaction.

JOE   Disgust.

HARRY   Concern. At the handling of the October fourth issue
and that we make it clear that we consider that anything other
than an all-out demo against Mosley, officially organised by the
Party on a local level, could be seen as an evasion of

responsibility and might result in some loss of credibility in this area. Shall we vote?

(Everyone looks surprised. Joe is delighted)

DANNY   Hang on, hang on, I'm still writing it all down.

JOE   Don't bother writing - all we need is a seconder. Great stuff, Harry.

JIMMY   I'll second it - on one condition.

HARRY   What's that?

JIMMY   That you give me the recipe for chopped herring.

RACHEL   Are you sure we aren't making too much trouble? Perhaps it would be better to stay at home. My father says, sometimes it is better to be a mouse than a lion.

JOE   Then tell your father he's wrong.

RACHEL   I mean perhaps we should leave this kind of thing to the police ... after all, that's what they are paid to do, isn't it?... to protect the people.

ZELDA   I think you'd better ask Harry.

DANNY   Come on. Let's vote! All those in favour ...

(Joe, Harry, Jimmy, Zelda, Phil, Madge, raise hands)

DANNY   Against? *(Rachel raises hand)* Abstentions?

HARRY   The vote's carried. Six in favour. One against. No abstentions. I'll write the letter myself.

DANNY   Can we go home now? Please?

(Everyone starts getting up, picking up papers, etc.)

JIMMY *(to Zelda)* I'll walk you home.

ZELDA   No - I'm going with Harry.

HARRY   I got to do the letter. I'll catch you up.

ZELDA   Phil - fancy a walk?

PHIL   Nah - Think I'll get an early night.

JIMMY   It's no use Zelly. You ain't got no-one to protect you, and I won't go away. I'll keep on trying. It'll drive you mad. Give in gracefully. Do yourself a favour. Come on ... I won't lay a finger on you. Promise. I tell you - I'm only interested in your mind.

ZELDA   And the recipe for chopped herring.

JIMMY   Right.

ZELDA   It's easy really. Some people use apple *and* onion. Some people only use onion ...

They exit together.
Lights change.

SCENE 10

The 1990's : Zelda, Harry, Phil and Clare are looking at photos.

ZELDA   It's the gang. Y.C.L. Young Communist League.

CLARE   Were you lot *really* Communists?

HARRY *(looking up)* Some of us still are.

CLARE *(sings)* The Workers' flag is deepest red ... all that stuff? What a hoot! What happened? How come you all vote Tory now?

ZELDA   Don't be ridiculous, Clare. Nobody in this house votes Tory!

HARRY   And nobody votes communist neither.

PHIL   What communist? You show me a communist and I'll vote for him!

ZELDA   Anybody fancy a tea or coffee?

HARRY *(to Phil)* You haven't voted communist for years and you know it.

PHIL   Do me a favour, Harry. I'm an old man. *(he gets up)*

CLARE *(returns to the photographs, suddenly holds up a photo)*
Hey - who's this? It looks just like my father.

PHIL   How can it be your father? He wasn't even born.

CLARE   But it looks just like him. Except for the suit. Daddy
would never be seen dead in a suit like that. Look ... *(she holds it
out to Phil. Zelda snatches it from her. Pause)*

HARRY   Zelda, what on earth?...

CLARE   It's that Jimmy, isn't it? The mysterious Jimmy.
Mmm ... sexy! Look at those eyes. Have a look, grandpa. He's got
real bedroom eyes.

HARRY   Your grandpa's not interested in no bedroom eyes.
Not at his age. Come on schmendrick ... *(pause)* Put the
photograph away, Zelda. There's a good girl.

ZELDA   No. And please don't call me a good girl.

HARRY   I said put it away.

ZELDA   And I said no.

PHIL   Leave her be, Harry.

*He exits slowly. Harry follows. Clare makes a tentative move
towards Zelda.*

ZELDA   I'll be alright. Just give me a minute.

*Clare stops, looking at Zelda, disturbed. Zelda still studies the
photograph. Lights change.*

*The sound of young voices singing comes up, faint at first, growing
louder, more raucous.*

SCENE 11

1936: Harry, Phil, Danny, Joe enter singing as they walk.
Zelda in the 1990's sees this and is still dimly lit.

1ST SONG   I'm a rambler
                  I'm a gambler
                  I'm a long way from home
                  And if you don't like me
                  Then leave me alone!
                  I eats when I'm hungry
                  And I drinks when I'm dry
                  And if the moonshine don't get me
                  I'll live till I die ... *(laughter)*

2ND SONG   *(Tune: John Brown's Body)*
                  We'll hang old Mosley on the red apple tree
                  We'll hang old Mosley on the red apple tree
                  We'll hang old Mosley on the red apple tree
                  When the red revolution comes
                  Glory, glory what a helluva way to die
                  Glory, glory what a helluva way to die
                  Glory, glory what a helluva way to die
                  When the red revolution comes
                  Glory, glory what a helluva way to die
                  Glory, glory what a helluva way to die
                  Glory, glory what a helluva way to die
                  When the red revolution comes.

As they walk past the watching Zelda and off, Jimmy's voice is heard
singing a bad version of 'Top Hat'.
Lights change.

SCENE 12

1936: The top of Box Hill. Enter Jimmy and Zelda. They are both singing and dancing playfully. Old Zelda watches .

JIMMY *(sings)* Top hat, I'm putting on my top hat.
I'm dusting off my white gloves ...
I'm putting on my tails ...

ZELDA *(sings very softly)* Top hat ... I'm putting on my top hat. I'm dusting off my ... Nobody knows all the words. *(looking round)* We've been here before ... I'm sure we have ... I recognise those trees ... look ...

JIMMY *(making a mock telescope)* Trees ... I see no trees.

ZELDA   We're lost aren't we?

JIMMY   Speak for yourself. *(trying to pull her into a song and dance)* Come on, Ginger. *(sings)* Top hat ... I'm putting on my ...

ZELDA   I don't know all the words.

JIMMY   Nor do I. Nobody does.

ZELDA   Not even Fred Astaire!

JIMMY   Right ... Come on ... Top hat, I'm putting on my dee da ... I'm putting on my .... white gloves ...

ZELDA   Top hat ... I'm putting on my whatsit ...

JIMMY   I'm putting on my something or other ...

BOTH   Chasing all the girls ... *(they loon about being Fred Astaire and Ginger, until they eventually collapse in a heap)*

ZELDA   We'd better try and find the others.
JIMMY   Why?
ZELDA   We might miss the train.
JIMMY   So what?
ZELDA   There might not be another one.
JIMMY   There's always another one. *(pause)*

ZELDA   Lovely view. Miles and miles and no houses. And
the air smells really fresh, don't it?... *(pause)* Why don't you look
at the view?

JIMMY   I am ... *(he reaches out and touches her hair)*
ZELDA *(moving slightly)* Don't Jimmy.
JIMMY   Why not?

ZELDA   I don't know ... (*she moves away a little*) Standing
here ... all this space ... great big trees that've been here for ages
... I feel as if I could do anything ... anything in the whole
world ...

JIMMY *(never takes his eyes off her)* I never knew no-one like you
before.

ZELDA   That's what they all say.
JIMMY   All who?... who else?
ZELDA   I was joking.
JIMMY   I wasn't.
ZELDA   I know. *(pause)* Harry'll be wondering ...

JIMMY   Harry's little sister ... *(pause)* You're a grown-up,
Zelly. You can do what you want.

ZELDA   I don't know what I want.

JIMMY   Well, I do. *(he takes hold of her, his arms round her
tightly)*

ZELDA   It'll only cause trouble.

JIMMY   I like trouble. Sometimes trouble is worth it. *(he
kisses her, it starts gently. Soon becomes more passionate)* See?

ZELDA   Yes.
JIMMY   I wanted to do that since that day at the Jumble Sale.
ZELDA   So did I.
JIMMY   Why didn't you then?
ZELDA   I didn't dare ...
JIMMY   And now?

ZELDA   I just want to touch you. I keep wanting to touch
you.

JIMMY   Well?... *(she reaches out, touches his face, very tentatively. He begins kissing her again, very urgently. Zelda pulls away. Pause)* What are you thinking?

ZELDA   What if you don't love me?

JIMMY   Who says I don't? *(pause)*

ZELDA   Alright, Jimmy Harris. *(she kisses him very passionately, deliberately. He is a bit bemused but responds eagerly)*

The lights change.

SCENE 13

The 1990's: Clare and Zelda stand opposite each other in two spots. An announcement is heard around the space, an echoing, scary announcement:

'Violent clashes between police and teenagers in the Hackney area this morning resulted in one hundred and twenty-five arrests ...'

CLARE   We've been to loads of demos, Jack and me. Crowds of people out in the sun, singing, shouting and waving things. *Save the Whale, Kill the Bill, Stop the Road.* It never seemed to matter what we were shouting about ... It was just great to be out there together, in the street, all wanting the same thing. It always gave me a great feeling, as if we could really make a difference, really change things for the better, just by being there. Today started the same as always. We'd heard there was going to be a march for racial unity through Hackney, ending up with a big rally with Asian bands. Very important issue, Jack said, and the music'll be great too! We were walking along next to these Asian boys and they'd got all these little drums and I said - Let's have a go, so they showed me how to play one and it made a really nice sound, gentle and sweet. The sun was shining and there were women in bright saris, orange, gold and turquoise, out getting their Saturday shopping with their little kids. They'd stop and smile and wave at us from the pavement. I felt proud and special. I was out there stand-ing up for what I believe in. And I felt the world could be a better place if only everyone tried a bit harder. Suddenly out of the crowd comes this gang of white boys with dangerous haircuts and stupid T-shirts, Union Jacks, skull and crossbones. They're shouting and yelling - *Kill the Pakis, Britain for the British,* banging empty cans with bits of rough metal. Their faces are very, very white and their lips very pale and they come marching towards us like a crazy army; their eyes are cold and full of hating. The women in the saris run away with their pushchairs. The kids are crying and screaming. Then the Asian boys put down their little drums, and move towards the rough kids; they're shouting ugly things in their own language, and their sweet faces are suddenly all shadowy with fear, with anger. It was like the sun had been blotted out in that one moment, and the sky was black as night. Like a nightmare vision of the future. But I thought: This isn't the future ... it's now ... it's happening here in our streets, now. *(pause)*

ZELDA *(to Clare)* Well?

CLARE   Well what?

ZELDA   Are you going to tell me what happened or not?

CLARE   I don't know what happened ... that's the point. It's all going round and round in my head and I can't make sense out of any of it ... you think you know someone and suddenly they're behaving like a total stranger. Then the whole world starts turning inside out and all the things you thought you really understood, suddenly you don't understand a bloody thing. People coming at you from all sides ... you get so you don't know what the hell you *do* believe in ... you get so you don't know *what* you want ... you ...

Lights down.

ACT TWO
SCENE 1

In the blackout, Clare's voice overlaps with the singing.

CLARE   So then the whole world starts turning inside out and all the things you thought you understood, suddenly you don't understand any of it. You get so you don't know what the hell you *do* believe in ... you get so you don't know *what* you want.

1936: The voices of Harry, Zelda, Phil, singing. The following should create a sense of preparing for the demonstration.

THEY SING   When the white guards invaded
And the Donbas was raided
In those grim, unforgettable years,
Swift our columns assembled
How the earth heaved and trembled
And we galloped with song and with cheers
With Budyeny to lead us
Like a thundering chorus
As the army that never gave way. *(laughter)*

Lights up towards the end of the song. In the street. Zelda and Phil are painting the words 'They shall not pass' in huge letters on a banner.

ZELDA   You think it's big enough? Perhaps it ought to be bigger?

PHIL   In case he's short-sighted? No - I reckon Mr Mosley should see this one alright. *(reads)* They shall not pass!

ZELDA   Not if we have anything to do with it!

Harry runs on with a pile of leaflets.

HARRY   These have been printed over with the new
   instructions.

ZELDA   Let's see *(she takes one, turns it this way and that,
   reads)* Alteration:- Rally to Aldgate, Two pm. Thats better! *(to
   Harry)* Thank God the D.P.C. changed the line, eh Harry!

HARRY   Don't thank God. He ain't in the party.

PHIL   Are you sure?

HARRY *(plonks a pile of leaflets onto Phil)* Come on ... let's put
   these leaflets into batches of a hundred then one of you can do
   Whitechapel and the other can go down Commercial Road.

Lights fade on them as they busy themselves with this.
*The lights come up on another area where Madge is painting a large
red banner. It reads:- 'Paradise Road Young Communist League'.
Zelda comes in. A pause.*

ZELDA   That's nice.

MADGE   Thanks. It's practically finished.

ZELDA   You're good at most things, aren't you?

MADGE   Not really. I used to be hopeless at maths. I never
   could get the hang of quadratic equations. *(she carries on with
   the banner, then looks up)* You don't like me much, do you?

ZELDA   I don't know what you mean.

MADGE   Don't you? *(pause)*

ZELDA   Got any idea where Jimmy is?

MADGE   No ... should I have?

ZELDA   I just wondered ...

MADGE *(puts down the brush)* Look, I'm sorry if he's giving you a
   hard time ...

ZELDA   Don't be stupid ...

MADGE   But don't blame me. I mean, I wouldn't touch him
with a barge-pole which isn't to say he hasn't tried. Cocky little
bastard. No ... don't worry ... he's not my type and quite frankly,
I'm rather surprised to hear that he's yours.

ZELDA   You rotten little cow ... you lousy stuck-up little ...
swanning down here once a week like Lady Muck, then running
home for a nice hot bath ... Why don't you go back to Chelsea
where you belong? After all, it's a long way from Aldgate East to
Sloane Square. We don't need your sort. Let's be honest
comrades, the rich *are* different - never mind about their politics.
We can fight our own bloody battles, thank you very much.

Danny comes in, catches the end of this.

DANNY   Spoken like a true comrade. *(pause)*
Not interrupting anything am I?
(Zelda pokes out her tongue and stalks off)
What the hell was all that about?

MADGE   Sex and politics. Nothing important ... come on, let's
get this finished.

*They return to the banner, work on in silence as the light fades on
them. The lights come up on the Breadshop. A woman is making
bread. Harry pleads with her.*

HARRY   It'd only be for a few hours.

WOMAN   What about my bread? Tomorrow I got to do six
dozen bagels, four dozen platzels ... oh and a couple of dozen
plavas also.

HARRY   There's nothing to stop you baking bread.

WOMAN   What with people dying all over the place? Do me a
favour!

HARRY   A first aid post, I said ... not a mortuary. Just the odd cut or bruise maybe, nothing serious.

WOMAN   Tell me, why don't they go to the hospital? Is what they there for ain't it? Bleeding all over my breadshop.

HARRY   They don't go to hospital, because our friends the police have a nasty habit of keeping a list of names of people involved in so-called disturbances - Jews, that is. You don't want comrades to have their names on no lists, now do you? *(pause)*

WOMAN   Why you come to me now, put guns to my head, kind of thing?

HARRY   Because we were going to use Mr Cohen's work-shop ...

WOMAN   So?

HARRY   His wife died last night.

WOMAN   Who Rosa? About time. She been dying as long as I knowed her.

HARRY   And anyway ... you got a telephone.

WOMAN *(grabs the telephone)* You don't go using my telephone. What you think? I a millionaire or something?

HARRY   Every call will be paid for. I promise. Please.

WOMAN   Alright ... but don't start joining me up to no communist parties, understand. Go on ... get out of my way ... schmoozer ... go on.

Lights change. To the street.
Enter Harry, Zelda and Phil. Madge and Danny emerge carrying the banner. Zelda goes up to touch it, avoiding Madge's eyes.

MADGE   Careful ... the paint's still wet.*(looking round)* Where's Jimmy?

PHIL   Probably gone to see the new Chaplin.

MADGE   Funny. He promised to take me next week (*Zelda looks across sharply*) All property is theft:- isn't that what they say? (*Zelda turns away*)

DANNY   What's next?... *(sees leaflets, mock horror)* Oh no ... not leaflets! I ain't doing no leaflets.

HARRY   Defying party orders again, eh, boychick? We've got to get this lot out tonight, like it or lump it.

PHIL *(picking up a bundle)* I'll take Richard Street and Jane Street, then I'll work my way down Commercial Road.

DANNY   I got to get home ... I promised my mother. Look, I'll see you all tomorrow ... promise! (*Harry looks disgusted*)

Danny exits.

HARRY   Typical!

ZELDA   I hear Lansbury's advising people to stay away.
(Harry nods)

PHIL *(looks very thoughtful)* Perhaps he's right? (*Harry looks at him sharply*) Perhaps we are sometimes guilty of provocation? It does tend to escalate - one incident on top of the other. Well don't it?

HARRY   Listen - first of all you're worried we ain't doing nothing to stop them, now you're telling me we ought to stay away on Sunday and leave Mr Mosley to take over the East End without opposition?

PHIL   No - of course not! It's just ... sometimes I ask myself - who's going to draw the line?... That's all.

HARRY   Write a letter to Franco and ask *him.*

PHIL *(turning)* It's a serious question Harry. Don't make me look like a meshuggeneh just because I raise a serious question.
(Jimmy's voice off)

JIMMY   Whitewash! Whitewash!

Enter Jimmy carrying whitewash, a brush and a bucket. He goes up to Madge and pretends to paint her. She pushes him away.

MADGE   Get off!

HARRY *(to Jimmy)* We *said* seven o'clock sharp.
   (Jimmy imitates Chaplin's walk)

JIMMY   Great film! Terrific!

MADGE   I thought you said we were going next week. You and me ... remember?

JIMMY   Did I say that? Never. *(he goes across to Zelda)* Alright? *(she turns away from him)* What's up with you, po-face? *(pause)*

HARRY   There's a couple of thousand leaflets. If you've got the time that is ...

JIMMY   Leaflets? Nah, not my style! *(brandishes whitewash brush)* I fancy a few slogans:-Fascists get lost! Mosley go to hell! Free Johnny Rivers!

PHIL   Who's Johnny Rivers?

JIMMY   My best mate. Got married last week and his wife won't let him out of her sight.

HARRY *(coming up to Jimmy)* This ain't a joke, you know.

JIMMY   Did I say it was?

HARRY   What we need round here is a bit of discipline.

JIMMY *(gives Nazi salute)* Your word is my command. *(Jimmy goes and examines banner - then picks it up, waves it)*
   (sings) The Workers' flag is deepest red ...
   Who's going to carry this?

HARRY   That's still got to be decided.

JIMMY *(to Danny)* Where's comrade Joe? Skiving off as usual?

ZELDA   Joe's fighting.

JIMMY The big one, eh? *(he goes up to Harry, pretends to box with him. Harry ignores him)*

PHIL *(to Harry)* I'll make a start with the leaflets.

JIMMY I'm going to paint the town! *(shouts out)* You girls can hold the paint!

They all exit except Zelda and Jimmy. Pause.

ZELDA Why don't you *say* something?... you can't just ...

JIMMY It weren't just me ... remember? It's like suddenly it was all my fault. I never saw you complaining ...

ZELDA Who's talking about fault? It's just ... there was all that, and then ... *nothing ... I feel so ... stupid* ... and Madge ... I mean ... what the hell's going on?

JIMMY Do me a bloody favour?

ZELDA Well, how should I know?

JIMMY *(comes up to her)* Marry me, Zelda ... the day after tomorrow. Ask your dad. *(she moves away, totally confused)*

Enter Rachel, running. She has blood all over her clothes.

ZELDA Rachel ... what happened?... where's Joe?

RACHEL He won the fight ... it was easy for him ...

ZELDA So where is he?...

RACHEL We were walking back along Stepney Green ... it was very dark ... a few of the street lights not working ...

ZELDA Yes.

RACHEL There were three of them waiting ... out ahead of us

JIMMY Who ... who was it?

RACHEL   I don't know ... just boys ... They called out - Joe! They said -Joe Aronowitz.!

ZELDA   Blackshirts.

RACHEL   I don't know. I wouldn't like to say.

ZELDA   You *got* to say, Rachel.

RACHEL   It could have been anybody. Rough boys ... anybody.

JIMMY   What they do?

RACHEL   They hit at his head mostly ... with the belts. One of them used the bottle. When he fell down, they start to kick. They had big boots. Big boots.

ZELDA   Why didn't he?... I mean ... Joe ... he could have ...

RACHEL   This was the strange thing. He stood there like this *(she puts up her fists)* till they start to hit. Then he just ... I don't know ... I think he was crying.

ZELDA   Where is he?

RACHEL   I took him to the hospital ... it wasn't so far. Some men sitting on the steps ... they helped me on the last bit.

ZELDA   I'll get Harry.

RACHEL   He'll be alright. They said he'd be alright. Nothing so serious, they said. Only so much blood. Always looks worse ... *(she begins to sob. Zelda comforts her)*

ZELDA   I'd better take you home.

RACHEL   I have to do leaflets. Everyone has to do leaflets. Harry says.

ZELDA   Are you crazy? Come on ... I'll take you home. Then I'll go and find Harry.

JIMMY   What did they look like ... the boys?

RACHEL   It was dark ... like I said ... I never saw any faces.

ZELDA *(picks up the whitewash brush, hands it to Jimmy, looks at him very steadily)* Whitewash ... remember?

She puts her arm round Rachel. They exit.

JIMMY *(watches them go)* I'd kill them ... that's what I'd do ... *(suddenly shouts)* Why don't you kill the bastards? Why don't you fucking kill the bastards?... before they kill the whole fucking lot of you!

Blackout.

SCENE 2

1936: Lights come up on a hospital bed. Joe lies very still.
Joe talks to no-one in particular.

JOE   Thing is, I could've killed him. Easy. The bloke what hit me first. I was stood there, fists up and suddenly I could feel it stirring up inside me like a a saucepan of milk coming to the boil - this bloody great whirlpool of anger, getting hotter and hotter, spinning round in circles, waiting to explode. And I thought: I could reach out and smash him to pieces. Once I got started I'd never be able to stop. Because it wouldn't just be for me - Joe Aronowitz - it wouldn't even be for all them other kids they've beaten up, down Whitechapel and Mile End - or even for the poor frightened little shopkeepers - no - it'd be for Harry's parents running out of their village, the sky full of flames, it'd be for Rachel's father and mother and cousins and friends - and for all the poor devils in Spain and for all the little bastards every-where whether they're Jews or they're Catholics because it don't matter who they calls God - and then I looked at him - saw his face all twisted up with hating and suddenly I saw myself, like looking in a mirror - and I couldn't hit him. No. Because I knew if I hit him I'd never stop - I'd kill him ... I'd kill all of them. With all that hate we carry around inside ... him and me. No different. Members of the human race ... all end up ... killing ... destroying each other ... got to stop ... think of something

different ... must be something different. *(long pause)*
I'll be there ... the march ... watching, not fighting. No more
fighting. Watching. All going to kill each other one day ...
members of the human race. *(sings very softly)*
Internationale ... unites the human race ...
Tell them Danny ... tell them ...

Blackout.

SCENE 3

The 1990's: Zelda, Phil, Harry and Clare.

ZELDA   Remember Joe?

PHIL   Course I remember Joe. Handy little fighter, eh
Harry? Nasty little right hook. Joe ...

HARRY   Strong boy, Joe. Very strong boy.

ZELDA   I think somebody should reply to this letter, Phil.

PHIL   I told you. I don't remember nothing.

CLARE   Cable Street. Of course. I was trying to think ... It
was in that programme about the police. We all went round to
Jack's place specially to see it. What a bunch of pigs.
Unbelievable. Were you there, grandma?

ZELDA   We all were.

CLARE   Amazing. What happened?

ZELDA   Why don't you ask your grandpa?

PHIL   I told you ... I don't ...

ZELDA   Don't want to, you mean.

CLARE   Are you still a communist Uncle Harry?

HARRY   Course I am - what do you think?

ZELDA   Come on ... let's all have a nice cup of tea..

PHIL   No, not yet. I want to ask Harry about this
communist party he believed in so much ...

ZELDA   Phil ...

PHIL   No - I'm interested. The way he used to talk about
the Soviet Union back in the thirties, anyone would think it was
utopia, heaven on earth. As for Comrade Stalin ... well ...
according to Harry, he was God and Moses all rolled into one.

ZELDA   Phil, don't start. Don't get him going.

PHIL   And then there's what you might call the Jewish
problem. Now there's a bit of a tricky one, eh lundsman? I mean,
how do you account for rabid anti-Semitism in a state that was
supposed to be dedicated to the equality of all races and creeds?
(pause) Still ... perhaps things ain't always what they seem, eh,
Harry? I mean, people do get things wrong, don't they?...

HARRY   Pure emotionalism. All of it. The patent bias of the
Western media. I'm surprised at you Phil.

ZELDA   This is ridiculous; it's all in the past.

PHIL   You're the one who wanted to remember.

ZELDA   So we should ... but not this ... not all this.

PHIL   You can't pick and choose. Once you start, it all
comes back, whether you want it or not.

ZELDA   It was a great day. An amazing day. You know
it was. There's no need to pull it all down. Just because
afterwards ...

PHIL   No-one's pulling it down, Zelda. I was there too,
remember.

HARRY   So was I. We was all there. *(sings softly)*
We'll hang old Mosley on the red apple tree.
We'll hang old Mosley on the red apple tree.

ZELDA   We'll hang old Mosley on the red apple tree

PHIL   When the red revolution comes

HARRY/ZELDA Glory, glory hallelujah.
        Glory, glory hallelujah.
        Glory, glory hallelujah.
        When the red revolution comes.

*As the lights fade, the song is taken up by other, younger voices.
Lights change.*

SCENE 4

1936: In the blackout several loudspeakers are heard.

LOUDSPEAKER Men and women of the East End. Come out of
    your houses. The Blackshirts are marching! Rally to Gardeners
    Corner. The fascists shall not pass!

*As the lights come up a tremendous explosion of noise. Thousands of
marching feet, growing in intensity. General hubbub. The criss-
crossing of several different marching songs - including:
We'll hang old Mosley / The Red Flag / Solidarity for Ever.
Shouts of : They shall not pass / Mosley shall not pass / Ban the road
to British fascism.
Gardeners Corner, Whitechapel:- the whole area festooned with
flags and banners, mostly red.
Enter Rachel, Phil. They carry the banner.*

RACHEL   It's amazing! I've never seen nothing like it! There's
    thousands of us ... thousands!

PHIL   He won't get through this lot - not in a million years.

RACHEL   I never expected ...

PHIL   None of us did ...

The sound of a tremendous hubbub.

POLICEMAN *(over loudhailer)* Clear the route. Clear the route. Anyone obstructing the route will be arrested.

CHANTING VOICES They shall not pass. They shall not pass. They shall not pass.

(Harry, Zelda, amongst others, form a human barricade against the police. The chanting continues)

HARRY Don't move back ... stand firm ... don't move back. Don't forget ... they're solid at Gardener's Corner.

ZELDA They'll mow us down. There's thousands of them.

HARRY You should've stayed back with the others. I told you.

ZELDA I wanted to see what was happening.

HARRY So see ...

ZELDA The horses ... they're terrified. Look at their eyes. They'll never be able to control them.

HARRY Don't worry about no horses ... Stand. Don't let them through. There's thousands more behind us. We're not on our own. *(shouts)* Ban the road to British Fascism. Mosley shall not pass! No violence ... remember what we said. Just stop them getting through. No violence.

Lights change. The chanting continues. Lights up on Micky, splendid in complete B.U.F. uniform. He stands grandly to attention. Enter Jimmy carrying bricks. A policeman calls out.

POLICEMAN *(to Jimmy)* Hey sonny, what are you doing with them bricks?

JIMMY I'm building the new Jerusalem.

POLICEMAN What's wrong with the old one?

JIMMY It turned into a police state. *(sees Micky, puts down bricks)* Hello Micky. What a nice surprise!

POLICEMAN You two mates?

JIMMY   Not exactly.

MICKY   Ask him where his Jew-boy friends are now. Hiding under the bed, are they? - Oy vay, oy vay. I told you ... you won't stop us that easy. How's the girlfriend? What's her name?... Becky ain't it? Hot bit is she? (*Jimmy hits him in the mouth. They begin to fight*)

POLICEMAN (*breaking it up*) Come on, come on, or I'll arrest the pair of you.

Lights change. The chants continue.

JIMMY (*running towards Zelda and Harry*) There's millions of them ... they're arriving in coachloads.

ZELDA   Police or blackshirts?

JIMMY   Both ... it's like a ruddy army ... There's no way we're going to stop them.

ZELDA   People are going to get hurt, Harry.

HARRY   You can't make a bubbeleh without breaking eggs. Remember?

ZELDA   People, Harry. Not eggs. Broken people.

HARRY   People are already broken. This'll be an end to it.

ZELDA   The end justifies. Is that what you're saying?

HARRY   They shall not pass. That's what I'm saying. That's what we're all saying, comrade. That's all we need to say. We got to stand firm ... stand together ... they shall not pass.

(The chanting continues)

VOICE OF POLICEMAN (*over loudhailer*) Will you get back all of you?... Permission has been granted by the Home Secretary for the march to pass. Clear the route ... this route will be cleared.

CHANTING VOICES They shall not pass. They shall not pass.

VOICE OF POLICEMAN This is your final warning ... get back ... get back ... Clear the route. People are going to get hurt. Get back.

CHANTING VOICES *(intensifying)* They shall not pass! They shall not pass!

(Thundering of hooves as the horses charge. Loud screams. General mayhem. Chanting)

ZELDA   No!... No!...

*Lights change to reveal Zelda on the ground. Harry is face to face with two policemen, with batons raised. Phil stands by.
Jimmy is close enough to see what follows.*

1ST POLICEMAN   Well, Mr Cohen ... Are you going to get back, Mr Cohen?... Or are you going to have a very sore head?...

(Harry stands, doesn't move. The policeman flicks him with his baton, hitting the side of his head)

PHIL   He never did nothing. He never touched nobody!

(The policeman continues his assault on Harry, intensifying it)

JIMMY *(approaches, shouting)* Hit him Harry ... don't just fucking stand there. Christ all bloody mighty! ... why don't you hit him?... *(pause)*

2ND POLICEMAN *(to Harry)* Will you get back?

HARRY   No.

1ST POLICEMAN Are you asking me to arrest you?

HARRY   I'm asking you to let me defend my own territory.

2ND POLICEMAN Your territory? Diabolical cheek! *Your* territory? Why you dirty little foreign bastard ... I'll show you whose territory ... (*he grabs hold of Harry as if to bodily throw him out of the way. Suddenly, Harry turns and lashes out at him with great force. He hits him, and continues to hit him)*

ZELDA   No, Harry ... No! Phil ... stop him ...

The 1st Policeman takes hold of Harry from behind, subdues him and then cuffs him . Both policemen drag him off. A long pause as Phil and Zelda look on exasperated.

PHIL   He always said people had to change but ...

ZELDA   He's just a human being, Phil. He ain't God all-bloody mighty.

(Suddenly a great cheer is heard from the crowd and shouting)

VOICES   They're going back! The Blackshirts ... look ... he's telling them they got to go back.

(An even bigger cheer and shouts of -)

They're turning back!!... they're turning back!!... they're turning back!!... The march is abandoned!!...

(A spontaneous outburst of The Red Flag -)

VOICES SING Then raise the scarlet banner high
              Beneath its shade we'll live and die
              Though cowards flinch and traitors sneer
              We'll keep the red flag flying here ...

(Then other songs break out - great jubilation They sing.)
Tune:Tipperary Its a long way to fight for freedom
              It's a long way to go
              It's a long way to fight for freedom
              But we'll get there soon you know
              Goodbye Mr Mosley
              Goodbye B.U.F.
              It's a long, long way to fight for freedom
              But we'll get there I know *(more cheers)*

PHIL *(embracing anyone)* We done it! We done it! See, comrades ... We done it! *(Zelda finds herself next to Madge. Madge grabs her, hugs her. They both begin to laugh)* They did not pass, eh comrades?

*They all begin to embrace - then slowly around them the crowd
begins to break up. People go arm in arm, laughing, calling out.
More singing. As the celebrations continue the lights change.*

SCENE 5

*The two following speeches should intercut and at some points could
be spoken together. Clare's speech is in the 1990's and Rachel's is
set in 1936. They should both be seen from the perspective of the
1990's*

CLARE   Jack, he's usually such a gentle person - you know
they say - oh, he wouldn't hurt a fly - well ... there's these two
blokes slugging it out on the pavement. One of them's an Asian,
quite small and weedy looking, and the other's a big white guy,
all flabby, with a pale, piggy face. He's calling the Asian kid all
the names under the sun - Black bastard, Paki pig, Foreign scum.
The Asian kid is definitely getting the worst of it. Then this
young policeman barges in and gets the Asian kid in a sort of
neck-lock, and shoves the white kid away. 'Scarper', he says ...
'Push off' ... and the white kid disappears into the crowd. Jack
and I see all this. Then suddenly without saying a word, Jack
pushes forward and starts hitting out at the policeman till he's let
go of the Asian kid. The kid runs off. But Jack doesn't stop there.
No. He keeps on hitting and hitting, till the policeman's nose
starts pouring with blood, still he doesn't stop. Jack, Jack stop ...
Jack, what the hell are you doing? But he can't hear me, or else he
doesn't want to. Then a couple of older policemen come up and
grab hold of him, put handcuffs on him and take him away. The
young policeman takes out a dirty hanky and starts wiping the
blood away. I see that he's crying. Something happened out there.
It was like he became a different person, Jack. He went mad,
completely out of control! And I thought: I don't know you ... I
thought I did, but I don't. I don't know you at all. I've never seen
so much hatred. Jack's face all twisted up with hating, he didn't
look like a human being, more like a wild animal, worse even.
Grandma, I'm scared, I'm so scared ... so bloody scared.

RACHEL   I was afraid ... I was one of those who was afraid. I
heard footsteps behind me in the street, I was afraid. Always
worrying in case someone should ask: 'Are you a Jew?' and I
have to answer: - 'Yes, I am a Jew.' And nightmares ... I had a
few nightmares. Breaking glass. A boot against wood ... the door
flies open and a man stands there, perhaps with a gun. Will every
Jew stand up, come out? We go outside. There is no-one there to
help us. So he shoots us, one by one. One by one we fall to the
ground. Afraid. Always afraid. *(pause)* When they tell me Mr
Mosley should march in Whitechapel, I said: 'So, leave him
march. Don't ask me to come out and stop him.' Probably I get
my face smashed in. My Jewish face. *(pause)* They jumped on my
friend. Black-shirts. Fascists. They beat his head and he stood
there gentle like a lamb. Joe Aronowitz ... used to be a boxer.
Lies now in a London hospital, tubes coming out of his nose.
Listen to me Joe ... don't die, ok? Don't die thinking there isn't no
hope. Because there *is* hope, Joe ... I saw that today. There *is*
hope. *(pause)* I never knew, comrades, how strong we could be if
we stood together - not just Jews - Catholics - Protestants -
people with religions I don't even know the name of. Not just
communists - Labour too - ex-servicemen, trade unions, young,
old ... workers, all of us ... we stood up and joined hands against
our common enemy. And, yes, Joe, we were strong. Jew and
Gentile together, we showed we could be strong. I was proud,
comrades, proud of myself, proud of all of us. *(pause, gathers
strength)* So listen to me, Joe ... don't give up hope. Because there
is nothing, nothing that can defeat us, just as long as we stand
together. In our unity we need never again be silent. In our unity
we need never again be afraid. In our unity is our strength.

Blackout.

SCENE 6

The 1990's. During the next scenes the past and present intercut at a rapid speed. It is possible for characters to speak across time to their counterparts and to other characters.

PHIL *(almost to himself)* I believed in you Harry Lazarus. Just as much as I believed in the Soviet Union - maybe more. Just as much as I believed in Comrade Stalin. We all did. Even poor little Danny running off to Spain just so that Harry wouldn't keep calling him a coward. Running straight into the front line and straight out of it again, scared shitless. Killed in a bloody car accident trying to get away - still carrying his bag of platzels, before he even had time to find out what a war is ... While Harry stood there in Cable Street, hitting policemen - Harry who never broke the rules.

Lights change.

SCENE 7

1936: Lights up on Zelda, Harry, Phil in the street.

HARRY   Who put up my bail? *(Zelda looks at Phil)* It was Tatta, wasn't it?... Zelda who told you to?...

ZELDA   Nobody *told* me to do nothing. Anyhow, it weren't my idea .... it was *his*.

HARRY   I was in the wrong.

PHIL   But Harry ...

HARRY   I was in the wrong Phil. The Party laid down a set of guidelines and I disobeyed them ... A policy was drawn up and I ignored it. It was completely unforgivable.

PHIL   Emotion exists, Harry. Why don't you admit it for once? You can't live your life with your head stuck in the manifesto. You try to toe the party line ... we all do. But sometimes ... like on Sunday ... you find yourself breaking all the rules. I'm not going to blame you, - any more than I'm going to blame myself because I was too scared to do anything. *(pause)* We joined the party because there was things we felt strongly about. It was something here ... burning ... a sort of *passion*. Don't try and stamp that out. Not in yourself or no-one else. That burning can't be taught how to behave itself. Because, if it could, there wouldn't be no Party, there wouldn't be revolution ... we'd all be dead from the neck up ... frightened little yes-men ... we'd all end up as bloody Tories!

HARRY/ZELDA Me ... a Tory! Do me a ... Do me a favour!

They all laugh, the tension broken. They freeze.
The lights change. Cut to the 1990's

HARRY: You said emotion exists, a sort of passion, you said ... a kind of burning ... you said ...

Lights down on the 1990's, up on 1936. Unfreeze. Enter Jimmy.

JIMMY   Did you speak to your old man?

ZELDA   My father? Yes. Yes I did.

JIMMY   And?

ZELDA   He showed me how to wet my lips.

JIMMY   Do *what*?

ZELDA   He said if you try to whistle with dry lips it's like a nightingale with no neck.

JIMMY   Is that translated from the Polish, or what?

ZELDA   Russian.

JIMMY   Sorry, Russian. Zelly - will you stop talking Russian
or Yiddish or double-dutch and give me an answer to the question
I asked you ... *(pause)*

ZELDA   I didn't think you was serious.

JIMMY   Of course I was serious.

ZELDA *(looks at him very straight. Pause)* Then the answer's no.

JIMMY   The old git ...

ZELDA   It's *me* that's saying no, Jimmy.

(It sinks in slowly)

JIMMY   You mean you don't want to ...

ZELDA   That's right.

JIMMY   But I ... but I thought ... I mean, it was lovely,
wasn't it? ... Or don't you remember?

ZELDA   Of course I remember. Part of me can't stop
remembering ... I been lying awake at night remembering ...

JIMMY   Then why?...

ZELDA   Because afterwards there were all them other
feelings - and they made me weak and useless and scared.
Because I know if I choose that, there'll be too many other things
I'll have to stop wanting. Because suddenly I can see there's a lot
of work for me to do. *(pause)* It's as if there in't the time ... there
just in't the time.

Lights fade to blackout.

SCENE 8

The 1990's: Lights up on the living room of Zelda and Phil.

CLARE *(to Harry)* It was only under extreme provocation, wasn't it
Uncle Harry? What Jack did. He wouldn't have done it otherwise.
I mean he's such a gentle person.

HARRY　　　Of course it was.

PHIL　　　Two wrongs don't make a right, Harry.

HARRY　　　Did they ever?

Zelda comes in with a cake, candles lit.

ZELDA　　　Happy Birthday.

(She begins to sing 'Happy Birthday'. Clare joins in. Harry and Phil still looking at each other. Slowly Phil begins to sing)

ZELDA *(to Clare)* Hand me that parcel, will you?

(Clare fetches the parcel, gives it to Zelda, who hands it to Harry. He opens it, looks at it very hard. It is a painting of some geraniums, red, very vivid)

HARRY　　　Geraniums. Isn't that what you call them? Big red flowers.

ZELDA　　　Yes.

HARRY　　　Red geraniums. Just like down Plummers Row. *(pause, looks at picture)* You know, I went back there not so long ago - just to have a look. It's all disappeared of course - all of it - just the name of the street, that's all that's left. It's all gone. That's the truth.

ZELDA　　　Okay. So we didn't change the world and that makes us feel a bit bitter and a bit tired and very disillusioned - specially after all the work we put in, eh Harry? But for that one day, we believed we could. Isn't that amazing! Isn't it?*(she goes to the geraniums)* Have you ever seen geraniums in the winter?... how they wither away to nothing more than a dry stump, a dead-looking twig? Then, suddenly, they shoot green, and in the summer you get all these incredible flowers again. You just have to believe.

(The phone rings, several times. Clare goes to answer it.)

CLARE   Yes. Yes. Of course. I'll come straight away. *(she puts the phone down)* I've got to go now. That was Jack.

PHIL   Never believe everything you're told, schmendrick.

CLARE *(stands in the doorway)* See you then ...

ZELDA *(goes to Clare. They hug each other)* Are you alright?

CLARE   I think I might be. Eventually. *(pause)* *(she speaks to them all)* You will answer that letter, won't you?

They all look at each other, smile. Harry picks up the painting, carries it to his chair, sits looking at it. Phil goes to the letter, looks at it, folds it carefully and places it in his shirt pocket. The lights fade slowly to blackout.

End

Sheila Yeger has written extensively for the theatre, radio and television. She is a published poet and the author of **The Sound of One Hand Clapping** (Amber Lane Press.) Theatre includes **Self Portrait** (Amber Lane Press), **Variations** (Methuen) and two community plays: **The Ballad of Tilly Hake** and **A Day by the Sea**. Radio includes **Heart of England** and **Yellow Ochre**. She is the mother of Ben and Sam and the grandmother of Naomi Starr and lives near Bristol with her partner Roger Stennett. There she teaches meditation, embroiders, practises T'ai chi ... and grows geraniums.

GLOSSARY OF YIDDISH WORDS AND PHRASES

bubbele. Pancake made with eggs and matzo meal.

choochka. Term of endearment. e.g. little darling.

lokshen pudding. Traditional milk pudding made with vermicelli.

lundsman. Someone from the same country of origin.

meshuggenehs. Madmen.

mumser. Bastard.

noch. Now.

noo. So...

platzel. Round bread roll with seeds on top.

plava. Sponge cake made with almond flour. (pronounced: play-va).

pupick. Affectionate insult (Lit: belly button).

schmendrick. Idiot.

schmerel. Fool, idiot.

schmoozer. Flanneler.

schwitzing. Sweating.

sehr shan. Very nice.

shobbos. Sabbath.

tatta. Daddy.

yok. Non-Jew (term of abuse).

Out of their Heads
by Marcus Romner

Out of their Heads

This is a play about drugs with a serious difference. I felt that a spin and a twist on the current surge of 'drugs education' plays was sorely needed. I often found myself uninspired by existing work and found current forms predictable.

It was kick-started by the 'Sorted' billboard campaign with Leah Betts pictured in hospital. I wanted to find out what she would have said. I wanted to find out the stories that came from 'out of their heads.' The central character, Jelly, is in persistent vegetative state; the thrust of the narrative is to discover how this occurred. The story unfolds in strands with time-shifts and gradually the picture becomes clear - the reason for his hospitalisation is not directly related to drug misuse but to betrayal by his best friend.

This is a story of love, betrayal and revenge. It is a triangular love-story which draws its themes from influences as diverse as **Othello, Trainspotting** and **Seven**. The parallel worlds of the club and the intensive treatment unit were tied together with a design that included fluorescent strip lights and rostra that were adapted to suit the variety of locations.

A continual sound-track of contemporary music was incorporated and this served to punctuate the action as well as providing a 'mix feel' to the piece that allowed the emotional points to be highlighted. The style was very fluid, allowing the action to be halted at any point, as each character took over the baton of the storytelling by addressing the audience directly. This style, which incorporates thought-tracking and monologue is a very powerful and potent way of addressing the issues within the piece.

Marcus Romer

'a bold, forthright and brutally honest play about drug and substance abuse. Solidly crafted with a riveting narrative and believable characters, it maintains a fierce pace in the compulsive, brilliantly choreographed style.'

Kevin Berry *(The Stage)* February 1997.

Out of their Heads

by Marcus Romer

Originally produced by *Pilot Theatre Company*, toured nationally 1996 / 1997 to 118 venues and two national festivals at Nottingham Playhouse and Darlington Arts Centre.
Directed by Marcus Romer.
Designed by Ali Allen and Marise Rose.

Devoy	Denny James Smith
Jelly	Karl Haynes
Mandy, Jelly's mother	Kate McGregor
Eugene, Jelly's father	
Frances, Devoy's mother	
Patrick, Devoy's father	
Mary	
Jonesy	
Adrian	
Biker 1	
Biker 2	
Crash Nurse	

(The play can be performed with 3 actors doubling.)

The club.

DEVOY	I went down to *Storm.*
JELLY	It was Friday night.
DEVOY	Looking for my mates.
MANDY	Jelly and me, Mandy.
JELLY	James Elliot, Jelly to me mates ... he's Coco.
MANDY	Coco was King that night.
DEVOY	Colin ... although I don't tell many people that. Cos it's Coco.

JELLY   Coco Devoy.

MANDY   Jelly is my man though. He's top.

DEVOY   I mean don't get me wrong. I love a good drink. Drink it out of ya system lad ... Drink it out of ya system.

JELLY   Drink while you're alive.

DEVOY   Cos you can't when you're dead!

MANDY   Into the toilets, check me hair, check me mascara ... lipstick's right glossy shiny, glitter, hair alright get out of there!

JELLY   Mandy my best girl. Four years ... I loved her.

MANDY   It's the best most beautiful night of the week.

DEVOY   She's like made of glass, gorgeous do you know what I mean?

MANDY   My head was spinning.

JELLY   Everything was spinning.

DEVOY   There were lights.

MANDY   There were music.

JELLY   There were everything.

MANDY   It was the best.

DEVOY   I'd had about four whisky and cokes, and I got chatting to some lass.

JELLY   Regular Friday night.

MANDY   Everybody were in, beautiful people.

JELLY   Beautiful lights.

DEVOY   Kicking tunes.

JELLY   The music's coming up.

MANDY   And so is the crowd. I'm feeling great.

DEVOY   It's getting louder, we're all going with it. I felt boss. You know what I mean? It's good for business ...

JELLY   I remember the sound of rain, the smell of beer ... blue lights ... sirens

(All shouting)

DEVOY   Burning.

JELLY   Running.

MANDY   Screaming.

JELLY   Falling.

Movement sequence into coma with music and lights.

CRASH NURSE Crash the doors ... On my count ... three ... Blood
pressure one hundred over fifty ... find a line ... stand clear ...
quickly we're losing him ... stand clear ... check the signs ... find a
line ... stand clear ... crash the doors ... find a line ... he's back ...
come on ... saline ... adrenaline ... check the signs ...

The hospital.

MANDY   He's been in a coma for three months now ... I visit
him at the hospital about four times a week ... I've taken over his
flat as well, I've settled in quite nicely ... keeping it cosy for when
he comes home ... He looks beautiful doesn't he?... pale and lost
... I bet he's having the best bloody trip of his life ... I tried to get
him some flowers you know, but that nurse, that snotty cow in
there won't let me bring 'em in here ... they're contaminated, full
of disease ... I threw them in the bin right in front of her stuck-up
face and she looked at me as if I were dirt. I just walked straight
past her, cos you've got to stick up for yourself ... Now that I
think on it, our relationship has never been better. Well we argue
less, and he listens to everything I say, he's very supportive ...
Sometimes I blame myself ... you see no-one really knows what
went on except the three of us, that's me, Jelly and Devoy ... Well
Devoy's gone now ... and so has Jelly really ... so it's just down
to me to tell you my version of events ... The first time all three of
us met it were a beautiful day ... sun was shining, sky was really
blue ... I ran down to meet Jelly at the bins at back of school ...

First meeting of Jelly, Mandy and Devoy.

DEVOY   Alright?

JELLY   Fine thanks.

MANDY   Who's he?... I mean suddenly this bloke just waltzed
right in and started talking to Jelly.

DEVOY   How you both doin?

JELLY	Fine, been down the arcade, playing the machines.
DEVOY	Do you know seven seven seven?
MANDY	It was that lad from the fairground, I recognised him now.
JELLY	Yeah! /seventh heaven.
DEVOY	/seventh heaven ... Top game that.
JELLY	Yeah Top!
MANDY	Where have you come from eh?
DEVOY	Birkenhead ... its near Liverpool ... where are you from?
MANDY	None of your business!
DEVOY	Here James.
MANDY	His name's/ Jelly ...
JELLY	/ Jelly ... I can speak for myself you know ...
DEVOY	Jelly ... what I wanted to say was ... ta for the other night like ... at the fair and that.
MANDY	Yeah , he really went out of his way for you.
DEVOY	Yeah, yeah ... I appreciate it ... that's what I'm saying
JELLY	It's OK ... it was nothing ...
DEVOY	No no ... I mean it ... honest.
MANDY	Then it all went quiet.
DEVOY	I liked these two, I mean well Jelly had helped us the other night and Mandy?... well there was something about her ... I didn't know many people round here ... I wanted to get to know them better like ... So ... what do you do at night?... Do you like a drink?
JELLY	I do.
DEVOY	Do you smoke?
MANDY	Yeah, why what's it to you?
DEVOY	Just asking.

MANDY   Is it true what we've heard about you?

DEVOY   What?

JELLY   We've heard this stuff.

MANDY   about you.

JELLY   Why you left ...

MANDY   Got kicked out!

JELLY   Your last school ... is that right?... You took a load of acid, and jumped out of the window and ran round the playground?

MANDY   Stark naked!

DEVOY   None of that was true ... Yeah it's all true ... all in one day that was ...

MANDY   Get out.

DEVOY   It's true!... honest ... I'll do it tomorrow if you like at school ... to prove it!

MANDY   Can you get hold of stuff?

DEVOY   Yeah.

JELLY   Like what?

DEVOY   Have you ever had strawberries? tabs? trips? acid!... can you keep your mouth shut?

JELLY   Yeah ... course I'd heard of them ... screwed your head up, I didn't want any of that.

DEVOY   You're not going to go screaming to your mum are you?

MANDY   No!

DEVOY   OK then ... I'll meet you here ... tonight ...

MANDY   How much?

DEVOY   It's a freebie ... it's on me ... a sort of thankyou for the other night like ... it's only a one-off though, next time it'll cost you ...

JELLY   Eight o'clock.

MANDY   We'll see you ... That were Jelly ... always needed an extra push before he'd agree to something ... Me? I'd jump in with my eyes shut if it promised a laugh and drag him after me ... umming and ahhhing, wanting to think things through, use his head ... But I loved him for that ... although on our first date, if I hadn't made the moves we'd never have got it together.

Jelly and Mandy's first meeting in a churchyard.

JELLY   She was late ... so I was grave-hopping, you know jumping from one headstone to the next.

MANDY   I'm sorry I'm late ... I was doing stuff ... getting ready.

JELLY   It's alright ... she looked gorgeous ... she was wearing a mini skirt with a small denim jacket and this sort of red top ...

MANDY   I couldn't believe it ... he were dead fit but he was wearing this tacky old leather jacket ... and it stank.

JELLY   It were my dad's ... He'd seen the *Rolling Stones* in it ... I looked ace.

MANDY   Have you got a cigarette?

JELLY   No!... Shit! I should have bought some ...

MANDY   Great night this is turning out to be!

JELLY   Sorry I forgot ...

MANDY   Have you got any alcohol?

JELLY   No.

MANDY   Oh great!

JELLY   She's gonna leave I know it ...

MANDY   I hate it when you spend all that time getting ready and it just feels like a complete waste of time ... Still I was here, there was nowt on telly and he were not bad-looking, so ... how far do you want this to go?

JELLY I couldn't believe what I'd just heard ... pardon?

MANDY Sit down.

JELLY I was crapping myself ...

MANDY Look Jelly ... you're a year older than me. Have you had many girlfriends?

JELLY I'd never been with a girl properly before ... yeah loads!

MANDY Are you seeing anyone else?

JELLY No ... are you?

MANDY I've got a lot of offers like ... but it's your lucky night!

JELLY Yes!... I was in! Stay cool son, stay cool.

MANDY So are we going out then or what?... cos if we are you've got to ask me properly.

JELLY So I picked up these flowers.

MANDY Off this dead person's grave!

JELLY Red Roses.

MANDY All withered and manky.

JELLY And I give them to her ... on one knee.

MANDY He were a nutcase, old red roses ... I fell in love with him instantly! It were brilliant ...

DEVOY They were inseparable ... all day everyday, in school and out ...

Coco's first day at school.

DEVOY My first day at Greenbank School was a laugh ... what I did, was go straight through the schoolgates and ask where the Headteacher's Office was, making sure that loads heard me. Then right, I went into his office and asked him if he could give me a lift home that night!... Honest to God, his reaction was the surest way of sussing out the school ... just by the way he'd tell you to get lost. Not only that though, cos all the kids would have found out about me, they knew my name, Coco Devoy, and that I wasn't to be messed with ... Respect from day one ... We'd moved into this new house, you see me dad, well he'd gone and got this new contract, another one like, and me mam says that we were going with him again, so we moved up here ... He was always doing this my dad, he gets these jobs, although they're not really what you'd call lasting jobs cos well he doesn't last long in them like ... he always gets sacked ... been there a few weeks like. Me dad was getting pissed that night, smoking loads, shouting at me mum ...

We hear Coco's parents' voices.

PATRICK   When's tea ready?

MARY   Shut your face!

PATRICK   Where's me dinner?

DEVOY   ... I had to get out ... straight through the kitchen ... emptying the jar of ten pence pieces, five pounds worth into me pocket and I set off out down the estate ... at the bottom of the hill was this fairground. It was fully open now ... I headed for the arcade bit, I saw a few faces I recognised from school and that, no-one said hello like, then these lads, bikers, started taking the piss out of my accent, my clothes and that ... then they started slapping me round the back of my head, slapping me ... about six of them ...

The fairground.

BIKER 1   Oi!

BIKER 2   Oi Scouser.

DEVOY   I haven't done anything.

BIKER 1   Where are you going?

BIKER 2   Where are you going new boy?

DEVOY   I haven't done anything.

BIKER 1   Where are your mates?

DEVOY   I haven't done anything.

BIKER 2   We'll be your mates.

BIKER 1   We'll show you around.

BIKER 2   Scouser.

DEVOY   I haven't done anything.

BIKER 1   Where do you think you're going?

DEVOY   Help!
                 (Devoy ends up on the floor. He is motionless)

JELLY   Get off him!!! This group of lads kicking, chasing
beating this one in the middle ... I had to stop them ... They
scattered ... I ran over ... Mandy was scared.

MANDY   I just stood there ... watching, it was awful.

JELLY   I reached him .. .Can you hear me?... Can you?...
Quick, Mandy go and get some help, he's hurt bad ... go on ... can
you move your hands?

DEVOY   Help me.

JELLY   I am mate, just hang on ... I'll look after you don't
worry ... What's your name?

DEVOY   Duuuh!

JELLY   I knew I had to keep him talking ... Come on what's
your name?

DEVOY   Devoy.

JELLY   Is your name Devoy, yeah?

DEVOY   Yeah ... them lads.

JELLY   Don't worry they've gone now. You're OK ... you're
safe now.

DEVOY   Cheers ... Ow!

JELLY   Where do you live?

DEVOY   Greenbank estate.

JELLY   Near the school?

DEVOY   Bestwick street.

JELLY   I know it ... don't move eh? We'll get you help, we'll
get you sorted.

DEVOY   Thanks mate, I owe you for this I really do.

JELLY   No worries.

DEVOY   Dont tell anyone about this ... will you?... please

JELLY   Sure don't worry mate ... you can trust me.

MANDY   That's how Jelly and Devoy met ... they were like
brothers from then on ... Devoy was always there you know,
when you needed him ... good times.

JELLY / DEVOY The best!

JELLY   It was great, out every night ... I felt safe with Coco,
he was a real laugh and he fitted in with me and Mandy straight
away ... he was the first mate I had who owned a car, he used to
take us anywhere we wanted ... service stations to play the machines ... sometimes to the coast, we'd sleepover in the car it was
brilliant ... It meant me and Mandy could spend more time together ... he was a real nutter behind the wheel but I loved the speed,
the danger.

Into club movement scene.

JELLY   We started clubbing, just threw ourselves straight in ... headfirst ... Mandy got well into it ... the music, clothes and she looked fantastic, blokes would stare at her ... and she was on my arm, I felt like a king ... Good times ... in fact the only bad time I can really remember ... it was early on with Devoy and his strawberries ...

Acid trip in the park.

JELLY   So we went down to meet Devoy like we'd arranged.

MANDY   At eight o'clock.

DEVOY   I turned up on the dot!

MANDY   How's it going?

DEVOY   Sound.

JELLY   You alright?

MANDY   Coco just nodded.

DEVOY   So you want your freebie then?

JELLY   Mandy was well up for it but I didn't want to ... I was scared ...

DEVOY   Here you go then.

MANDY   Ta...Coco.

JELLY   He just handed us these little bits of card ... with pictures on ... little strawberries.

JELLY   They looked so small, it was hard to believe that they'd do anything.

MANDY   You just swallow them yeah?

DEVOY   Chew vigorously and swallow and in fifteen minutes you'll be off your head!

JELLY   Devoy and Mandy were straight in, no messing.

MANDY   Come on Jelly get it in your gob.

DEVOY   Come on, do it, /do it, do it.

MANDY   /do it, do it, do it!

JELLY   I couldn't stand it, them both going on, so I did it

DEVOY   Yeah!

MANDY   Wow!

JELLY   Then I really started to panic ... I thought what if somebody comes.

DEVOY   What if?

JELLY   What if they see me and they know what I've done?

MANDY   Paranoia, paranoia!

DEVOY   They won't know, honest, it'll be OK.

MANDY   You'll be OK Jelly, I'll look after you ... I'll still look after you ... Oh God Devoy look at him, he's off his chump!

JELLY   It kicked in ... everything.

MANDY   So bright.

JELLY   Colours.

DEVOY   Blue flashing lights.

MANDY   Beautiful ... everything that Jelly saw, I saw too.

JELLY   This tree ... strong and green.

DEVOY   Where? I can't see it.

JELLY   In the leaves, hiding ... a small pigeon.

MANDY   What's it doing?

JELLY   Just lying there, quite still. It was all scruffy and tattered.

MANDY   I can see it now ... it's beautiful.

JELLY   It's got some of its feathers missing and it can't flap one of its wings ... it's got a weepy eye ... cat must have got it or something.

DEVOY   Can't see it.

MANDY   I'll look after you.

JELLY   Hold my hand.

DEVOY   It was tremendous.

MANDY   Best feeling ever.

JELLY   I'm burning!

DEVOY   I'm laughing.

JELLY   I'm falling.

MANDY   I were nearly killing myself.

JELLY   He's running.

DEVOY   Top night out ... good mates.

MANDY   Three of us ... on this ride ... I didn't want it to stop.

JELLY   I'm turning, someone's turning me over and over.

DEVOY   Just stay there ... enjoy yourself.

JELLY   I want to lie down.

MANDY   Beautiful flowers.

JELLY   Red roses ... Can't bring them in ... full of germs.

DEVOY   Just running ... moving all the time ... no-one can
    stop me.

JELLY   I trusted everyone.

MANDY   Jelly!

In the hospital.

MANDY   I miss him ... I miss him talking to me. I come down
every day ... to talk to him, I need him to listen to me ... I want
him to give me some advice ... It's ironic isn't it? Going out with
him for ages and this is the first time that he's all mine and he
can't see me. I spent loads of time on my mascara and stuff and ...
Look I've lost weight, I've never looked this good and he can't

even see me ... I couldn't believe it when I first went to see him ... there were all these tubes and that coming out of his body ... I felt so scared ... I was so grateful that Devoy were there, looking after me ...

DEVOY   Hiya Jelly ... you alright mate?... how's it going?... Can you hear me?... He looks great doesn't he?

MANDY   Yeah.

DEVOY   He looked like death ... I'd never seen so many wires and tubes going into one person before ... it was like something off the X-Files.

JELLY   Someone's here. I can hear noises, talking and that.

MANDY   I want to get him out of here. He shouldn't be in here.

JELLY   Mandy! It was Mandy, I knew that sound, that voice ...

DEVOY   Look, Mandy do you want me to get you anything?
MANDY   No I'm OK ... I felt awful ... so sick.
JELLY   It was Coco with her too ...

MANDY   He looked beautiful ... Jelly ... Jelly can you hear me?

DEVOY   It's alright Jelly lad ... It's Coco, I've come to see you mate ... Everyone's asking about you down at *Storm* you know ... Oh and you've no need to worry ... I 've put the word out ... to find out who got you into this mess. We're going to get you sorted aren't we, Mand?

MANDY   Yeah ... Devoy's going to sort it out ... he's a good friend.

JELLY   I want to tell her things but I can't ... I can't move.

MANDY   How do you stand that hospital smell? I'm sure they pump it in just to annoy the visitors. It's like tippex.

DEVOY   You what?
MANDY   Tippex /on your arm!
JELLY   /on your arm!

The school flashback.

MANDY   From a bottle?

JELLY   No, on your sleeve.

DEVOY   What are you two on about?

JELLY   Tippex thinners. It was ages ago.

DEVOY   Oh that!... I wouldn't do that shit now, rots your brain, sends you daft.

JELLY   Yeah but in maths, there was this lass Rachel Thomo.

DEVOY   Head case.

MANDY   I know her, what about her?

JELLY   Little green bottle on her sleeve, poured some on and put her mouth round it ....

DEVOY   And away!

JELLY   Made her face go bright red.

MANDY   So did you have a go?

JELLY   Course well, only a couple of times. Gives you a massive headache.

DEVOY   A real thumper. It really kills you that.

MANDY   I remembered Christine. Her eyes seemed to sink into her when she did it. She said there were a noise in the back of her head ... Voom Voom.

JELLY   What were it?

MANDY   It were that stuff you got plasters off with.

DEVOY   Zoff, good stuff that.

JELLY   Smells like hospitals.

MANDY   Yeah, it were like when I had some teeth out, right. They gave me gas, and they put this like Darth Vader mask on me face. I can see it, it were all black and had a pointed nose thing.

And this smell, it were sweet and when I breathed it I could feel me head going to explode and I could hear this noise like going Voom Voom in me head ... Voom Voom ... it were awful ... that smell ...

Back to the Hospital.

MANDY   I had to get out of there.

JELLY   I can picture her ... she looks like the first time I met her ... I want to hold her ... to touch her, to tell her how sorry I am.

MANDY   I've got to go now Jelly ... I'll come back and see you again ...tomorrow ... I will I promise ... I'll make myself look right nice for you ... I'll see you.

DEVOY   That was the way it was ... He loved her and she loved him ... together, always ... I was always jealous of him, cos he had everything ... everything going for him ... he had smart clothes, money, a Panasonic TV ... he got taken to school, by car, he had somewhere to go in the summer holidays, abroad like ... he had all that ... but most of all he had people who took care of him ... to look after him, to love him ... Mandy, his mum and dad ... whenever anything happened, they'd sit down and have a chat with him ... sort it out ...

Jelly at home.

FRANCES   James ...

JELLY   What?

EUGENE   James, is that you son?

JELLY   Yes mum!

FRANCES   Would you mind turning the TV down please James, while we have a word with you?

JELLY   Oh God! I hate it when this happens ... What?

EUGENE   Now just turn that down and listen.

FRANCES *(to Eugene)* I've found this bag of powder, white powder in his jacket pocket ... when I was going to wash it.

EUGENE   Look son ... It's yer mother, she's concerned about you ... she heard you come in, late again last night ... she'd been sitting up half the night worrying about you ... I told her there was nothing to worry about ... there isn't is there? James?

FRANCES   It's just that you're not yourself at the moment.

EUGENE   Look love, our son doesn't do drugs see, he's not like that, he's a good lad, he's got prospects. You've been a bit quiet lately son ...

JELLY   I've been working hard, just a bit tired. Something's happened I know it has, this is different.

FRANCES   I've read that you've got to look for the signs, the tiredness, and, and being disorganised and erm ... listlessness and I've got an article on it somewhere. You're not eating properly ... what's the matter?

JELLY   Nothing ... something's going on I just know it ... look just leave me alone.

EUGENE   Don't speak to your mother like that, she's worried. I mean you treat this place like a bloody doss-house coming in at all hours and then sitting here all day watching TV and if you're not doing that you're making all that racket upstairs with that bloody Colin Devoy.

FRANCES   I hate that lad, I'm sure it's him that's been influencing, changing our James.

EUGENE   How come Colin Devoy can afford that car of his eh? I'm talking to you.

FRANCES   Look love ... we've found something.

EUGENE   In your room.

JELLY   Shit ... Coco's stuff.

EUGENE	We don't know what it is.
FRANCES	We want to know where it came from.
JELLY	It was from the club!

Dealing in the club.

JELLY   I was feeling great, cos I'd got Coco and Mandy into the club that night ... knew a mate of mine on the door.

DEVOY   Cheers for getting us in Jelly lad!

MANDY   Yeah, it's a brilliant club.

DEVOY   Stormin'.

MANDY   It was like nowhere I'd ever been before ... the music was loud ... tons of people ... with this new gear on. I felt great.

JELLY   What do you reckon?

MANDY   I love it!

DEVOY   Jelly!... come over here mate ... good place for business this lad.

JELLY   What do you mean?

DEVOY   Me and you ... together like ... Dealing!

JELLY   What?

DEVOY   Wheelin, dealing ... duckin and divin ... a team!

MANDY   What are you two on about?

JELLY   Shearer!

DEVOY   Two nil!

JELLY   Top corner of the net!

MANDY   Shut up ... what's going on ... all those signals and that?

DEVOY   Can she be trusted?

MANDY   Shut your face, course I can.

DEVOY   All I'm saying is ... what I want you to do is help me
out.

JELLY   Keep your voice down ...

DEVOY   It's alright ... It's nothing!.. No worries about that
stuff ... I mean Ecstasy sealed in a plastic bag can't be tracked
down ... sniffer dogs can't smell 'em.

JELLY   Really?

DEVOY   Not if its sealed down ... I told him that and he
believed me!

MANDY   Jelly?

JELLY   What?

MANDY   I want to try something else ... in here ... it's
brilliant!

JELLY   Don't be soft.

MANDY   I'm not ... I want to try an E ... just half a one then ...

JELLY   Look, not now eh?

MANDY   Hey ... that acid were great, you enjoyed it too.
What's wrong with you?

JELLY   It was alright ... nothing special ... I'd hated it.

DEVOY   What do you reckon eh?... Come here, look I've got
a bit of a problem.

JELLY   What?

DEVOY   Well, I've got a bit of gear on me like ... you know
off Jonesy ... it's not much, just a few E's and a bit of speed ... but
what it is right, people are watching me ... they're not watching
you.

JELLY   Look I don't know.

DEVOY   It's true ... Look, listen to me ... what do you
reckon? ... if you hang onto it ... just for a while like... I'll take the
money. I'll come and get the stuff off of you and at the end of the
night I'll give you a cut like ... what do you say?... I mean the risk
is all mine isn't it?

JELLY   Is it?

MANDY   Devoy threw ideas round his head, confusing him ... Jelly didn't know what he were getting into ...

DEVOY   Imagine the business we could do Jelly. It'd be better than winning off a poxy scratchcard!

JELLY   I could see it ... with a bit of money I could get my own decks, tunes ... everything ... to be up there ... playing music ... leading it all, mixing it ... feeling like God.

DEVOY   We've got it sussed ... Thursday, Friday, Saturday nights ... what do you reckon Jelly? Three nights a week ?

MANDY   Three nights a week what?

DEVOY   We'd be laughing!

JELLY   I don't know.

DEVOY   I'll do all the worrying for you.

JELLY   What if we get caught?

DEVOY   We won't.

MANDY   It all falls into place now doesn't it?... I mean if I hadn't asked him to get the E's ... then maybe he wouldn't have listened to Devoy ...

DEVOY   It was the perfect situation ... everyone trusted Jelly ... He was an ideal partner ... he wasn't soft ... and neither was I ... don't get me wrong, I didn't want him to get caught ... but if push comes to shove you've got to look after number one haven't you?... I'm not going down for drugs ... drugs is a mug's game.

JELLY   He made it sound so simple ... he'd do the selling and take the money, I just had to look after the stuff, nothing to it ... and I'd get sorted, get a bit of money together ... Mandy, she were well into it, Coco saw to it that she got her cut too ... if you know what I mean ... I loved her ... I thought I was helping her ... OK then lets do it.

DEVOY   Put it there, Jelly man, shake on it.

MANDY   And that was how it started ... good times ... fun times ... I felt great, out every night, doing what I wanted ... and Jelly, Jelly was in control and so was I ... I knew exactly how I wanted to look ... I had this image in my head you see and I knew exactly how I wanted to feel ... sometimes, a lot of the time I just wanted to feel able to sod off somewhere else and leave me behind ... leave this fat lass lying on her bed, head stuck in a magazine fretting over the lack of cellulite on some supermodel's arse, leave the bits of cheap make-up scattered on the floor, leave the pile of sweaty lycra, laddered tights and high-heeled shoes that cut into my ankles, leave the bank statements and application form for a bloody new job unopened ... and just laugh, dance, talk bollocks and feel beautiful ... so I took E ... made perfect sense to me then ... These were the best days of our lives, that's what everyone kept saying ... and who was I not to believe them?

In the pub.

JELLY   It started off just at weekends, you know what I mean? Then one Monday I was in the local.

MANDY   With me.

JELLY   When Devoy came across.

DEVOY   Alright Jelly lad?

JELLY   What?

DEVOY   I need some help.

JELLY   There were a couple of lads.

DEVOY   Over at the top bar.

MANDY   They needed some stuff.

DEVOY   Give us an hand.

JELLY   I'm clean you know that!

DEVOY   Here I've got the E's.

JELLY   I didn't want to do it.

MANDY	Don't be soft.
JELLY	I was getting hassle off her too.
DEVOY	Mandy was well into it now.
JELLY	I just want a quiet night out ... no hassle.
DEVOY	Just stand by me eh ... You see I don't know them.
JELLY	Neither do I!... It was all happening fast ...
MANDY	Keep up Jelly.
DEVOY	Got to keep ahead of the crowd.
JELLY	More and more stuff to keep at my house?... Mandy?
MANDY	What?
JELLY	I can't see you tonight.
DEVOY	He's busy.
MANDY	When can I see you?
JELLY	I dunno.
DEVOY	When he's done ...

Later that night.

JELLY   I tried the stuff, sure ... The thing is with most E and speed you never know what you're taking, it's cut with all sorts of crap ... too dangerous ... The stuff we sell, well Coco says it's the best around, I feel safe taking it ... And Mandy? Well as long as we got her sorted she gave us the space to get on with it ... as for the people we sell to, well that's their choice isn't it?

DEVOY   Where do I get it from? It's easy that ... from Jonesy ... First time I went to his house I was crapping myself ... what if my dad saw me? Or the police? I could get done there and then ... I used to go round to Jonesy's house every Thursday ... he kept it behind the back of his mam and dad's freezer in the garage ... he told his mum that he and his mates were going in to fix his moped!... People got to know me then, I'd sort them out in school, in the youth clubs, in the pubs and then in the clubs ... 'Hey Coco have you got any gear?'... Now don't get me wrong, I'm not a drug pusher ... people come to me, that's different is that ... Look if it wasn't me it would be someone else ... I'm not a junkie, I'm everyone's mate ...

Jelly's parents visit him in the hospital.

EUGENE   Morning son ... You're looking ... well this morning.

FRANCES   He's a grand lad ... Doctor says he's stable ... it's good news is that.

JELLY   There's times that being stuck here really pisses me off.

FRANCES   You tell him about it Eugene.

JELLY   Normally it's when my mum and dad come to visit ...

EUGENE   I'm going fishing next week, it's the competition season.

JELLY   Because I can hear but I can't bloody move.

FRANCES   Your dad can't wait till you're up and about again, and you can go with him.

EUGENE   I'll get you some new wellies ... Oh come on, this is useless!

FRANCES   No, come on, we've got to keep talking to him ... Doctor says ... look, I've tidied your room.

JELLY   Bless them, they try so hard but I'm lying here absolutely bored rigid.

EUGENE   He looks so peaceful doesn' t he?

FRANCES   He does ... I've done some baking ... freezers full for when you get out.

JELLY   Oh aye!...

FRANCES   Come on ...

EUGENE   The cat was really sick this morning.

FRANCES   Don't!... that'll upset him will that!

EUGENE   She'd had some of that new *Choosy*, liver and heart, your mother gave it to him.

JELLY   This is what it is like every single time they come to see me.

FRANCES   We're taking him to the vet don't you worry about that James.

JELLY   Now that is a weight off my mind!

EUGENE   Hey, you missed a cracking game of hockey on TV yesterday.

JELLY   The other thing about my dad is that he's into really crap sports ... hockey!... fishing!

EUGENE   And the table tennis championships start next Tuesday.

JELLY   Purrrlease!

FRANCES   It's all my fault ... I should've phoned the police when I found that white powder.

EUGENE   Don't blame yourself again love ... I've told you, you did all you could ...

JELLY   Its not what they think it is ... It wasn't Ecstasy that was to blame, not directly ... Coco knows the truth.

MANDY   His mum and dad really did care for him in their own way. Parents do I suppose ... It was at this time that my mum started giving me an hard time ... looking back on it I know she were just anxious but I didn't need it. Devoy and I got talking more and more like ... he told us about his home and that ... he made me laugh even though it wasn't funny, because his dad were a right sad case ...

Devoy and his dad.

PATRICK   Here son, can you lend us a fiver?... Well a couple of quid then ... don't tell yer mam.

DEVOY   Why? What's happened to your money?

PATRICK   Ahh ... you know how it is lad ... its your mum's birthday next week and I thought I'd get her something special.

DEVOY   No it's not! Where's your money gone?... It's only Tuesday?

PATRICK   Alright ... look, it's your uncle's fault, dead cert he said, and if it had won I was going to treat you and your mum to a ...

DEVOY   Shut up dad! Just shut up ... look ... why don't I just buy you a bottle of whisky eh?

PATRICK   Yeah that'd be nice that son ...

DEVOY   To think I used to look up to him, I used to love him in fact. Once right, I split me chin open and I ran into the house and he picked us up and put me straight down on the worktop on the kitchen and he wiped all the blood away ... and I looked into his eyes as he was cleaning me up and I thought, 'that's my dad, is that, he cares for me,' and all the blood went away and so did the pain ... I loved him ... until the time he punched me in the face and broke my nose ... funny ... I didn't look up to him after that. *(pause)*

MANDY   You know what got me right? My mother thought I was anorexic. Well then again if I had an headache she thought I was pregnant, or if I got up late she thought I was a heroin addict. She reads all this stuff in the papers and files it all in her head. But I'm telling you right, I'm not anorexic ... So one Sunday she cooks this big meal you know, roast joint, all the trimmings. So I sat back and I thought, I'll show her ... so I ate all my roast potatoes, I ate all my mash, carrots, double portions the lot, and it were all swimming in gravy. Then I had a massive trifle, three lots and I drank a full bottle of coke, not diet coke but fat coke, loads of sugar coke. And after all that I said, 'See mum? I'm your healthy daughter, your fat healthy daughter' and then I went upstairs and put me fingers down me throat ... because I'm in control.

DEVOY   Here you are Mand, take this, it 'll make you feel really good.

MANDY   Ta Coco. *(she takes a tablet from him)*

A couple of weeks later.

JELLY   I was spending more time on my own, away from Mandy, trying to make as much money as I could ... I didn't notice the signs, the changes in her. I didn't notice just how much she was taking ... she looked different, still great but just different ... knackered all the time ... I was just too busy.

MANDY   Where were you last night?

JELLY   Shit, I was gonna phone you.

MANDY   Why didn't you call me ... let me know?

JELLY   I'm sorry.

MANDY   Do you know how I felt, stood there all tarted up waiting for you? Girls looking at me ... she's been stood up.

JELLY   Look I was busy.

MANDY   Busy! I don't know where you are, who you're with.

JELLY   I was with Coco last night ... so what?

MANDY   Look Jelly, if you're seeing someone else I want to know ... I'm not making a fool of myself.

JELLY   I've told you before, I'm not seeing anybody else, you're paranoid!

MANDY   I'm scared.

JELLY   What about?

MANDY   All this, Devoy, you ... everything ... It started off as a laugh, it were wonderful but now ... it's getting out of hand ... What am I going to do if something happens to you?

JELLY   Nothing's gonna happen.

MANDY   You're not a fighter.

JELLY   I am ... it's not going to be for long.

MANDY   What do you want?

JELLY   A life ... *(pause)*

DEVOY   I saw that her and Jelly were having a bad time ... I tried to help her, in my own way like ... I thought I'd have a chat with her. Tell her a few things ... some of them were true. Well what had I got to lose? Nothing, but I had everything to gain.

MANDY   Coco, can I have a word?... Look, you're his best mate ... I think you know what's going on in his head sometimes better than I do ... If I ask you something will you be honest with me?

DEVOY   Course I will.

MANDY   We've just had another argument, it's like he doesn't want to see me any more ... he doesn't look at me, he just snaps ... and if he's been seeing someone else that would really mess me up ... and so ... if he's said anything to you like ... I want to know and ... I hope that you'd be able to tell me about it, cos like the three of us, we've been close you know ...

DEVOY   Sure, I know that ... For the first time I had a chance and I took it ... I wanted her ... Look I'm afraid he's seeing someone else Mandy.

MANDY   No ... I don't believe it.

DEVOY   Well course it wasn't true but she didn't know that ... Yeah, ever since that party, you know, when we all got wasted over at Sean's ... I'm sorry.

MANDY   I didn't say anything for ages ... I just felt so angry.

DEVOY   If there's anything I can do ... I mean if you want anything or if you need somewhere to stay then it's fine I'll look after you ...

MANDY   Thanks Coco, you're a real mate, you're sound ... I held him.

DEVOY   She felt so fragile ... *(pause)*

JELLY   Devoy's a laugh ... makes me feel safe. With a mate like that he'll always protect you ... you can trust him. I'd trust him with my life.

MANDY   I wanted to know what was going on ... I want it to stop! I wanted it to all stop ... Jelly ... I need to talk to you.

JELLY   What ...?

MANDY   I've sorted it out ... in my head and I don't want to see you any more.

JELLY   Why?... I don't understand.

MANDY   Stuff.

JELLY   What stuff?

MANDY   Stuff I've heard, and that I've been thinking about.

JELLY   Mandy come on tell me what's going on.

MANDY   I can't trust you ... I don't know where you are, I don't know who you're with, I don't know what you're up to ... I don't know who you are any more ...

JELLY   I know ... look ... please Mandy!

MANDY   I've had enough.

JELLY   I was doing it for you Mandy ... for us.

MANDY   You haven't ... you've been doing it for yourself ... I know exactly what you've been doing.

JELLY   What do you mean?

MANDY   You've been seeing someone else.

JELLY   You what?...

MANDY   You've been seeing someone else, behind my back and other people know about it.

JELLY   Who?... I mean ... I don't know what you're talking about.

MANDY   ...and I'm embarrassed and I don't want to see you any more.

JELLY   I haven't ... I haven't seen anybody.

MANDY   Who is she? Do I know her? Is she better than me eh? Is she? Come on I can take it.

JELLY   Mandy!

MANDY   How could you?

JELLY   I'm not seeing anybody else ... I've told you ... not since I first met you.

MANDY   You liar! You've been with her and you've been laughing about it with Devoy ... I know you have.

JELLY   Mandy listen to me ... where's all this stuff come from?

MANDY   A friend ... a good friend.

JELLY   Mandy, look ...

MANDY   Using all the time, E, speed ...

JELLY   No more than you. You're just paranoid.

MANDY   I don't believe you!... I don't trust you ... and I'm leaving you ...

JELLY   Mandy please!

MANDY   That was the last conversation we had ...

JELLY   She turned and left ... I called Devoy, he'd be able to help ... Coco ... please ...

DEVOY   Sure. I'm sorry to hear that Jelly, lad. Listen I'm sure she'll come round given time ... look we'll have a drink tonight eh?

JELLY   Yeah thanks mate ...

DEVOY   After work maybe?

JELLY   I'll see you ...

DEVOY   Course I was the best friend in the world that night ... perfect shoulder to cry on ... after all I understood ... everything. *(pause)*

MANDY   It was a couple of nights after that, that it happened ... I was at home in my bedroom ... My mum came in at five in the morning and said that the hospital were on the phone ...

Devoy's betrayal.

JELLY   We were in the car park. Look Coco I need your help mate ... it's Mandy.

DEVOY   I know mate, no problems. Look will you take care of the stuff and the money tonight?

JELLY   OK yeah ... when we heard this car pull up.

ADRIAN   Where do you think you're going?

JELLY   Going home ...

LEE   Don't think so.

DEVOY   I knew what they wanted ... What's your problem?

ADRIAN   Which one of you's Devoy?

DEVOY   I was shit scared.

LEE   Which one of you two is Coco Devoy?

JELLY   Why?

ADRIAN   Cos he's been selling dodgy gear, that's why.

LEE   And we want to teach him a lesson.

DEVOY   It's him.

JELLY   What?

DEVOY   He's Coco. He's got the gear.

JELLY   What's going on?

ADRIAN	What's your name?
DEVOY	James.
LEE	You, turn your pockets out.
DEVOY	Do as he says Coco.
JELLY	Hang on, I'm not -
ADRIAN	Hurry up.
LEE	Or we'll do it for you.

DEVOY Look he's got the stuff, I'm clean man ... just a wallet ... no money in it ... just a video card with my name on ... James Elliot.

JELLY He'd got my wallet ... my head was spinning. I didn't know what was going on.

ADRIAN	Yeah, he's the one alright.
LEE	Get him.
DEVOY	Look I've got to go now.
JELLY	But wait, it's not true ... what are you doing?
DEVOY	Going home. It's nothing to do with me, is this?
JELLY	You bastard.
ADRIAN	Come here.
LEE	It's you we want.
JELLY	Help me!
DEVOY	Sorry mate.
ADRIAN	Get him!

Devoy watches the scene and then walks away. See crash scene again from the beginning. Movement sequence into coma.

CRASH NURSE Crash the doors ... On my count ... three ... Blood pressure hundred over fifty ... find a line ... stand clear ... Quickly we're losing him ... stand clear ... check the signs ... find a line ...

stand clear ... crash the doors ... find a line ... he's back ... come on ... saline ... adrenaline ... check the signs ...

Mandy at the hospital.

MANDY   The hospital were really great. I could go in anytime ... and Devoy had been looking after me ever since ... He were brilliant. He'd found Jelly, he'd been lying there, on the ground for two hours bleeding ... he thought it were a bundle of rags ... It felt weird ... felt like I was still Jelly's girl ... I was dead confused.

DEVOY   Come on Mand ... you need something to take your mind off all of this ... get out of it for a bit ... enjoy life.

MANDY   It seemed like the right thing to do at the time ... I thought Devoy was good times ... good times in a bottle and I wanted to drink it all down ... *(pause)* I'm going out tonight Jelly.

JELLY   She's seeing Devoy.

MANDY   I just need someone at the moment.

JELLY   I wanted to say something ... to tell her.

MANDY   He takes me places ... we're going to a party.

JELLY   He's a liar.

MANDY   He understands.

JELLY   He knows nothing!

MANDY   You've got to make the most of life.

JELLY   Mandy!... I wanted to be able to scream ... to move to let her know, give her a sign, signal, anything ... Don't go with him.

DEVOY   You've got to work out what's important in life see. For me it's two things. First it's me and second, it's me again. No-one else gives a toss. 'You'll come a cropper Colin Devoy, you'll come a cropper'. Drink it out of your system, get smashed, enjoy life, do it all ... Right then, I will. Don't get me wrong, I'm not complaining, life's a rollercoaster and you've got to hold on tight or you'll fall off ... I'd sorted my own life out ... I didn't mean for Jelly to get done over so badly but that's life and right now Mandy needed me ... we had living to do!

Devoy and Mandy at the party.

MANDY   I got out of my head that night, smashed ...

DEVOY   Wrecked!

JELLY   Wasted ...

MANDY   I didn't know what I was doing.

DEVOY   I did. We were out of our heads, having a storming good time ... we'd taken loads of stuff.

MANDY   Devoy started mixing some drinks.

DEVOY   Whisky and coke Mand! We were having a brilliant night.

MANDY   I wanted to go home.

DEVOY   Come on Mand, have another.

MANDY   I've had enough.

DEVOY   It was coming on for about two o'clock ... I felt that this would be the night.

MANDY   I want to get back.

DEVOY   Sure Mand, I'll take you ... we'd been really close since Jelly had had his ... accident.

MANDY   Coco ... I'm feeling a bit out of it.

DEVOY   I'll look after you Mand.

MANDY   I remember getting into this cab.

DEVOY   Back to her place ... well Jelly's really ... felt a bit strange but I was well up for it ... she was too.

MANDY   I just wanted to sleep.

DEVOY   Mand here have another one ... this 'll make you feel
better.

MANDY   No.

DEVOY   One more E would do the trick ... it would bring her
round, get her in the mood like.

MANDY   I need some water now.

DEVOY   I put my arm round her.

MANDY   No ... I just want to crash.

DEVOY   I love you. *(Devoy puts his arm round Mandy)*

JELLY   Mandy. No! *(pause)*
Next day she came to see me. She held my hand, she told me
everything ... She'd woken up in the late afternoon.

MANDY   My head was pounding.

JELLY   Devoy's jacket was draped -

MANDY   Over the end of the bed and in it was your wallet ... I
felt used, cheated ... I couldn't remember all the details but I
could put two and two together alright.

JELLY   I wanted to squeeze her hand, to let her know I was
trying.

MANDY   I love you.

JELLY   She kissed my forehead.

MANDY   Turned and headed straight to see ... Devoy!

DEVOY   What?

MANDY   What happened last night?

DEVOY   What do you mean?

MANDY   Did you spike my drink? Drop a tab in my water?
Eh?

DEVOY   What would I do that for?

MANDY   You tell me.

DEVOY   Come on, we were having a laugh.

MANDY I blacked out, I can't remember when, but I remember your face.

DEVOY Now look Mand.

MANDY Did you sleep with me?

DEVOY No.

MANDY I don't believe you.

DEVOY I didn't.

MANDY How come your jacket was on the bed.

DEVOY I was helping you.

MANDY You planned this, didn't you?

DEVOY What if I did? We've been close lately.

MANDY Not like that.

DEVOY It was just a matter of time.

MANDY That's not the point ... I don't want you taking advantage of me.

DEVOY You need me Mandy ... the last couple of months have been great ... In fact, Jelly being in the coma has suited me just fine

MANDY What are you saying?

DEVOY It's allowed us to be close ... he was always in the way. It was fate that did this ... You were ready enough to believe that he was seeing someone else.

MANDY What do you mean?

DEVOY You wanted to believe it so you could be with me.

MANDY I trusted you ...you lied to me.

DEVOY Yeah ... you believed me, everyone always believes me! I'll tell you I'm glad it wasn't me in the coma. ...

MANDY Were you there?... come on tell me the truth.

DEVOY Course not ... but if I was I'd make sure I'd look after number one.

MANDY   You selfish bastard.

DEVOY   You've got to take what comes your way.

MANDY   I know ... and you did, that night didn't you?

DEVOY   I told you Mand, I never touched you.

MANDY   I'm talking about the night Jelly got beaten up.

DEVOY   What do you mean?

MANDY   I know you were there that night.

DEVOY   Don't be stupid.

MANDY   It's true, isn't it?... You'd been selling dodgy gear?

DEVOY   No, I'd have told you Mand, you know me.

MANDY   I thought I did ... just tell me the truth. Were you there when he got beaten up?

DEVOY   No.

MANDY   How come you were there to find him?

DEVOY   Look Mand, he's my mate.

MANDY   Then how come you stole his wallet?

DEVOY   Eh? I don't know what you're talking about.

MANDY   How come you've got his wallet in your jacket pocket?

DEVOY   Just looking after it for him ... Look Mand.

MANDY   Don't you come near me. You are nothing but a liar Devoy ... You're a user ... you use people in the same way as you pop your pills, chew them up and when you've had enough, spit them out and try some more ... I thought you were great, a breath of fresh air, a bit of danger ... but it's all clear to me now. *(pause)*

DEVOY   You've got it all wrong.

MANDY   No! I've got it completely right. When I took E, I looked up to you. Jelly did too ... and all the time it was just words from you, games with people's heads and people's lives ...

DEVOY   I'm going ... leaving here, I've had enough.

MANDY I don't think you've had a moment of reality since we met you.

DEVOY You don't know what you're missing out on. Good times Mand remember. Hey look, none of it was my fault. Hey do you want something, just to bring you down a bit?

MANDY Get out! Just get out! You cowardly bastard. You've got to face up to your life you know ... you can't hide behind lies and bullshit forever ... sooner or later you'll learn that ... *(pause)* And he was gone ... I called the police, but there wasn't anything they could do, as far as everyone was concerned, here was my boyfriend in a coma, involved in drugs, done over for dealing, and me with a story about his mate ... So it was just down to me to sort it out.

Back to the present.

MANDY It wasn't Ecstasy that put Jelly in a coma, it was his best mate ... I still can't believe all the attention we got ... local and big time newspapers, his picture on billboards all cheesy and healthy ... didn't even look like him ... so I'm determined to clear his name for him ... You know the greatest irony of all? After years of wanting to be noticed I am suddenly the most popular girl in the world ... last night at *Storm* everyone were looking at me, asking if I were alright ... 'Are you coping Mandy? You're looking really good ... Do you want a drink?'... It's a cheap night out when your boyfriend's in a coma!

DEVOY I've just met these great new mates, down in Brighton ... they said I could stop with them like, just til I get myself sorted

JELLY Apparently I'm making good progress ... these machines over here are making more beeping noises than ever ... I've got significant brain activity ... I could have told them that ages ago ... My dreams? I still want the decks, the DJ'ing, the club ... only in here they're bigger and better.

DEVOY   There was no proof ... I'd no gear on me, and the wallet?... Well it was my word against hers wasn't it?...

MANDY   I still go clubbing, paint my face, squeeze my body into something indecent ... I just don't mess with my head ... my choice ... up to now all my best memories are when I've been high on something and that sort of scares me ...

JELLY   Life's never been easier in a way ... got food and drink on tap, well from a tube! And I don't have to worry about showers or shaving ... the nurses do that for me, three times a week in here ... I'm exercised regularly, turned twice a day, so I imagine I look pretty good ... I don't feel any pain, I'm constantly pumped full of drugs in here ... ironic that isn't it?

DEVOY   I'm too smart to get caught, especially when there's always someone willing to give me a hand like ... if you know what I mean ...

MANDY   I took a tablet, stuck my head in the sand and waited for that warm flirty feeling to kick in and then ... Why?... because I thought it took my mind off my problems.

DEVOY   I'm off now, maybe see you around sometime.

JELLY   I felt so angry ... for her ... she deserved better than this ... I thought Devoy was great to begin with ... I'm not blame-less, just unlucky ... I knew what we were doing was dodgy ... but I just loved the buzz it gave me.

MANDY   No-one is going to take me for a ride ever again ... I don't care what crap I've got to deal with ... from now on I'm not going to block stuff out any more. I'm going to face it with a clear head ... my choice, my decision ... and for the first time I'm really in control.

Lights down.

End.

Marcus Romer

Born in Blackburn. Following his degree from Leeds University he has worked as an actor, director and writer for a variety of companies. These include Major Road, Red Ladder, NTC, Cleveland and Theatre Foundry. As Artistic Director of Pilot Theatre Company he has directed all their recent award-winning work - including **Taken Without Consent, Who's Breaking?** and **Out of their Heads**; as well as several projects with the West Yorkshire Playhouse and the Theatre Royal, Wakefield. He will direct the first ever tour of **Lord of the Flies** in 1998.

He lives in Yorkshire with Susie Hargreaves and their son Christy.

OTHER TITLES BY AURORA METRO PRESS

MEDITERRANEAN PLAYS BY WOMEN

ed. Marion Baraitser

A collection of astonishing plays by women from countries geographically linked but politically divided.

Twelve Women in a Cell, (trans. Marion Baraitser / Cheryl Robson) a play written after a period of captivity in Egypt by dissident writer **Nawal el Saadawi.**

The End of the Dream Season, (trans. Helen Kaye) a woman doctor outwits her friends and relations to retain her inheritance, by Israeli writer **Miriam Kainy.**

Libration, (trans. Lola Lopez Ruiz) a mysterious, intense and comic two-hander about two women who meet in a city park at night, by Catalan writer **Lluisa Cunillé.**

Mephisto, from the novel by Klaus Mann, (trans. Timberlake Wertenbaker) the story of a German actor who sells his soul to Nazi ideology by the eminent French writer/director **Ariane Mnouchkine.**

Harsh Angel, (trans. Rhea Frangofinou) a gentle Chekhovian tale of a family torn by the partition of their native land, written by Cypriot writer **Maria Avraamidou.**

Veronica Franco (trans. Sian Williams / Marion Baraitser) describes the life of a sixteenth century Venetian courtesan and poet, by Italy's foremost woman writer **Dacia Maraini.**

a great opportunity for those who don't see much live theatre by women to know what they've been missing. Everywoman Magazine

Price: £9.95   **ISBN 0-951-5877-3-0**

SIX PLAYS BY BLACK AND ASIAN WOMEN WRITERS

ed. Kadija George

A landmark collection of plays for stage, screen and radio showing the range and vitality of Black and Asian writing.

My Sister-Wife by Meera Syal, a taut thriller about two women who discover they are both married to the same man.
'A phenomenal talent.' Sunday Times.

Running Dream by Trish Cooke, tells the story of three generations of West Indian women with warmth and humour.
'the author's promise ripens.' The Times.

Song for a Sanctuary by Rukhsana Ahmad, explores the painful dilemma of an Asian woman forced to seek help from a women's refuge.   'perceptive and moving.' Morning Star.

Leonora's Dance by Zindika, four women share the house of a ballet dancer, whose contact with the supernatural lays the ghosts of the past to rest.
'a compelling show.' Caribbean Times.

Monsoon by Maya Chowdhry, is a poetic account of a young woman's sexual awakening.
'evocative and sensual.' Radio Times.

A Hero's Welcome by Winsome Pinnock, a tale of misplaced loyalty, longing for escape and early love.
'terrific new play' The Independent.

'showcases a wealth of talent amongst Black and Asian communities... often neglected by mainstream publishers.' Black Pride Magazine

Price: £7.50   ISBN 0-9515877-2-2

SEVEN PLAYS BY WOMEN: Female Voices, Fighting Lives
ed. Cheryl Robson

A bumper collection of award-winning plays by a new generation of women writers together with short critical essays on theatre today.

Fail/Safe by **Ayshe Raif**, 'a most disturbing lament for the way that some family ties become chains from which there will never be escape...' The Guardian

The Taking of Liberty by **Cheryl Robson**, 'the extraordinary tale of a town in the French Revolution: when the women take offence at an improvised statue, the incident escalates into savage retribution.' What's On.

Crux by **April de Angelis**, follows four women who follow their own doctrine of pleasure and hedonism in opposition to the stifling dictates of the Church.
'stimulating and humorous new play.' Time Out.

Ithaka by **Nina Rapi**, 'theatrically inventive, often surreal, witty and funny... sensitive charting of a woman's quest for love and freedom.' Bush Theatre.

Cochon Flambé by **Eva Lewin**, explores the sexual politics of waitressing in a comic, one-woman play.

Cut it Out by **Jan Ruppe**, a sharp blend of humour and pathos, tells the story of Laura, a self-lacerator.

Forced Out by **Jean Abbott**, a powerful drama of a lesbian teacher's confrontation with her community's prejudices, unleashed by a newspaper's gay witchhunt.

'a testimony to the work and debate that is going on among women, artistically, theoretically and practically. It is an inspiring document.' What's On

Price: £5.95   ISBN: 0-9515877-1-4

THE WOMEN WRITERS' HANDBOOK

eds. Robson, Georgeson, Beck

An essential guide to setting up and running your own writing workshops.

Creative Writing Exercises

Extracts from workshop writings

New poetry and fiction

Contact Directory

Essays on writing and dramaturgy by

CARYL CHURCHILL
JILL HYEM
BRYONY LAVERY
AYSHE RAIF
CHERYL ROBSON

A gem of a book. Everything a woman writer might need in one slim volume.
Everywoman Magazine

PRICE: £4.95 ISBN: 0-9515877-0-6

HOW MAXINE LEARNED TO LOVE HER LEGS
and other tales of growing-up
ed: Sarah Le Fanu

A sparkling collection of short stories exploring a host of female parts - rites of passage, revelations, strange relationships, love, loss, danger - the pleasures and pains of growing-up female in one entertaining volume.

Featuring 23 new and established authors including:

HILARY BAILEY   **KATE PULLINGER**
BONNIE GREER   **RAVI RANDHAWA**
KIRSTY GUNN   **MICHELE ROBERTS**
GERALDINE KAYE   **ELISA SEGRAVE**

'Being a clerical officer wasn't a bad job but April was a girl, who at 12 years of age had re-upholstered a 3-piece suite without a pattern.'

'she only went to school to please her mum, because looking after mum was the most important thing... she felt more like her mum was her and she was her mum. A pity they coudn't swap.'

'Auntie Poonam always thought things were worse when done in broad daylight... in front of the whole world, sister. Shameless!'

'I have a young erotic mother...'

PRICE: £8.95   **ISBN: 0-9515877-4-9**

A TOUCH OF THE DUTCH, plays by women

ed. Cheryl Robson

Internationally renowned and award-winning writers.

The first ever collection in English of modern Dutch drama, demonstrating the range and sophistication of new theatre writing by women in the Netherlands.

Write me in the sand by Inez van Dullemen (trans. Anthony Akerman) is a poetic portrayal of a family where layer upon layer is removed to reveal the painful secrets within. Performed to acclaim throughout Europe, available in English for the first time.

The Caracal by Judith Herzberg, Holland's leading woman writer, (trans. Rina Vergano) is a comic one-woman show about a teacher whose complicated love-life is revealed through fragmentary telephone conversations.

A thread in the dark by Hella Haasse, internationally renowned novelist, (trans. Della Couling) is a profound retelling of the myth of Theseus and the Minotaur, from the viewpoint of Ariadne. Widely acclaimed at home and abroad, the play won the Visser Neerlandia prize.

Eat by Matin van Veldhuizen, (trans. Rina Vergano) is a darkly humorous exploration of the lives of three sisters who come together to eat, drink, reminisce and celebrate the anniversary of their mother's death.

Dossier: Ronald Akkerman by Suzanne van Lohuizen, (trans. Saskia Bosch) is a highly topical two-hander, detailing moments between a patient suffering from AIDS and his nurse.

Introduction by Mieke Kolk, senior lecturer in Theatre Studies at the University of Amsterdam, former critic and cofounder of the women's theatre group Persona.

Price £9.95   **isbn 0-9515877-7-3**

ORDER FORM

- THE WOMEN WRITERS HANDBOOK   £4.95
- SEVEN PLAYS BY WOMEN   £5.95
- SIX PLAYS BY BLACK AND ASIAN WOMEN   £7.50
- HOW MAXINE LEARNED TO LOVE HER LEGS   £8.95
- MEDITERRANEAN PLAYS BY WOMEN   £9.95
- A TOUCH OF THE DUTCH   £9.95
- YOUNG BLOOD   £9.95
- BEST OF THE FEST   £12.99
- EASTERN PROMISE   £11.99

ADD 10% UK / 20% INTERNATIONAL POST AND PACKING

NAME   _____

ADDRESS   _____

_____

_____

POSTCODE   _____

PAYMENT BY CHEQUE OR POSTAL ORDER IN £ STERLING TO:

AURORA METRO PRESS
4 OSIER MEWS
LONDON W4 2NT. UK. TEL. +44 (0) 181 747 1953
www.netcomuk.co.uk/~ampress   email ampress@netcomuk.co.uk

TRADE DISTRIBUTION:
UK: CENTRAL BOOKS TEL: 0181 986 4854 FAX: 0181 533 5821
USA: THEATRE COMMUNICATIONS GROUP TEL: 212 697 5230
CANADA: CANADA PLAYWRIGHTS PRESS TEL: 416 703 0201